TIME AND MIGRATION

TIME AND MIGRATION

How Long-Term Taiwanese Migrants Negotiate Later Life

Ken Chih-Yan Sun

CORNELL UNIVERSITY PRESS   ITHACA AND LONDON

First published 2021 by Cornell University Press

Library of Congress Cataloging-in-Publication Data

Names: Sun, Ken Chih-Yan, author.
Title: Time and migration : how long-term Taiwanese migrants
    negotiate later life / Ken Chih-Yan Sun.
Description: Ithaca [New York] : Cornell University Press, 2021. |
    Includes bibliographical references and index.
Identifiers: LCCN 2020030343 (print) | LCCN 2020030344 (ebook) |
    ISBN 9781501754876 (hardcover) | ISBN 9781501754883 (pdf) |
    ISBN 9781501754890 (epub)
Subjects: LCSH: Taiwanese—United States—Social conditions—21st century. |
    Older Asian Americans—Social conditions—21st century. | Older immigrants—
    Family relationships. | Generations—Social aspects. | Old age—Social aspects. |
    Taiwan—Emigration and immigration—Social aspects. | United States—
    Emigration and immigration—Social aspects.
Classification: LCC E184.T35 S86 2021 (print) | LCC E184.T35 (ebook) |
    DDC 305.26086/912—dc23
LC record available at https://lccn.loc.gov/2020030343
LC ebook record available at https://lccn.loc.gov/2020030344

For my family

Contents

Preface

Questions regarding time, aging, and migration are deeply intertwined with my own biography. During my fieldwork and after almost every presentation of this research, scholars, respondents, and laypeople asked why a younger person like me was interested in older people. Implicit in this question are assumptions about age, age-related activities, and generational differences, but the question also prompted me to reflect on my curiosity about the experiences of older migrants. For me, studying older immigrants who are long-term residents in the United States is both professionally intriguing and personally significant. As a sociologist, I am interested in the experience of living in a host society for an extended period and especially in the issues that migrants encounter nationally and transnationally. As someone raised by grandparents, without the company of parents, I also found the stories of my respondents both new and familiar.

My grandparents relocated to Taiwan during 1949, when the Kuomintang lost the civil war in mainland China.[1] Although my grandparents were not part of a racial minority, Taiwan presented a foreign experience to them. They did not speak the local language (i.e., Taiwanese/Fujianese). They did not know the environment well and had no local connections. Their economic situation drastically and rapidly deteriorated, largely because they had left most of their savings, properties, and financial means in their hometown in Donghai County, Jiangsu Province, in mainland China. Because they did not work for the KMT government in Taiwan and lacked a salary and access to public benefits (e.g., subsidized public housing that the KMT government provided to public servants), my grandparents had to find a way to survive and support their family. Like many migrants, they had left behind family members, including their own parents and their first daughter. They had expected eventually to return home, after the war was over, but instead, they settled, died, and were buried in Taiwan.

My grandparents resembled many newcomers. Life in a new society meant both developing cross-cultural friendships and experiencing intergroup conflicts. In the eyes of some native-born Taiwanese, they were intruders and a threat to the local population.[2] Yet they also received timely help and fostered friendships with local people. My grandfather always remembered that, when they first arrived in Taiwan and almost starved to death, a Taiwanese woman—who later became our neighbor—offered them free meals. As he related to me, she even spoke a different dialect, and they could not at first communicate.

Growing up surrounded by my grandparents' friends planted the seeds for my sociological curiosity about the experiences of older people who had crossed borders when they were younger. The stories I heard from my grandparents and their friends taught me much about the complexity, malleability, and adaptability of older generations. My grandmother, for example, had bound feet (*guo jiao*), a status symbol for women of her generation. Only women from wealthy families could afford to bind their feet, she explained, because they did not have to work under the sun. Binding her feet had caused bone fractures and made walking difficult and painful. She had managed, however, to travel hundreds of miles from her hometown to Taipei and give birth to my father during the journey. She had been used to having servants, both before and after her marriage, and had rarely done housework, but after 1949, in Taiwan, she had to clean and cook for her family, tasks that she hated, as she finally told me, on her deathbed.

My grandmother had been unaccustomed to interacting with people outside the family (especially men). Women from "good" families, she told me, were supposed to confine themselves to the private domain and refrain from appearing in public. Yet she and my grandfather established a small business, a grocery store, in Taiwan. To talk with local customers, she even learned Taiwanese/Fujianese. Although she suffered constantly from the damage of foot-binding, she walked twenty to thirty minutes from her home to her store every day for almost four decades. Life never treated her kindly. She had contracted smallpox in mainland China and was infected with tuberculosis in Taiwan. She lost most of her eyesight when I was three years old because she devoted all her time and attention to caring for me while I was suffering from chicken pox and had no time to rest and recover from eye surgery. The rapid decline of her eyesight, however, never stopped her from working or taking care of her family. Her story inspired this project. Her resilience alerted me to the complicated life histories of older generations and to their adaptability to changing and challenging circumstances.

Talking with my respondents offered me a new perspective on my grandparents, who died in 1996 and 2000. When I was younger, I could not relate well to the many stories they told me and often found their experiences surreal or confusing. For instance, growing up after Taiwan's economy took off, I could not imagine Taiwan as an underdeveloped, agricultural society, where cows, rather than cars, traveled the streets. I also failed fully to understand why my grandparents were so often in tears as they chatted with other migrants from their hometown and when they finally reunited with their left-behind daughter, my aunt. I knew that they were nostalgic and missed family and friends in mainland China. Yet I wondered why they rarely visited their homeland after the KMT government lifted the travel ban in 1987. While some of their friends returned frequently to visit or even to settle, my grandparents were uninterested in going back. As I recall, they explained to me their feelings about their forty years' absence: "People die. Places change. We cannot even find where our ancestral tombs are. What is the point of going back?" Their hometown had become a different place; the idea of going "home" was painful because it reminded them of what they had lost. But as a child, I also wondered why so many of their friends were eager to travel back and forth between Taiwan and their hometowns and why some of them even bought houses in mainland China and planned to move there.

Spending time with my respondents, I reconsidered the experiences of older migrants like my grandparents and the reasons for their varying responses to home and host societies. Writing this book made me reflect on the scholarship on aging, families, and migration in relation to my own past, present, and future. Sociological research has sharpened my analytical abilities. As C. Wright Mills (1959, 161) argues, "the life of an individual cannot be adequately understood without references to the institutions within which his biography is enacted." Having become a migrant myself, living in many places, away from my grandparent since I was twenty, I now recall what I learned from them. Their stories sensitize me to the complexities of cross-border ties and the temporalities of migration.

Acknowledgments

If my grandparents planted the sociological seeds in my heart, many people have helped me grow, cultivate, and harvest the fruit. This book would not have been possible without the respondents who generously shared their life stories with me. For ethical reasons, I cannot thank them here individually, but I appreciate their generosity in opening themselves and, in many cases, their homes to me. I am also deeply grateful for the inspiration they provided.

This book began at Brandeis University, and my colleagues there provided valuable feedback that shaped its development. I am blessed to have had Karen V. Hansen as my mentor. Karen had incredible faith in me, more than I sometimes have in myself. She reassured me during periods of self-doubt and guided me through difficult professional transitions. I want to thank Wendy Cadge for teaching me to organize data, construct a sociological argument, and navigate the discipline. She has always been there for me. I am grateful as well to Sara Shostak for teaching me to be a professional sociologist; as a graduate student, I secretly dreamed about being as sharp as her one day. I also extend my sincere gratitude to Nazli Kibria, who was generous with her knowledge, insights, and professional connections, even when she was stretched thin with professional and personal commitments. I am indebted as well to Mary C. Waters for her insightful comments. She is the first person who alerted me to the potential for bridging the areas of aging and international migration.

I also wish to extend my gratitude to a few people who provided critical support for this book and for my professional development. Nadia Kim introduced me to the field of migration and taught me the importance of thinking about the complexity of race/ethnicity, class, and gender. From the first day of graduate school, Laura Miller helped me handle many difficult moments and recover from many setbacks. David Cunningham and Peter Conrad set great examples of excellence in both teaching and research, and I am thankful for their generous time and insights. I was lucky to have Kathleen Jenkins and Kelly Joyce during my first job at the College of William and Mary; both were mentors who supported me selflessly. Bandana Purkayastha consistently reminded me that my book will be an important contribution to the field; without her encouragement, I might have dropped this manuscript.

Collegiality is essential to the completion of any book. Anita Chan, Russell King, Peggy Levitt, Yao-tai Li, Lake Lui, and anonymous reviewers at Cornell University

Press offered constructive feedback on the manuscript. My analysis also benefited tremendously from the insightful comments of the following colleagues: Sealing Cheng, Cati Coe, Joanna Dreby, Sara Friedman, Elaine Ho, Kathleen Jenkins, Miliann Kang, Sarah Lamb, Pei-chia Lan, C. N. Le, Jennifer Bickham Mendez, Margaret (Peggy) K. Nelson, Nicole Newendorp, Bandana Purkayastha, Wendy Roth, Kevin Roy, Kristy Shih, Robert C. Smith, Judith Treas, Leslie Wang, and Min Zhou. In addition, I received helpful comments from my presentations in the Fairbank Center of Harvard University, Sociology Department of the University of British Columbia, Anthropology Department of the Chinese University of Hong Kong, Sociology Division of Nanyang Technological University, Sociology Department of National Taipei University, and Institute of Sociology at Academia Sinica.

Institutional support provided a material foundation for researching and writing this book. I received generous funding from the Chiang Ching-kuo Foundation, the Andrew Mellon Foundation, Brandeis University, Hong Kong Baptist University, the Subvention of Publication Program at Villanova University and the 2020 Taiwanese Overseas Pioneers Grants (TOP Grants) for New Scholars from Taiwan Ministry of Science and Technology.

I also appreciate the postdoctoral fellowships I was granted at Academia Sinica and at Nanyang Technological University, which gave me time to conduct follow-up research and analyze the data. In Taiwan, I wish to thank Holin Lin, Yen-fen Tseng, and Chia-ling Wu for bringing me to the world of sociology, and I am grateful to Yu-Yueh Tsai and Alice Yen-Hsin Cheng for their friendship and words of encouragement. I also appreciate Chin-Hua Chang for having faith in my academic potential. At Hong Kong Baptist University, Adrian Bailey and Gina Lai supported my research in every possible way. I also wish to thank Anna Lo, Yinni Peng, Danching Ruan, and Day Wong for various forms of assistance. At Villanova University, I thank Robert (Bob) Defina and Thomas Arvanites for all of their helpful guidance. I also gratefully acknowledge constructive feedback from Meredith Bergey, Glenn E. Bracey II, Lance Hannon, Melissa Hodges, Heidi Grundetjern, Rory Kramer, Brianna Remster, and Kelly Welch. I feel amazed every day that I have such wonderful colleagues.

I thank Cornell University Press for giving me the opportunity to transform this book from an idea to a reality. I greatly appreciate the keen editorial eyes and clear guidance of Jim Lance. I published portions of this book in "Reconfigured Reciprocity: How Aging Taiwanese Immigrants Transform Cultural Logics of Elder Care," *Journal of Marriage and Family*; "Transnational Healthcare Seeking: How Ageing Taiwanese Return Migrants View Homeland Public Benefits," *Global Networks*; "Negotiating the Boundaries of Social Membership: The Case of Aging Return Migrants to Taiwan," *Current Sociology*; and "Professional Remittances:

How Ageing Returnees Seek to Contribute to the Homeland," *Journal of Ethnic and Migration Studies*. I gratefully acknowledge the feedback of anonymous reviewers for these journals. Both Jill Smith and Nathaniel Tuohy provided helpful editorial assistance on different chapters. Baiyu Su helped format and fact-check the final draft. Debra Osnowitz merits a special thank-you: the writing in this book would not be as polished without her meticulous final editing. Of course, all the errors are my responsibility.

Friends made writing this book a less lonely journey. In Boston, Guy Abutbul, Robyn Blair, Casey Clevenger, En-chieh Chao, Nicky Fox, Judith Hanley, George Hu, Ruth Lin, Tom Mackie, Erin Rehel, Ashley Rondini, Jill Smith, Mrinalini Tankha, Miranda Waggoner, and Jacob Yang are the best friends that I could ever hope for. I am grateful to Erin and Miranda for helping me anchor my first few years in the United States and my first year of teaching in a rural locale here. I also appreciate having had Jen-Hao Chen as a loyal and supportive friend; he provided timely help no matter how busy he was. For their friendship and support, I thank Ting-Hua Chang, Yiuchun Chen, Chiwei Cheng, Ying-chao Gao, Elisha Huang, Kim Ling Lau, Karen Lee, Yi-Hsuan Li, Chia-wen Lin, Frankie Ng, Sau Ching Sek, Cheng-Shi Shiu, Chaoching Wang, Harry Wu, Yung I Wu, Wing Wah Yick, and Meng-sung Yu. Words cannot describe how wonderful you are to me.

I dedicate this book to my family members in Taiwan. My sister, Ching-I Sun, has supported my career aspiration without hesitation. She also took care of the entire family in Taiwan when I was abroad. Ching-ting Sun passed away before I published this book, but she will always live in my memory. I am often touched by the sweet gestures of Ching-ying Sun, although I rarely thank her explicitly. My mother, Rui-liang Huang, and my aunt, Yao-pei Lin, always believed in me and fullheartedly supported my decision to study and work abroad, even though they had only vague ideas about the world of academia.

Beyond my birth family, I am grateful to my families by choice. The Lin family has been a wonder since the day we met. Pastor Sekiong Lin and his wife, Hsiu Ching Lee, welcomed me into their lives and treated me like their son. Shirley Lin helped me better understand myself and the root of my struggles. Douglas Lin showed me a way to be caring and critical at the same time. I am also deeply grateful to Dennis Chang and Mao-chen Chang for their long-term support and loyal friendship. Despite the physical distance, Dennis was emotionally and spiritually there for me whenever I needed him. And not least, I want to thank my partner, Jerry Fu, for his unconditional love. He is my anchor. He teaches me to love. I am truly blessed to have him in my life.

Note on Transliteration and Naming

This book uses the Pinyin system to romanize Chinese words, expressions, and names of the respondents. In addition, all the names of my respondents cited in this book are pseudonyms. I use "Mr." and "Mrs." as prefixes to surnames to conform to the cultural practice of addressing elders through more formal and honorific language in Taiwan and other Chinese societies.

TIME AND MIGRATION

INTRODUCTION
How Time Complicates Migratory Experiences

The midsummer afternoon in Boston became less hot and humid after the thunderstorm. I was on the way to Mrs. Chou's house, where I planned to interview her and her husband (separately). She had come to the United States during the mid-1960s, when she was in her midtwenties, and had spent most of her life in the Boston area. She had not, however, settled in Chinatown and now lived in a colonial house in a middle-class neighborhood. She and her husband had moved to this neighborhood to enable their children to attend good schools, which they believed would increase their children's life chances, and they had continued to live there even after their children moved elsewhere after graduating from college. Back then, the area had few Asian faces, so that Mrs. Chou and her husband were pioneers in a predominantly white neighborhood.

During the interview, I asked Mrs. Chou about differences she had experienced since relocating to the United States. She frowned and looked at me as if she had many things to say but did not know where to start. Initially, she said, "If I never left Taiwan, I would probably never get accustomed to the suburban lifestyle—I mean, living far away from city center and driving everywhere." She continued, "Obviously, I would also never learn how to speak English if I never moved to the US, and my husband and I would certainly have a different career trajectory." Appearing dissatisfied with the answers she had given me, she paused for a while. Then she seemed to think of something really important and said, "Without coming to the US, I would *not* end up becoming the parents and grandparents of Americans!" Implicit in this statement was a transformation in family relations. Yet trained as a sociologist, I found Mrs. Chou's use of "American" puzzling. The

1

United States is a complex, stratified, and multilayered society. Soon, however, I realized that unpacking what "American" or "American society" meant to my respondents would constitute the crux of this book.

Two years later, in 2014, Mrs. Chou and her husband returned to Taiwan for an extended visit. Knowing that I was there too, they invited me to dinner with some of their extended family, where Mr. Chou asked many questions about my experiences relocating to Williamsburg, Virginia (where I had my first job), and about my feelings working as a new professor. He was particularly thrilled to share his experiences of navigating the rural and urban United States as a migrant newcomer during the 1960s. But as we talked in Taiwan, the conversation precluded the Chous' siblings and in-laws, none of whom had lived in the United States. Their inability to join our conversation suggested that our experiences of migration created a social world that might not be immediately relatable to people who never lived abroad, even to the siblings with whom we had grown.

In addition to sharing his experiences of migration and relocation to the United States, Mr. Chou talked at length about changes to the hometown he had left. We met in a modern Taiwanese restaurant in one of Taipei's most bustling areas; the cuisine was traditional, but the facility and infrastructure were contemporary. When Mr. Chou grew up, this area had been full of farms, shabby flats, and vacant lands that were now supplanted by fancy stores and restaurants. Mr. and Mrs. Chou thought highly of these drastic developments in Taipei. They loved taking subways to meet friends, go sightseeing, and attend medical appointments, which they scheduled in Taiwan, with its excellent health care and prices that were much more affordable than in Boston. For them, Taiwan might have become a different place, but they enjoyed many new features of their evolving homeland—changes they deemed great for older people.

The stories of long-term immigrants like Mr. and Mrs. Chou point to the need to integrate time and the experience of aging into the analysis of immigrant adaptation, assimilation, and transnationalism. Relocating to a new society involves loss: downward mobility, life outside familiar racial homogeneity, and the imperative to give up familiar habits, lifestyles, customs, languages, and cultural norms. Immigration also means reclassification within the US middle or working class, new racial and ethnic membership, and resocialization with new habits, lifestyles, rituals, language skills, and ways of knowing. Much research has demonstrated the myriad ways in which immigrants and their family members adapt in host societies, navigating both obstacles and opportunities across borders (Alba and Nee 2003; Levitt 2001; Portes and Zhou 1993). Yet few studies offer insights into the long-term consequences of immigration. How, for example, does the passage of time change or complicate immigrants' experiences? What happens to "newcomers" who spend several decades living in a place that might no longer be "foreign"? How do they feel about experiencing life transitions, transnationally, in an adopted country?

A focus on older, long-term immigrants also pushes us to rethink their connections to their homelands. Between the 1960s and the 1990s, rapid economic and social development in Hong Kong, Taiwan, South Korea, and Singapore—the so-called Asian dragons—stunned the world. Later economic and social progress in India and China once again attracted global attention (Feenstra and Hamilton 2014). With economic growth, these later-developing societies began to establish public benefits programs and infrastructures for public services (J. Wang 2004). For immigrants from these countries, therefore, homelands may well have become drastically different since they left. How, then, do they feel about these developments? Are they proud? Does the unfamiliar seem strange? How do they rethink the decision to migrate and the possibilities for returning to an evolving homeland? What motivates the decisions they face now?

Aging and Immigration in the United States

This book examines a group understudied in social scientific research: long-term immigrants in a later stage of life and their complex relations with home and host societies. According to the US Census Bureau, nearly 4.3 million immigrants in the United States are age sixty-five and over. This figure represents an all-time high (Purkayastha et al. 2012). Research predicts that with the rise of foreign-born populations migrating to the United States, the number of non-white elderly immigrants will double, growing from 16 to 36 percent of the senior population by 2050 (Choi 2012; Yoo and Kim 2014; Newendorp 2020).

Among older foreign-born individuals, nearly two-thirds have lived in the United States for more than thirty years (Brownell and Fenley 2009). Yet despite this unprecedented increase in older migrant populations, the experiences of elderly immigrants remain understudied in current analyses of both aging and international migration. Although roles, issues, and challenges at different life stages have a differential impact on immigrants' identities and practices (Levitt 2002), the logics, rationales, and strategies through which long-term senior immigrants assess and address life issues and life transitions remain marginalized in scholarship on aging, migration, and race/ethnicity.

To date, a growing number of studies have attended to hardships—cultural displacement, language barriers, family conflicts—with which older immigrants struggle (Ajrouch 2005; Angel and Angel 2006; Guo et al. 2016; Jackson, Forsythe-Brown, and Govia 2007; Mui 1996; Parikh et al. 2009). Scholars have paid particular attention to the ways aging immigrants recently arriving in host societies—typically through family reunification—grapple with family intimacy and intergenerational reciprocity across social and cultural worlds (Guo et al. 2016; King et al. 2017; Lamb 2009; Newendorp 2020; Treas and Carreon 2010; Zhang and Zhan 2009; Y. Zhou 2012). Yet the experiences of long-term aging migrants who relocated to the United States during adulthood have largely eluded scholarly analysis. This inattention is surprising because US-based immigration scholars argue that immigration reform in 1965 changed the social and cultural landscapes of US society (Alba and Nee 2003; Massey 2008; Portes and Zhou 1993) and immigrants who arrived as adults during the 1960s and 1970s are entering or have already entered a later stage of life.

These older migrants might have encountered similar issues, but they may be differentially equipped to respond to the changes and challenges of a later life stage. In particular, the interaction between temporalities and migratory experiences—length of stay in the United States, different paths of incorporation into US society, and cross-border ties maintained at different life stages—may profoundly shape the ability of aging, foreign-born populations to address the changes and challenges that they encounter during life transitions. Because current studies have yet to examine the complex lived experiences of long-term immigrants, we have only a preliminary understanding of the ways longitudinal migration and settlement in the United States influence immigrants as they address their needs, desires, and roles in a later phase of life.

As immigrants age in host societies, their home societies may undergo profound transformation. In particular, the global south, developing societies, and the so-called third world have experienced what scholars have termed compressed modernity—a mix of social, cultural, economic, and political changes that take place extremely quickly—over the past three to four decades (Kyung-Sup 2010; Lan 2018). These changes, while raising the positions of these nation-states in the global order (Hoang 2015), may provoke ambivalence among local, nonmigrant people (Cohen 1994; Lamb 2000). For migrants overseas, however, the evolving homeland contexts may offer a constellation of social, political, and economic opportunities (Tsuda 2012). While many scholars have underscored the ongoing circulation of goods, people, ideas, capital, and information between immigrants' home and host societies (Basch, Schiller, and Blanc 1994; Levitt 2001; Smith 2006), few have paid close attention to the impact of changing homelands on the everyday lives of older migrants. As a result, we know surprisingly little about the meaning of an evolving homeland to long-term emigrants in general and long-term older emigrants in particular. Nor do we know much about long-term migrants who must consider aging and life transitions in both a national and a transnational context.

To address these questions, this book explores the experience of long-term migration, coupled with the temporal variation of homeland contexts, as it shapes the ways aging migrant populations consider, construct, and fulfill their needs and desires. The mutual shaping between temporalities and migratory experiences, I argue, is essential to understanding the ways globally dispersed aging immigrants rethink and reconstruct their social worlds. Here I offer the concept of *temporalities of migration* to trace the trajectories through which aging immigrants draw on the social and cultural norms they learn transnationally and transtemporally to reestablish relationships with families, friends, home locales, and host societies. Temporalities of migration are central to understanding the ways migrants (re)write their biographies, not only because major life events have "both temporal and spatial attributes" (Pred 1977; see also Ho 2019, 28–30) but also because temporal and contextual forces complicate each other's influence on human experience.

Temporalities of migration, as a concept, build on the notion of an aging-migration nexus, developed by Russell King and his colleagues (2017). Temporalities of migration, however, are broader. Human aging constitutes only some of the temporalities that explain the experiences of older migrants. Because it is social, time manifests differently at individual, professional, and familial levels, and its intersection with structures and culture affects our self-perception and our management of daily lives (Erel and Ryan 2019; Hansen 1996; Levitt and Rajaram 2013). The effects of time on migratory experiences are also persistent. As Purkayastha and her colleagues (2012, 10) argue, migrants' encounters with different social structures and belief systems at each life stage have cumulative effects on their experiences as older adults. Older migrants' *life paths*—individual biographies deeply embedded in and shaped by specific historical, structural, and cultural contexts—significantly affect the ways these people respond to later-life transitions socially, symbolically, and emotionally (Hägerstrand 1982; May and Thrift 2001). An analysis of migrants' lived experiences, therefore, should be conducted not just "along the spatial cross-section but along the time axis and in the particular sequence of events which makes up the life of each individual human being" (King 2012, 141).

Combining insights from literature on both the life course (Carstensen, Isaacowitz, and Charles 1999; Elder 1994; Hareven 1994) and international migration (Cwerner 2001; King et al. 2006; Levitt and Rajaram 2013; Purkayatha et al. 2012; Smith 2014), the concept of temporalities of migration includes three foundational elements: (1) individual and familial transitions in home and host societies (e.g., children growing up, leaving home, and establishing their families; becoming grandparents; retirement from work); (2) cross-border socialization (e.g., memories, education, labor market history, and acquisition of cultural norms); and (3) historical changes at subnational, national, and transnational levels (e.g., changes in sending and receiving societies). Moreover, rather than assuming that aging individuals are passively or only negatively influenced by these complex time-migration configurations, I contend that they actively anchor themselves and their intimate relations by reacting to the intersection of various temporal and structural-cultural factors. Therefore, the concept of temporalities of migration not only pushes us to rethink the interplay between place and space but also underscores the reflexive management of intimacies at familial, communal, and state levels as aging migrants grapple with their sense of national and transnational belonging.

In this book, I adopt what scholars have termed a subject-oriented approach (Lee and Zhou 2015, 148). Rather than using normative assumptions to measure the effects of long-term transnational relocation on migrants, I seek to understand the processes through which older migrants assess and address the impact of time-migration configurations on their intimate lives. Of course, immigrants' stories might be biased, as "the production of 'longitudinal' qualitative data often relies upon interviewees 'remembering' and requires researchers to impose a degree of logical progression on the lives of individual migrants that may, in fact, not exist" (J. Waters 2011, 1122). Here, however, I use not only retrospective life-history interviews but also ethnographic observations as data to explore my respondents' evaluations of long-term migration and its effects on themselves and their intimate relations, whether or not they accurately describe their pasts (Cwerner 2001, 9–10; Sun 2017). Their accounts might be "*post hoc* constructions" but nonetheless reveal the worldviews that guide their feelings, emotions, and decisions (Shia and Tuan 2008, 271). Perception, in this sense, is reality.

This study draws on the accounts of fifty-eight older Taiwanese immigrants in the United States, fifty-seven older return migrants living in Taiwan, and ethnographic observations of the intimate lives of both groups over two years of observation in each society. Throughout this book, I underscore the interaction between temporal and other contextual factors that shape the processes whereby these older immigrants reflect on belonging, mutuality, and reciprocity with their families, communities, and societies as they reconsider social and cultural norms nationally and transnationally. This book thus enriches scholarly and public understanding of graying, post-1965 immigrants to the United States. It underscores the interaction between manifestations of time and contextual features of relocation that shapes the perception, perspectives, and practices of foreign-born populations.

How Aging Individuals Navigate Temporalities of Migration

Near the end of the summer of 2010, I attended a church retreat in Greater Boston. There I hoped to locate and recruit potential respondents for my research on aging immigrants from Taiwan. The guest speaker for the retreat, Pastor Lu, was in his late sixties and originally from Taiwan. He started his talk by thanking the consistory for inviting him to Boston, and he then alluded to *The Taste of an Apple*, a well-known Taiwanese novella by the novelist Chun Ming Huang, to illustrate perceptions of the United States broadly shared by Taiwanese people of his generation.

The story is situated between the 1950s and early 1960s, when the US military still had bases in Taiwan. The main character, A-Fa, is a male factory worker who is struck by an American soldier's car on his way to work. Even though he survived the accident, A-Fa and his family are worried about sustaining themselves with the family's breadwinner seriously injured. They are therefore relieved, even pleased, after an unnamed American soldier comes to visit and promises to do everything he can to compensate the family—including covering all related expenses and sponsoring A-Fa's mute daughter for study in the United States. Most notably, A-Fa and his family are excited about the basket of apples brought by the American soldier because apples are luxuries that most Taiwanese families in the 1950s and 1960s could not easily afford. As Chun Ming Huang wrote in the novella,

> The kids and A-Kuei [A-Fa's wife] started biting apples. The room was silent, and only the crisp sound of biting apple could be heard here and there. They tasted the apples slowly and nervously. People who tasted the apple did not know how to describe the taste of apple at the first bite. They felt that the taste of apple was not as sweet as they imagined. The taste of apples was actually bittersweet. The texture of apples was powdery and made them feel a bit unreal. Yet the second bite of apples became so much better when the kids thought of what their father told them: "the value of an apple is worth 4 kg rice." (Huang 2009, 69)

As Pastor Lu explained to the participants at the retreat, apples in the story symbolized the American dream shared by many Taiwanese people of his generation. He joked sarcastically, "Fortunately, the Taiwanese worker was hit by an American. Therefore, he and his family have plenty of apples to eat!" Most people laughed at the joke. Some sighed.

During my fieldwork, I came to realize that these older immigrants had laughed or sighed not only because they were thinking of the past but also because they had experienced disrupted biographies that unfolded in unexpected ways after they emigrated to the United States. Just as the apples, money, and cars in Huang's novella symbolize the US prosperity desired by many Taiwanese in the 1950s and 1960s, many of these older Taiwanese immigrants thought of the United States as a land of opportunities unavailable in Taiwan. Much as characters in the novel began to feel differently about the apples after the first bite, my respondents' views of the United States had changed as they adapted to life there. For them, the experience of migrating and settling in a new place required ongoing learning and the development of new connections to their homeland. The immigrants I met during my research had, over time, reconsidered and reconstructed their intimate lives, and as they aged, they had faced life transitions and navigated multiple changes, both in their lives and in their host and home societies.

To date, scholars of social gerontology and public health are the key knowledge producers identifying the needs and desires of older migrant populations. Most of their research, however, has focused only on the vulnerability of these populations. Unaddressed in most of this research is age at migration, length of stay in host society, and path of incorporation into new social contexts—all factors that affect the course of aging for immigrants (King et al. 2017). Oriented by the assumption that older individuals are vulnerable to changes and challenges, much gerontological and public health research seeks to measure the process by which migrants can "successfully" or "healthfully" grow old in the host societies. This research has identified protective and risk factors at familial (Jackson et al. 2007), communal (Litwin 1997; Mui and Shibusawa 2008; Tam and Neysmith 2006), institutional (Okafor 2009), and cultural (Newbold and Filice 2006) levels that can affect the physical, social, and psychological well-being of older immigrants. What eludes us, however, is migration as a continuous process, often beginning early in life. For long-term immigrants, experience in host societies accumulates, potentially affecting responses to opportunities and constraints encountered later in life. How, then, does long-term migration shape the ways senior immigrants desire, define, and seek "aging well"?

The experiences of older migrants remain underexplored in social scientific research (cf. Dossa and Coe 2017; Horn and Schweppe 2015; Walsh and Näre 2016). The significance of "place/space" (i.e., the changing structural, cultural, and contextual features involved in relocation) and its intersection with the "immigrant generation" (i.e., the foreign- and native-born divide) often trumps the differences between age groups and informs sociological analyses of immigrants' experiences (Jiménez 2017; M. Waters 2014; Waters and Jiménez 2005). Migration scholars, especially those in North America, have addressed the ways in which immigrants and, later, native-born generations are socioeconomically, ethnoracially, and politically incorporated into (or excluded from) host societies (Alba 2005; Bloemraad 2006; Jiménez 2010; Kasinitz et al. 2008; Massey 2008; Portes,

Fernandez-Kelly, and Haller 2005). These studies, however, focus primarily on younger immigrants during adolescence or early adulthood and offer limited insights into the experiences of aging migrant populations, especially those who are long-term residents in host societies. We thus lack a sophisticated understanding of the interplay among temporalities (human aging, life transitions, life histories), place/space, and human agency as factors that mold immigrants' incorporation or exclusion in their adopted countries across life stages.

Recent social scientific research has been increasingly attentive to aging immigrants and their intimate lives. Some of these pioneering studies examine the influence of international migration on children of immigrants and their responses to the needs of their aging parents (Chung 2016; Sommer and Vogel 2015; Vallejo 2012; Yoo and Kim 2014). For example, as Pei-Chia Lan (2002) explains, many Chinese immigrants in Northern California use markets to satisfy the care needs of older generations by hiring "coethnics" to expand networks of support for their aging parents. These Chinese immigrants foster new strategies to fulfill rather than abandon ethnic traditions that emphasize intergenerational reciprocity. Grace Yoo and Barbara Kim (2014) use the concept of "linked lives" to demonstrate that the lives of children of Korean immigrants in the United States are intimately and intricately tied to their aging parents. As they convincingly argue, the experiences of immigrants' children as linguistic and cultural brokers for their parents, their understanding of the sacrifices that older generations have endured, and their interpretation of Korean cultural norms have prepared many children of Korean immigrants to take care of their ailing parents in their twilight years. These studies point to the enduring influence of ethnic conventions on the children of immigrants in a foreign land, although the practice of homeland traditions regarding elder care varies across national borders.

As some pioneering studies have demonstrated, aging migrant populations may be guided by factors beyond homeland traditions and expectations for children to resolve their problems or provide care (Gardner 2002; Lamb 2009; Purkayastha et al. 2012). Rather, this research suggests that aging immigrants display an ability to reconstruct homeland traditions and address daily issues. For example, older immigrants may provide much-needed support, such as caring for grandchildren (King and Lulle 2016; Xie and Xia 2011; Y. Zhou 2012), and they may remake traditional intergenerational relations as they respond to cultural norms (Horn and Schweppe 2015; Treas 2008; Walsh and Näre 2016; Zontini 2015). As Sarah Lamb (2009) astutely observes, many aging Indian immigrants who move to reunite with their children in the United States actively seek to adapt to new social and cultural conventions, despite some ambivalence. As Lamb (2009, 210) chronicles, "after spending some time in the U.S., most older immigrants, along with their families, end up self-consciously taking on practices, values, and modes of aging they regard as American, although often ambivalently with both eagerness and misgivings." Implicit in her analysis is time (i.e., length of stay in the host society), which potentially transforms the ways aging migrant populations think about homeland traditions governing family relations. Purkayastha and her colleagues (2012, 10) further argue that older migrants' temporal reflexivity across borders can profoundly affect their life prospects, including "ideas about independence, relationships with their children as possible care providers, relationship with the state as an old-age support provider, and so on."

Building on these insights, this book explores the crossroads between time and migration—what I term temporalities of migration—as an influence on the perspectives, perceptions, and practices of older long-term immigrants. This focus allows us better to understand what happens to the millions who migrated to study, work, and marry when they were younger (Mahler and Pessar 2006, 34). Theoretically, this work contributes to knowledge of immigrants' experiences of moving, settling, and adapting over time by examining their worldviews, ways of living, and sense of belonging. Attention to older long-term immigrants makes "time, timing, the life course, cohorts, and generations central to transnational migration, when considering how these issues shape migration decisions, cultures of migrations, and the social and emotional effects" of relocation on globally dispersed older immigrants (Dossa and Coe 2017, 5).

Rethinking a Transnational Social Field through Temporalities of Migration

When moving to the United States during the 1970s, Mr. Leung wanted to make a lot of money. He had always planned to use the money he earned in the United States for a comfortable retirement in Taiwan. Unfortunately, his dream never came true. For most of his life, he worked as a waiter in Chinese restaurants. He never married. He did save some money from the tips he received during the thirty years he worked abroad, but he lost much of it by gambling. Single, childless, almost bankrupt, and close to retirement age, Mr. Leung felt lost. By 2010, in his midsixties, he had talked with friends and decided to move back to Taiwan.

Mr. Leung was ambivalent about returning to Taiwan. He was deeply disappointed with the result of his journey to the United States. Unlike many of his friends, he never joined the American middle class. Whereas many Taiwanese Americans could convert their incomes from employment into respectable wealth in their homeland, he was instead poorer than many local people who had never migrated. He also returned to a country that had undergone several decades of development and today has a world-class infrastructure. Taipei was no longer the city he had left in the 1970s, and it was also completely different from the Chinatown neighborhood in which he had lived in the United States. Returning "home" thus felt strange.

Yet Mr. Leung also felt that his life was somewhat easier after he returned to Taiwan. Through a friend, he found a job working as a janitor in Taipei. There, the cost of living was significantly lower than in the United States, and his remaining savings could stretch much further. In addition, as a Taiwanese citizen, Mr. Leung gained access to public benefits, including subsidies for low-income senior citizens and publicly financed health insurance. These benefits significantly improved his living conditions. After moving back, for example, he received root canal procedures to address dental problems with which he had been struggling for years, at a cost of about forty US dollars. A social worker then helped him apply for the municipal government's monetary assistance to qualified elderly needing dentures and implants. To Mr. Leung, as an elderly person, Taiwan was much better than the place he had left decades earlier.

Mr. Leung's story highlights the need to investigate the experiences of older long-term immigrants beyond a single nation-state (Näre, Walsh, and Baldassar 2017). As research has shown, migrants might return to their homeland after spending many working years in their host societies (Coe 2017a; Gilbertson 2009; Hunter 2011). They might return to pursue the lifestyle they miss, to reunite with their families and friends, or to convert their savings abroad to an economically secure life (Coe 2017a). Nonetheless, returning home is never an easy decision. Although the development of information and communication technologies offers the possibilities for migrants and their family members to be virtually "co-present" with each other (Baldassar 2016), living abroad for many years still transforms habits, behavior patterns, and cultural orientations (Ho 2019; Ley and Kobayash 2005). Moreover, relocating to home societies typically involves deeply felt tensions and complicated interpersonal dynamics (Constable 2014; Hunter 2018). Adaptation to life in host societies has often transformed migrants, distinguishing them from those who remained home (Fitzgerald 2013). The experience of return, therefore, pushes migrants to reflect on the impact of the host society and creates deeply felt tensions with nonmigrant populations (Erdal and Ezzati 2015; Tsuda 1999; Zontini 2015).[1] A significant period in a host society may also so transform cultural dispositions that return migration becomes undesirable and migrants no longer feel "at home" in the societies they once left (Ho 2019; Hunter 2018).

As Mr. Leung's story shows, the passage of time changes not only people but also places. Like people, places undergo fundamental transitions over time, but few studies have addressed the effects of changing homelands on the subjectivities of emigrants. My focus on temporalities, however, offers an analysis of the ways in which aging migrant populations—including those who remain abroad and those who decide to return and settle—position themselves in relation to their homelands over time. I underscore the tension that older immigrants encounter as they articulate rights, responsibilities, privileges, and entitlements in a homeland that has become significantly different as they worked for several decades in another country. Examining the experiences of older long-term migrants underscores the ways temporalities of migration—life transitions, length of stay, and changing homeland contexts—affect the consideration and management of cross-border ties.

More broadly, temporalities of migration complicate current scholarship on migrant transnationalism. Over the past two decades, a growing body of work on migrant transnationalism has demonstrated the ongoing circulation of goods, people, ideas, capital, and information between immigrants' home and host societies, prompting changes in both places (Basch et al. 1994; Fouron and Schiller 2001; Levitt and Jaworsky 2007; Vertovec 1999). Research on Chinese transnationalism has particularly shown that privileged Chinese families seek to convert economic capital to their children's human, social, and cultural capital across national borders (Ong 1999; Sun 2014a; J. Waters 2005). These immigrants live in a transnational social field and are embedded in multilayered cross-border networks (Levitt and Schiller 2004). I highlight the processes through which migration histories, modes of incorporation, and evolving homeland contexts influence the reconfiguration of cross-border relations. The development of immigrants' homelands, I argue, complicates what Peggy Levitt and her colleagues (2017, 6) call the resource environment—"a combination of all the possible protections available to them from our four potential sources (states, markets, third sector, and social networks)"—that aging individuals face. Focusing on the coconstruction between temporalities and the transnational lives of migrants, older migrants negotiate their well-being by accessing concrete and symbolic resources across the territories or nation-states.

Reconstructing Intimate Relations through Temporalities of Migration

The temporalities of migration are most salient in the ways migrants negotiate their intimate ties. Time matters, I argue, because the course of biological aging and the experience of living abroad for several decades prompt older immigrants to reflect on their connections to the individuals and institutions in their everyday lives. According to Viviana Zelizer (2005, 14), relations can be defined "as intimate to the extent that interactions within them depend on particularized knowledge received, and attention provided by, at least one person—knowledge and attention that are not widely available to third parties." Furthermore, Lynn Jamieson (2011, 1) defines intimate relationships as the process of establishing connections that "are subjectively experienced and may also be socially recognized as close." As she points out, "the quality of 'closeness' that is indicated by intimacy can be emotional and cognitive, with subjective experiences including a feeling of mutual love, being 'of like mind' and special to each other."[2] On the other hand, the processes of creating closeness (i.e., intimacies) often have much to do with stratifying forces such as race, ethnicity, class, gender, and culture, since few intimate "relationships, even friendship, are mainly simply about mutual appreciation, knowing and understanding" (Jamieson 1999, 482).

Aging immigrants in this study constructed and reconstructed intimacies in everyday life as they closely attended to their positions within webs of social relations. Like other senior populations approaching the last phase of life, my respondents considered the limited time they had and the types of intimacies they wished to sustain (Carstensen, Isaacowitz, and Charles 1999). At the same time, growing older as long-term migrants pushed them to reassess their intimate relationships, both nationally and transnationally. The ways in which these migrants evaluated intimacies were typically path dependent (Mahoney 2000). The decisions they made earlier in life, along with the knowledge, habits, and cultural logics they had absorbed over time, played a key role in shaping the ways they perceived and organized intimate relationships at different scales.

Rethinking intimacies also becomes central to the daily lives of aging immigrants who negotiate the support that they and their loved ones need (Zelizer 2005). To be sure, not all older people need to be cared for, and at other stages of the life cycle, such as pregnancy and childbirth, assistance might also be much needed. Yet the elderly are more likely than other age groups to arrange for support, either for themselves or for their loved ones. As my respondents reflected on their changing needs, desires, and roles, they (re)considered not only the constellation of resources they could activate but also the strategies they might use (Boris and Parreñas 2010; Friedman and Mahdavi 2015). This process often motivated creative and sustained efforts to deliberate, establish, maintain, transform, and/or terminate relations with families, communities, markets, and state aid (Zelizer 2012). Aging immigrants thus rarely take intimacies—with families, friends, or with nation-states—for granted. Rather, they consistently remake these intimacies in response to structural and cultural contexts, mediated and complicated by temporalities.

I highlight three types of labor through which my respondents managed intimacies: (1) emotion work (Hochschild 2003), through which they sought to control feelings, emotions, and thoughts; (2) boundary work (Lamont 2000), through which they established distinctions among groups of people, objects, and relations; and (3) cultural work (Swidler 2001), through which they strategized and manipulated competing frames of cultural reference. To maintain intimate relationships, my respondents carefully monitored, controlled, and channeled their emotional responses, further differentiating what they felt from what they believed they should feel (Hochschild 2003). This emotion work mitigated conflicts that could disrupt relationships they wish to maintain. Maintaining boundaries, in turn, allowed them to sustain intimacies by distinguishing between what they could expect or request and what they could not (Hansen 2005; Pachucki, Pendergrass, and Lamont 2007). Central to these emotion-laden, boundary-setting processes were meaning-making activities. Expatriates who reside in the United States for a long time are not merely exposed to different cultural norms and traditions. Rather, they actively evoke cultural repertoires—perspectives and practices—which they use selectively and reflexively to foster strategies of action. Learned and accumulated over time and across borders, these strategies allow them to address the opportunities and constraints they face in the later phase of life (Swidler 1986, 2001).

Why Migrants from Taiwan

Focusing on older Taiwanese immigrants, this study excludes Han Chinese who relocated to the United States from other parts of the world, such as mainland China. Because the US government had no formal diplomatic relationship with the People's Republic of China between 1949 and 1979, most citizens of mainland China were legally prohibited from entering the United States during that period (Tseng 1995). Han Chinese immigrants from Taiwan, therefore, came to the United States decades before those from the mainland (H.-S. Chen 1992). I recognized this distinction as I started this project in 2010. Then, the first wave of mainland Chinese immigrants who had initially arrived as student migrants after the United States reopened its national gate to China were mostly in their early fifties and were too young to be considered senior migrants. In contrast, the life trajectories of immigrants from Taiwan allow me to trace the intersection of time, migration, aging, and life transitions over a significant number of decades, a span of time now possible for contemporary Asian immigrants generally.

Place of departure is important in analyzing the lives of immigrants. In line with other researchers (H.-S. Chen 1992; Tseng 1995), I use the term "Taiwanese immigrants" to refer to immigrants whose country of last residence was Taiwan, even though some were born in mainland China. Sending contexts involve many forces that encourage remaining or leaving and affect migration and adaptation in the host society. For example, research shows that many Taiwanese migrants establish or participate in their own commercial, political, cultural, and religious organizations, in addition to joining institutions whose members are from mainland China and Hong Kong (C. Chen 2008; H.-S. Chen 1992). Like other migrants, they engage in familial, political, and social activities in their homeland (Lien 2010; L. Wang 2007; Zhou and Tseng 2001).[3] Recognizing significant differences in Chinese and Chinese American communities, I therefore distinguish Taiwanese from other Chinese immigrants.

Taiwan resembles many East Asian and Chinese societies in that it has undergone profound economic, social, and cultural changes over the past decades (Lan 2018). Between the 1960s and the early 1990s, Taiwanese society underwent rapid industrialization, exceptionally high economic development, technological innovation, and a transition from an authoritarian to democratic regime (Feenstra and Hamilton 2014). Despite the slowdown in its economic growth since the late 1990s, Taiwan has implemented public benefits programs—such as its National Health Insurance (NHI), established in 1996, and its National Pension Insurance (NPI), established in 2008—for vulnerable populations (including senior citizens) (Chen et al. 2008; Lin 1997). Because Taiwan recognizes dual citizenship, many expatriates can access public benefits in their homeland. Taiwan thus provides an excellent case through which to examine the relationship between a changing homeland and the life course of its expatriates.

Older immigrants from Taiwan also capture the class features of many Asian newcomers to the United States, one of which is educational selectivity. This selectivity, in turn, has significant implications for their life chances and life trajectories. Many of my respondents evidence what Jennifer Lee and Min Zhou (2015, 6) term hyperselectivity among contemporary Asian newcomers: "what makes contemporary Asian immigration unique is that Asian immigrants are, on average, not only highly selected but also more highly educated than average Americans, despite the tremendous heterogeneity in their countries of origin" (Lee and Zhou 2015, 18). This hyperselectivity is particularly salient among Taiwanese immigrants in the United States, who, on average, have significantly higher levels of education than Chinese immigrants from other areas, with nearly two-thirds having completed at least four years of college (M. Zhou 2009). This educational selectivity profoundly shapes their social and economic incorporation into the US society. Rather than living in ethnic enclaves such as Chinatown, my respondents resembled other middle-class Asian immigrants, living either in predominantly white suburbs or in what Wei Li (2009) calls ethnoburbs, suburban areas with some features (e.g., goods, services, and people) of an ethnic enclave but without a single ethnic majority.

My respondents represent hyperselectivity in their pre- and postmigratory educational backgrounds, but few became members of the US middle class on their arrival. Rather, many experienced downward occupational mobility because their educational credentials from Taiwan were nontransferable or their English fluency was limited (Gu 2017). Most respondents reported that, when they arrived, their families were in a precarious financial situation and they were unprepared for wage differentials and differences in costs of living. Many, however, experienced significant class mobility within a single generation. These experiences, I contend, can deeply influence immigrants' self-perception, identities, and daily practices. The hyperselectivity of the older immigrants I interviewed intersects with the upward socioeconomic mobility they experienced in the United States, further orienting their assessment of family relations, community ties, and notions of citizenship, nationally and transnationally. Becoming American, in many regards, transformed their sense of who they are, where they belong, and how they position themselves in a transnational social field.

The US-Taiwan relationship also constitutes a unique transnational context (Levitt and Schiller 2004). The United States has provided Taiwan various forms of aid, including economic and military support between 1950 and 1965. Even after severing formal diplomatic ties with Taiwan and recognizing the People's Republic of China (PRC) as the only legitimate representative of China in 1979, the US government continues to play a key role in Taiwan's self-defense, and the US immigration system maintains separate quotas for immigration from Taiwan and mainland China. These historical-social contexts, as I discuss in chapter 1, explain the reasons many of my respondents first aspired to relocate to the United States. Taiwanese immigration thus merits special attention.

Studying Older Immigrants Who Stay and Those Who Return

This book compares aging immigrants who relocated to the United States in their earlier adulthood and stayed with those who returned to Taiwan after retirement. Although recent literature has documented variation among long-term immigrants' decision making about location later in life (Coe 2017a; Erdal and Ezzati 2015; Gilbertson 2009), this study is the first book-length study that examines similarities and differences between those who "age in place" and those who "age transnationally." These two groups by no means represent or capture diverse patterns among aging migrant populations. Research shows that older immigrants include people who migrate to reunite with children, to work abroad, and to pursue affordable care or lifestyles. They also include long-term residents in host societies, those who return after spending most of their working years abroad, and those who travel regularly between their home and host societies (King et al. 2017; Näre, Walsh, and Baldassar 2017). Nevertheless, studying aging migrants in the United States and their returning counterparts in Taiwan—all of whom migrated during adulthood—serves important theoretical and methodological objectives.

First, talking with aging migrant populations in different countries helps us triangulate their perspectives and avoid the limitations of "methodological nationalism" (i.e., treating the nation-state as the taken-for-granted unit of analysis) (cf. Wimmer and Schiller 2003). These multiple vantage points further allow us to examine the meanings that elderly immigrants in the United States and their return counterparts in Taiwan assign to their ancestral and destination societies. Second, examining the decision making of aging migrants who consider returning to their first home enables us to delineate the myriad dimensions through which these people conceptualize their later lives. This broader lens helps us better capture key factors that shape the processes of aging as migrants grapple with later-life transitions.

Analyzing two distinct groups, I do, of course, recognize the possibility of cross-border networks (Levitt and Schiller 2004). Indeed, aging immigrants in this study traveled regularly between their home and host societies, even as they spent most of their time in either Taiwan or the United States. Distinguishing immigrants who stayed from those who returned, however, allows me to trace the directionality of their cross-border activities, as they pondered important life decisions with significant economic and social consequences. Because both immigrants in the United States and returnees in Taiwan are physically present in a specific society most of the time, the transnational exchange of people, capital, ideas, information, and practices that mark their lives not only flows in different directions but also requires distinctly different management strategies.

Comparing immigrants in the United States with return migrants in Taiwan—two groups with long-term residence in the United States—highlights not only their differences but also their similarities. To be sure, immigrants in the United States and those who returned to Taiwan had made distinct choices. Such decisions typically have much to do with negotiating individual, familial, and social needs in a transnational resource environment (Levitt et al. 2017). Here, however, the two groups share similar life paths, having spent decades working, living, and raising families in the United States. They are thus embedded in a cross-border social field spanning the United States and Taiwan. Despite residing in different societies, therefore, all of these migrants can reflect on their long-standing relationship to US society. Indeed, for some, returning to Taiwan had produced a heightened sense of "foreignness."

Research and Organization for This Book

This book draws on qualitative data collected through multisite fieldwork in the United States (Greater Boston and New York) and in Taiwan, primarily between July 2009 and December 2013. I began my fieldwork with the Taiwanese immigrant communities in Boston and New York. (See appendix A on why I chose to study both Boston and New York.) Between 2009 and 2012, I conducted interviews with fifty-eight Taiwanese immigrants, all over age sixty. Of the immigrants I interviewed, twenty-seven were male, and the rest were female. Most had come to the United States in the 1960s and 1970s, though a few had arrived in the early 1980s. Their ages ranged from sixty to eighty-eight. Most had children who had grown up in the United States, and forty-six had grandchildren born and raised in the United States. I also conducted participant observation, becoming involved with numerous activities organized by immigrant organizations or immigrants themselves, such as hiking, Bible study, dinner parties, tai chi sessions, and dance classes. I made three return visits to some of my key respondents in 2014, 2015, and 2017.

My second field site was Taiwan. Between January and August 2010 and between September 2012 and December 2013, I interviewed fifty-seven returnees ranging in age from sixty-two to eighty. Of the return migrants I interviewed, twenty-nine were male, and the rest were female. All but two had children, and forty-eight had grandchildren born and raised in the United States. Most of the returnees I interviewed lived in downtown areas of metropolitan cities, such as Taipei and Kaohsiung. A few lived in rural areas, such as Hua-lien, Taitung, Chi-ayi, and Chunghwa. Most interviews took place in respondents' homes, where I took detailed notes of the pictures, books, magazines, trophies, slogans, and national as well as religious symbols (e.g., flags and crosses). I made three return visits to several key respondents in 2014, 2015, and 2016.

Drawing on these 115 interviews, I explain the strategies through which aging migrants manage intimate connections with families, friends, and governmental infrastructure involved in their intimate lives. Chapter 1 explores the ways temporalities of migration are manifest in the intimate lives of my respondents. There I address the temporal, structural, cultural, and contextual factors that shape their changing relations to home and host societies at different points of their lives. I illustrate the historical backgrounds against which these aging immigrants aspired to migrate to the United States and their perceptions of "America" and "American" in relation to Taiwan. I further chronicle their views of the American dream. Documenting their stories, I examine their assessments of transnational opportunities and restrictions and their changing notions of membership in home and host societies in later life.

Chapter 2 traces the trajectories through which aging migrant populations navigate temporalities of migration as they reconstruct intergenerational intimacy. Aging immigrants, I argue, transform cultural ideals of aging and family in response to changes in their social worlds across life stages. I therefore offer the concept of *reconfigured reciprocity* to analyze the processes through which aging immigrants fashion cultural logics of intergenerational relations to sustain connections with their children and their children's families. While a small portion of these older immigrants embraced ethnic traditions regarding elder care, most transformed reciprocal relationships with their immediate kin.

Chapter 3 analyzes the temporalities of international migration as they shape conjugality between older migrants and their spouses. The interplay among international migration, acculturation into US society, and experiences of aging motivates immigrants to reconstruct these intimate relationships. As I explain, most migrant couples transform their intimate connections as they encounter new contexts and new cultures. Migration to the United States sets the stage for these changes by affecting socioeconomic standing and connections to kin in the homeland. For example, immigrants' perceptions of Americanization shape gender hierarchies, and entering later life leads older immigrants to rethink gender norms. Citing egalitarianism as the dominant cultural feature of spousal relations in the United States, many respondents emphasized the importance of maintaining harmonious relationships with their spouses through mutual communication, coordination, and respect. Nonetheless, symbolic gender inequality persists and is often evident in private, backstage interactions.

Chapter 4 reveals older immigrants' strategies for "doing" grandparenthood that testify to the significance of temporalities of migration. I analyze the interplay between the time my respondents spent in the United States and their observations of the changing global economy, which leads them to assign new meanings to intimate relations with their grandchildren. Welcoming grandchildren to this world, my respondents developed new rights, responsibilities, obligations, and entitlements. This chapter underscores gender as an organizing principle that informs the division of labor between grandfathers and grandmothers. Older migrant women and men might both value grandparenting, but they interpret their responsibilities, obligations, and commitments to a third generation in gender-specific ways.

In Chapter 5, I focus on the ways temporalities of migration can be observed through my respondents' relations with their communities. Both respondents who remained in the United States and those who returned to Taiwan developed strategies to organize their social relationships. Engaged in social networks, they often grappled with belonging and community. My two groups of immigrants, however, adopted different approaches to their cross-border networks. Those in the United States "knew their place" within their social relationships, but returnees in Taiwan tried to reacclimate to the communities they had once left. This chapter compares the processes through which these two groups of immigrants maintained relationships that transcended national borders. Cross-border ties motivated them to rethink membership in transnational communities. Navigating complicated interpersonal dynamics, they anchored themselves in a time-migration nexus.

In Chapter 6, I use temporalities of migration as a conceptual tool to explain its manifestation among Taiwanese immigrants as they consider intimate relations with their home and host societies. Most salient, I argue, is the way my respondents reconsider their worthiness for "social care" provided by both the US and the Taiwanese governments. Most of my respondents constructed moral boundaries to govern their use of public resources. By denigrating other migrant groups, many not only attempted to justify their right to government-sponsored entitlements for senior citizens but also claimed moral superiority over other newcomers. Temporal variation, however, offered some of these migrants new options and resources for organizing their lives across national borders. Specifically, public benefits programs—such as health care in Taiwan—offered older returnees a new means for overcoming the difficulties they had encountered in the United States. Given that they had spent most of their working years contributing to the United States rather than Taiwan, however, many returnees faced negative critiques in Taiwan and needed to justify their receipt of governmental support.

The book's concluding chapter revisits the concept of temporalities of migration, to consider the ways in which aging immigrants anchor themselves in a transnational social field. I review the mutual processes that shape temporalities and migratory experiences and their connections with the organization of intimate relations at the individual, familial, communal, and state levels. I also underscore the need for reassessment by scholars, applied researchers, and policy makers seeking institutional responses to the needs and desires of aging migrant populations.

EMIGRATING, STAYING, AND RETURNING

Older immigrants—in both the United States and Taiwan—assign meanings to emigration, immigration, and return migration by reflecting on their shifting priorities across life stages. Vesting their commitments in two places, they enact an *economy of belonging* to evaluate their needs, wants, and visions of themselves as they articulate material and symbolic motivations for emigrating, settling abroad, and returning. Here, the term "economy" differs from "economics" and goes beyond the production, distribution, and consumption of goods and services. Rather, my use of "economy" refers metaphorically to the criteria that not only structure people's feelings, emotions, and perspectives but also suffuse their behaviors and practices. This notion of economy of belonging extends what Arlie Hochschild (1989) called "economy of gratitude" and what Allison Pugh (2009) termed "economy of dignity." Hochschild uses economy of gratitude to examine the gendered standards with which couples measure and foster emotional responses to the division of labor at home, and Pugh (2009, 7) utilizes economy of dignity to analyze the ways "children collect or confer dignity among themselves, according to their (shifting) consensus about what sort of objects or experiences are supposed to count for it."

Building on these foundational works, I define economy of belonging as the evolving criteria that the respondents relied on to evaluate their own and their loved ones' social, cultural, and emotional well-being and sense of membership across life stages. These older migrants, I argue, constructed an economy of belonging mediated via temporalities of migration. The opportunities and constraints that they navigated in their transnational social field intersected with their needs, dreams, and desires at different points of life. These shifting concerns explain their reasons for emigrating to the United States when they were younger and, for some, account for a decision to settle in different places later in life. In other words, how migrants decide where to settle is by no means a cost-and-benefit calculation in a financial sense. Rather, temporalities and place/space are complexly intertwined, further shaping the ways in which older migrants made sense of their home and host societies and planned their life prospects at different life stages.

The interplay between temporalities and migration, as central to an economy of belonging, complicates current analysis of cross-border ties. To date, the relationship between temporalities and place remains understudied, even as the ways in which migrants develop connections to places have been the central focus for scholars of international migration (Ang 2001; Hall 1993; Levitt 2001). As the anthropologist Lok Siu (2005, 4) contends, the development of transnational attachment requires migrants to sustain "a sense of connection to both where one is from and where one is" and to become "part of a larger collectivity of people who share the same sense of displacement from a homeland and emplacement elsewhere in the world." Temporalities, however, further shape migrants' social, cultural, and national belonging. This chapter explores these processes by tracing the reflections of older Taiwanese migrants as they consider their goals, visions, and priorities across time and across borders. This investigation thus "illuminates the ways in which historical events and circumstances have affected the life experience of different age groups" (Hareven 1994, 438), highlighting ways the economy of belonging evolves and reconfigures at different life stages.

These older Taiwanese migrants constructed an economy of belonging across four different time-migration configurations: (1) the period before coming to the United States, (2) arrival in the United States, (3) working and child-rearing years, and (4) later phase of life. The immigrants I met had a sense of imagined belonging to US society before they arrived. For them, US support to Taiwan between the 1950s and 1970s, global mass media, and their interpersonal connections with earlier migrants had shaped an understanding of US society as superior to Taiwan. After their arrival in the United States, however, these Taiwanese immigrants adapted their sense of belonging to acclimate to life in both the United States and Taiwan, especially as they encountered US racial and ethnic hierarchies. As they began to raise children and establish careers, economic success and class mobility justified their decision to migrate. At this stage, the meanings of geographical and class mobility were intimately connected, and their desires to succeed as newcomers were salient characteristics of their working and child-raising years. Later, however, they reevaluated their social membership in relation to both the United States and the evolving structural and cultural features of

Taiwan, which profoundly shaped their decision to stay or return. Perceptions of home and host societies thus point to the myriad ways in which aging migrant populations construct their notions of belonging within the nexus of time and place. For them, the meanings of the United States and Taiwan not only change across time but also twist and turn alongside an evolving transnational social field.

Indeed, the respondents spanned a wide range of ages. While some were in their sixties and belonged to the group of so-called young old, some were in their eighties and beyond. Respondents of different birth cohorts may have unique life experiences as well as life paths because they grow up during different periods. At the same time, the older migrants I studied also shared important historical and collective memories about their situations and struggles nationally and transnationally. These memories, which might be selective and illusory, point to the social forces and cultural frames that mediate their construction of economy of belonging through the complex interplay between temporalities and place/space.

Before Emigration: Imagining an Ideal Future Home

Before arriving in the United States, the respondents constructed social belonging based on both their dissatisfaction with Taiwan and their imagination of US society. At the core of this time-migration nexus, idealization of life in the United States, together with an aspiration to migrate, featured prominently. When younger, these immigrants had struggled to create better professional, familial, and social environments for themselves and their children. The unique relationship between the United States and Taiwan further affected how the respondents envisioned their destination. While still in Taiwan, most had possessed vague but idealized notions about life in the United States, typically viewing the United States as economically prosperous, politically powerful, and socially progressive. With this view, they saw emigration as a wise decision.

Taiwan from the 1950s to the 1980s

As many respondents reported, Taiwan was still an underindustrialized, agricultural society when they left, and the United States presented a clear contrast. Those who came as international students typically regarded relocation to the United States as an opportunity to pursue professional careers. Those who came as economic migrants, with or without the sponsorship of family members, often saw the United States as a place for the easy accumulation of wealth. With the value of one US dollar equal to about forty New Taiwanese dollars between the 1960s and early 1980s, many of these respondents assumed that even a meager income in the United States might be readily converted into considerable wealth in Taiwan.

The oppressive political regime in Taiwan further motivated many Taiwanese immigrants. After losing its battle with the communist government and withdrawing from mainland China to Taiwan, the Kuomintang government imposed strict control over freedom of speech (Jacoby 1966). From 1951 to 1988, authorized by martial law, the Kuomintang government forbade new political parties and regulated news agencies and institutions. Even forty or fifty years later, many of the respondents still talked emotionally about their insecurity, anxiety, and dissatisfaction with the political situation in Taiwan. For them, it was as if these events had just happened. Migrating to a more democratic society in the 1960s, 1970s, and 1980s had offered a chance to escape their oppressive homeland.

Mr. Chen, who had relocated to the United States in his midtwenties during the mid-1960s, was in his midseventies at the time of our interview. He reported that one of his classmates in college had "disappeared" after criticizing Chiang Kai Shek (then president of Taiwan) for taking a third term. Mrs. Ma, in her midsixties and living in a middle-class neighborhood at the time of our interview, expressed continued despair that her brother had been arrested and sentenced to death in the 1970s, after having been accused of involvement in "antigovernment" activities. Mrs. Wei, a middle-class return migrant in her seventies, also recounted social and political oppression in 1970s Taiwan. She described feeling constrained and regulated in every aspect of her life. After graduating from college, she had immediately sought liberation by pursuing further study in the United States. "Taiwan was still under martial law [before we left]," she explained. "We did not have any freedom of speech in Taiwan. Zero freedom of speech. And everything in the newspaper was one-sided. You could not hear anything opposed to the government. You could only hear what the government wanted you to hear and think what the government wanted you to think. We felt really upset. I felt that someone was even spying on every breath I took. It was very constraining. And I felt that the only way was to get out of there."

Fear of discussing politics and public affairs in Taiwan between the 1950s and the 1980s had contributed to doubts about the fairness and integrity of Taiwanese society in general. According to the respondents, personal connections to political power, rather than skills and qualifications, had been the key to success in this period. Mr. Chang, in his seventies and recently retired from a prestigious biotechnology company in Boston at the time of our interview, recalled political elites in Taiwan manipulating a system rife with nepotism. For him, the need to use *guanxi* (personal connections) with people in power had been a factor in his decision to migrate forty years earlier, after finishing his PhD. Mr. Chang believed that living in a more democratic and meritocratic society could enable him to better realize his potential without undue worry about politics. Because he came from a family with few connections to powerful people, he had been skeptical about making a successful career back home.

Mr. Lee—a return migrant and successful businessperson who had moved from New York back to Kaohsiung in 2004—shared with me his observations of the ways some colleagues in Taiwan in the 1970s had manipulated their connections to obtain a position or get promoted. Even though he was very proud that he had managed to join his employer and perform well without turning to personal ties, he had decided to apply for a green card and move to the United States. He had become tired of consistently unequal treatment and unfair evaluation, which he attributed to an acutely felt but invisible tension between *benshengren* (native-born Taiwanese) and *waishengren* (Chinese who came with the Kuomintang government from mainland China to Taiwan in 1949). Waishengren, especially those with connections to government officials, he explained, were often at the top of a hierarchy:

> Back then, very few people without guanxi could enter [the company]. You definitely had to have some connections in order to enter that company. A lot of them were either waishengren with privileged backgrounds or people with connections to the Kuomintang government. A lot of them were siblings or children of the officials. There were only three Taiwanese people who did not have connections in that company. I was one of them. Unlike those people who had connections, we had to work really hard. Those people fooled around all day as if taking a vacation. You know, Taiwanese society was like that back then.

In contrast to native-born Taiwanese, the waishengren among my respondents were less critical of corrupt practices, nepotism, and ethnicity-based privileges in Taiwan. Instead, they placed more emphasis on their "outsider" status and corresponding vulnerability. Many of these mainlanders expressed ambivalence about whether Taiwan was truly their "home" and whether local people there might sincerely accept them as equals or peers. As "migrants" in both the United States and Taiwan, they had seen emigration as a route to broader career opportunities. As a return migrant, Mrs. Lam maintained,

> I think most mainlanders of our generation had the experiences of feeling dislocated. Unlike many native-born Taiwanese, we don't have an ancestral home that we can return to. Many native-born Taiwanese people have an ancestral home that they can return to during Chinese New Year. We don't. Our ancestral home and ancestral tomb are so far away. We also don't have a lot of land that our ancestors passed on to

us. We have to depend on ourselves because we don't have heritage passed on from our ancestors. A lot of mainlanders of our generation have an American dream. It is easier to survive or accomplish something in the United States because it is a wealthier country.

The oppositional relationship between Taiwan and mainland China, especially the fear that the communist regime in China might declare war against Taiwan, constituted another factor that had encouraged many of the respondents to leave Taiwan. War was a common theme among those who had witnessed World War II and/or experienced the civil war in China. Many remained traumatized by those experiences. The prospect of another war had thus been a source of anxiety pushing many of these immigrants overseas. For instance, the bombarding staged by the People's Republic of China (PRC) against Kinmen, one of Taiwan's outlying islands, in 1958, assured some respondents that China had never given up trying to take Taiwan by force. The shaky diplomatic ties between Taiwan and other countries during the 1970s had also made many afraid that Taiwan had lost international allies and might be isolated if war took place. With Taiwan's loss of membership in the United Nations in 1971 and the severing of diplomatic ties by the United States in 1979, which in turn established a formal relationship between the United States and the PRC, many respondents experienced an intensified sense of insecurity. By migrating to the United States, they had tried to avoid the afflictions of war for themselves and their families.

The educational system in Taiwan was another reason for overseas migration (Chee 2005; Ong 1999). Many of the respondents had been worried about the negative effects of Taiwan's educational system on their children. Those who had raised children in Taiwan pointed to the limited number of colleges and universities as a source of cutthroat competition for postsecondary schooling. Many were therefore worried that their children would be either trapped in a cycle of endless studying for exams or denied access to colleges altogether. Migrating to a country with a better-developed educational system, they had believed, would be a more desirable option for their children's academic and professional development (M. Zhou 1998).

Social Roots of an American Dream

The respondents reported that, before emigrating, they had imagined the United States as an international superpower where people enjoyed economic prosperity, political freedom, access to educational resources, and national security. Looming large in their premigratory images of US society was not only an escape from the structural constraints that Taiwanese society imposed but also a vision of a "better" life in the United States. Three key contextual factors during this historical period shaped the ways in which the respondents idealized the United States: US government support for Taiwan, global media and popular culture, and information conveyed through transnational networks.

Many respondents vividly remembered the various forms of support that the US government had provided for Taiwan from 1950 to 1965. Most had been children or adolescents, but they recalled loans, grants, food, expertise, and technological support for Taiwan's economic and social development. Before the United States established formal diplomatic relations with the PRC, the US military had maintained bases in Taiwan, a measure intended to prevent the intrusion of the mainland communist regime. Such generous material resources and military support had led many respondents to believe the United States to be a superior country.

Mrs. Chen, who owned and lived in a colonial house in a middle-class neighborhood, remembered the economic challenges of the 1960s. Support from the US government, she recalled, was not only indispensable but also a clear indicator that the United States was more economically and socially prosperous than a "third-world society" like Taiwan. "The US government provided us with a lot of resources, like dry milk, flour, and butter," she elaborated. "Back then, when we told people that we were moving to the United States, most people were really envious. Many people thought Taiwan was full of constraints and that America was like a land full of gold. There were opportunities everywhere in the United States. So Taiwanese people back then tended to think that if we came to the United States and worked hard enough, we could freely pursue what we wanted and easily succeed. That is what is called the American dream, isn't it?"

The presence of the US military in Taiwan between 1951 and 1979 also informed the respondents' collective memories. For older immigrants, Taiwan's infrastructure for US soldiers had stimulated interest and adoration for an American lifestyle. Mr. Liu remembered listening to the Armed Forces Network Taiwan—a radio station intended to serve the US military—which had been an important way he learned English during high school and college. Listening to the Armed Forces Network Taiwan had also exposed him to US culture. While still a high school student, he developed an interest in US professional sports, which, as he explained, later became an important part of his family life:

> When I was little, I always listened to the radio station for the US soldiers in Taiwan. They had various shows that introduced news, music, and sports on the radio. I think it was called American Forces Network Taiwan. It was an all-English channel. I listened to that channel to learn English and started to become interested in professional baseball in the

US. Back then, there was still no professional baseball league in Taiwan. And I always dreamed about watching baseball games in the US. Since then, I have been interested in professional baseball in the US. I am a big fan of the Red Sox. My wife and I just went to Fenway Park to watch a game yesterday.

What Arjun Appadurai (1990) calls global cultural economy further provided many of the respondents with materials for constructing an American dream. Before leaving Taiwan, they had some exposure to US popular culture in the form of music, television shows, and movies. Although the mass media representations of the United States were partial and even unrealistic, my respondents had relied on these cultural sources to construct their perceptions of US life. Mrs. Guo, who had lived in Boston for more than forty years, maintained that, as a teenager, she had relied on broadcast mass media to imagine life in the United States. Influenced by movies, she had often imagined the United States as a more civil, modern, and progressive society, especially compared to Taiwan. "When I was still in Taiwan," she recalled, "I very much enjoyed watching movies. I went to the movies all the time. . . . I watched lots of [US] movies like *An Affair to Remember* and *For Whom the Bell Tolls*. Watching these [US] movies made me feel like the United States is like a wonderland. It's so progressive and modern in every aspect, especially in comparison with Taiwan at that point. Taiwanese society was really backward then, and Taiwanese people's lives were difficult in general. We did not have fancy cars, clothes, high-rise buildings, and arts like those in the American movies."

Similarly, Mrs. Gui, a return migrant in her sixties, reported that her exposure to US popular culture, along with the support that the United States provided for Taiwan, had shaped her perception of the United States during her high school and college years in Taiwan. By observing and absorbing the images she watched on TV, Mrs. Gui had fostered an idealized image of US society and a fancy lifestyle that, she explained, she could not afford but could hope to pursue:

> Back then, my impression of the US mostly came from TV shows and movies. I remember everything in the movies was so pretty, and the girls were always nicely dressed and looked so graceful. . . . Since then, I thought living abroad seemed really good. Particularly, I always dreamed about living in the US. In comparison with other countries like Britain, Spain, Germany, or France, moving to the US seems like the most reasonable and ideal option for us. . . . And I even remember, one day after reading a geography textbook, I had a dream at night that I finally got to visit the US. . . . Then I woke up and realized I was not in the US. It was a dream.[1]

Information transferred through transnational social contact had offered the respondents important clues for picturing their prospective lives in the United States. Even hearsay from family members, friends, and acquaintances had led them to envision better lives after emigration. Mr. Tseng, in his seventies at the time of our interview, commented that, because of accounts from family and friends before he arrived in the United States, he had always assumed that earning money was much easier. "Before we came to the United States, we always heard people describe the United States as the place full of gold," he told me.

> We had a friend, Mark, who was an immigrant in the US and returned to visit Taiwan. And he donated one million Taiwanese dollars to his high school. He was not even in the US for that long. It seems like he moved to the US and suddenly became so rich. And he also told us that our kids would receive a better education in the US. And it's easier to enter prestigious colleges in the US. He told us that students in the US did not have homework and did not even have to bring books to school!

The information that Taiwanese immigrants gained from their cross-border connections was obviously partial and inaccurate. As many respondents joked, after working in the United States for many years, they realized that making a fortune was much more difficult than they had expected. Some also admitted that other aspects of their premigratory impression of the United States turned out to be wrong. Mr. Fong described thinking about opening a Taiwanese ice cream store in the United States, where he and his wife could serve their coethnics. He had a brother who ran an ice cream store in Taiwan and could teach him to make Taiwanese ice cream. But family members in the United States had then told Mr. Fong that cold weather keeps people from eating ice cream in winter, and he gave up learning to make Taiwanese ice cream and thus missed the opportunity to start his own ethnic business. "Before I came to the United States," he explained, "I called my family members here and asked for some information. Back then, I knew very little about life in the US. I thought about learning how to make Taiwanese cuisine ice cream before leaving in order to start a family business in the US. But I called my older sister in New York and asked her opinion about it. I still remember my sister told me, 'New York is so cold in winter. Who is going to eat your ice cream?' But now you can see there are ice cream stores in New York everywhere."

By contrast, Mr. and Mrs. Chao, a return migrant couple, both in their mid-sixties at the time of our interview, had restarted their business in New York. But the experience had led them to realize that making a fortune in the United States was not as easy as they had imagined. Before migrating, they had operated their own plumbing and electric maintenance company in Taipei and had drawn a fairly comfortable income every month. They had assumed that, because they were already very experienced and an increasing number of Chinese people lived in Greater New York, that they would have no problem reestablishing their business and making a profit. When they tried to set up their company, however, they came to recognize the limitations of their social networks and the business niche that they had depended on in Taiwan. Making a living and supporting a family in a new society, they realized, would not be as easy as they had imagined.

Some of the respondents did not expect to settle in the United States. As Yen Le Espiritu (2003) contends, migration is about both decision and indecision. Many respondents I interviewed did struggle in their younger years as they decided whether to stay or leave. Mr. Wu, an immigrant who had come to the United States as an international student, reported that he thought about moving back to Taiwan after receiving his PhD but ultimately stayed, surprising himself when he realized he had lived in the United States for more than forty years. "When I left Taiwan, I thought I was just coming here for two years for my master's degree," he recounted. "Then I thought perhaps another three years to get my PhD degree. I always felt like one day I would go home and I would reunite with my family members [*sigh and a long pause*]. I kind of wanted to stay and kind of wanted to return. I was prepared to stay, but I was also not prepared to stay at the same time. Then forty years passed." Like Mr. Wu, Mrs. Hung, a return migrant in her midsixties, remarked that she could not believe that she had spent forty years in the United States. When she was younger, she had been busy with work and family, but she had always thought that she would move back to Taiwan when all of her "missions" were done. When she finally relocated to Taiwan with her husband, she was in her sixties.

After Arrival: Encountering an Unequal Promised Land

A growing awareness of their subordinate status in the United States informed the economy of belonging, through which respondents assessed their social membership. Even if they had understood, prior to departure, that life in the United States would be different, the difficulties were greater than they had anticipated. Many described their arrival as a journey full of struggle. Central were encounters with inequalities that transformed their perceptions of the United States. On the one hand, most respondents deemed many features of US life modern, civilized, and progressive, especially in comparison to Taiwan at the time. On the other hand, they quickly realized that they had become part of a "racial minority" after setting foot in the United States (Espiritu 2003; Kim 2008; Roth 2012).

Some reacted strongly against stereotypes of Chinese immigrants, often those living in Chinatown, which they found disparaging.

After their arrival, most of these immigrants felt tension between their admiration for US superiority and their status as social outsiders. They continued to be impressed by the degree of modernization and "civilization" in the United States. Mrs. Chou, who had come as an international student in the 1960s, told me that she was amazed both by how modern San Francisco was and by the countercultural "hippie" lifestyle in Oakland, California. From her perspective, the modern buildings of San Francisco symbolized prosperity, and the hippie culture represented the pluralism and liberalism of US traditions: "I still remember that, when I arrived in San Francisco, my sister and husband came to pick us up. When we went over the Bay Bridge, we were so impressed. I was like, 'Wow, how could a bridge be so magnificent and so impressive?' I felt like this is just a great country. Then we went to the Berkeley campus, and we saw a lot of hippies on University Avenue. Their hair was so long. We were initially shocked but felt—'Wow, the US society is such a liberal society.' This really broadened our horizons."

Similarly, Ms. Ho, who had moved back to Taiwan in 2008, reported that she was very impressed by the arts education that she received in the United States in the 1960s and 1970s. Unlike Taiwan, she maintained, US education encouraged students to think independently and creatively. Referencing a painting course that she took in Boston, Ms. Ho depicted the United States as a progressive, liberal, enlightened society fundamentally different from Taiwan:

> Education in the US is really creative and teaches students how to think independently. I remember that I took one painting course at [name of university]. When I took painting courses in Taiwan, we always learned how to copy previous work or the teacher's own painting. Yet my professor at [name of university] just asked us to go to [a neighborhood] and draw whatever we liked best, using our own creativity. I also remember one class was about sketching a naked model. A girl came in and took off her coat. Then she was completely naked in front of us. I was shocked and could not even look at her, and my classmates asked me why I did not draw. I had a lot of enlightening and liberating experiences like that in the US.

Despite their admiration of US society, the respondents also faced racial inequality compounded by their status as newcomers. Encountering the racial hierarchy in the United States made them acutely aware of white privilege and caused them to wonder where they fit in the binary black-and-white classification system. Mr. Chang, in his seventies with completely gray hair, told me that after arriving in the United States in the mid-1960s, he was confused about defining his "race" in the US context. He had then been very poor and unable to afford a flight, so he took a boat first to Seattle, which took about three months, and then went on to Boston by bus. This bus route was meandering but was the cheapest ticket that he could find back then. The trip also had led him to consider his place in the US racial classification system. "I remember taking a Greyhound bus from Seattle to Boston," Mr. Chang explained.

> Most of the passengers were white. Then we went through Nevada and Alabama. When we arrived in Alabama, there were some black people getting on the bus. When the bus stopped in Texas, I went to the bathroom. I noticed the bathrooms were divided into white and colored. There were two bathrooms for white and two bathrooms for colored. One of them was for men, and the other was for women. And I did not know which bathroom I should use. I was not white or black. I was worried whether somebody would beat me up if I entered the wrong bathroom. Back then I did not know this was so-called racial discrimination. I finally decided to use the bathroom for the black people. On the bus, white people sat in the front, and black people sat in the back. I did not know where to sit, so I sat in between. I started to think, "What's going on, and where do I fit?"

In addition to confusion about racially and ethnically positioning themselves, many of the immigrants I interviewed had encountered unfriendly treatment. While the respondents often could not be exactly sure whether a hostile attitude could be regarded as racial discrimination, they did ask themselves whether they would have been treated better if they were white. Mr. Wang—a biologist trained in the United States who had moved back to Taipei in 2003—recounted white superiority as an implicit attitude. Although he was a recognized scientist in his own field, he still felt ranked, socially and culturally, below white Americans. "Sometimes racial discrimination is really subtle and [*long pause*] invisible," Mr. Wang reflected.

> It is not always explicit. It can be a very implicit, very subtle form of discrimination. Somehow you feel discriminated against, and somehow you feel like you have no evidence for it. Yet a lot of times, you have negative feelings about a certain situation. It might be the way someone looks at or interacts with you or the tone with which someone talks to you. . . . A lot of times, you wonder is it me or is it because I am an Asian? Like if a white American and I were both qualified for a job, would people prioritize the white person?

How the respondents arrived in the United States played a key role in facilitating the socioeconomic incorporation of respondents into US society. Unlike respondents who had come to the United States as international students, those who had come with the sponsorship of family members or as economic migrants typically reported more experiences of explicit racism. Respondents who had come to reunite with family members and to search for work had typically lacked opportunities to receive professional training in the United States and so lacked relationships with elite institutions or people outside their ethnic communities. Mr. Lin, who had owned a Chinese restaurant in Boston, bitterly told me that, while immigrants who came to the United States as international students had the chance to pursue advanced degrees, his job offered few opportunities to gain educational credentials or even improve his English, which might have led to a more prestigious job. Instead, white, native-born Americans paid attention only to his Chinese accent and failed to appreciate his hard work. In the eyes of most Americans, he assumed he was a just a diligent but "cheap worker who spoke terrible English," as his story illustrated:

> When I came to the United States, I worked in a club for three months. The manager there was originally from Germany. I remember telling him, "I'm sorry. I don't speak English well." And he told me, "I want you to work, not to talk!" You know what I'm saying. That means that the boss wanted you to work and doesn't need you to communicate much. So a lot of immigrants came here for work and did not have chances to speak English. But some Americans discriminated against our English, picking on our accent! How did we ever have the chance to speak English?

The stereotypical assumption that the Chinese should—or do—prefer to live in Chinatown further complicated the respondents' perceptions of themselves in the United States. For many, Chinatown evoked stalled mobility as well as cultural isolation from mainstream US society. Those who had come to the United States as international students expressed a particularly strong sense of resentment toward the image of Chinatown and sought to distance themselves and their families from people living there. As the historian Xiaojian Zhao (2010) documents, many (upper) middle-class and professional-class immigrants of Han Chinese descent have avoided Chinatown. One of Zhao's respondents, Kathy Yan, who came from Taiwan with her husband in 1967, recalled it as a "weird" time when "every Chinese was seen as associated with Chinatown" (Zhao 2010, 57): "One of my American friends got into the habit of passing on information about Chinatown events to us. I eventually told her that we didn't like Chinatown at all—I hated the way it smelled, and I didn't even care for the grocery there since my son wouldn't eat Chinese food. She was very surprised. She thought all Chinese are the same—that's frustrating!"

Like Zhao, I found that migrants who had come as international students and stayed to join the US middle class perceived Chinatown as the opposite of the American dream. They could eat and shop there, but they were reluctant to envision a future in an ethnic enclave associated with low-wage work and limited opportunities. Some who had briefly worked or resided in Chinatown were more neutral but nonetheless had moved away when their economic situations improved. Many of the respondents sought to create a category of Taiwanese or ethnic Chinese with communities elsewhere. More often than not, respondents' comments about Chinatown were infused with views of a cultural hierarchy.

Mrs. Hung, a return migrant who had moved back to Taipei in the mid-2000s, had lived in both Houston and New York City. She associated Chinatowns in both cities with economic, social, and cultural backwardness and had been unwilling to eat, shop, work, or see doctors there. Chinatown, she suggested, appealed to Chinese immigrants from other geographical areas. While talking with me in her modern apartment in one of the most expensive areas in downtown Taipei, Mrs. Hung stressed that "unlike the old and shabby houses in Chinatown," she and her husband used to own a Victorian-style house in a wealthy, predominantly white neighborhood near Boston.

My respondents also referenced dialect to differentiate themselves from residents of Chinatown. Mrs. Gao, in her early seventies, highlighted the linguistic differences between Taiwanese immigrants like her and Cantonese-speaking residents in Chinatown. For her, these differences were not neutral but marked a clear status hierarchy:

> These Cantonese-speaking Chinese can be really mean and rude. Typically, we think manners are important, right? For example, when we went to Chinatown, we need to line up, right? Back then, a lot of them did not stand in a line. Or sometimes we were waiting for a parking spot, and they just interrupted. If you chew gum, you should wrap it in your own tissues and bring it home. I mean, you need to change yourself and adjust to this society. When we tried to argue with them, they yelled at us in Cantonese. This is a kind of courtesy, you know? People should pay attention to courtesy.

Without considering differences in premigratory status and socioeconomic origins, Mrs. Gao focused on cultural features, such as language, and framed Chinatown as a place lacking in civility. By positioning herself in opposition, Mrs. Gao not only represented herself as someone with better manners and social skills but also distinguished the behavior in her community from what she had witnessed in Chinatown. These claims point to her anxiety to prove her deservingness in the context of racial discrimination and misrepresentation.

Settling, Working, and Establishing a Family: Class Mobility and Its Limitations

The respondents' desire to attain class mobility for themselves and their families was central to their construction of an economy of belonging at the juncture between their earlier adulthood and arrival to the United States. To maximize their own—and often their children's—life chances, these immigrants relocated and pursued upward social mobility. Like other Asian immigrants (Lee and Zhou 2015), many employed class-based resistance strategies to confront the disjunction between presumptions of white American superiority and cultural associations with Chinatown as shabby and lower class. Their aspirations thus constituted the defining feature of an economy of belonging, which my respondents had typically constructed after arrival, during time spent working and raising their children in a foreign society.

Taiwanese immigrants could not circumvent the white-dominated racial hierarchy in the United States, and so they regarded their markers of upward social mobility—income, education, neighborhood residence—as evidence that they were not inferior to white Americans. Mr. Zhang, in his sixties, connected his motivation to attain class mobility for himself and his family with his status as a foreigner: "When we were younger, we had the ambition to prove ourselves to the US. We wanted to prove that we were as good as white people. So we forced ourselves to speak English. We wanted to let Americans know we are well-educated and capable people, although we are not from here." Winning recognition from the mainstream society, he emphasized, had been important for him earlier in life. By the same logic, Mr. Ning—a return migrant in his seventies who had moved from Los Angeles back to Kaohsiung in 2004—reported that even after he had been granted US citizenship in the 1980s, he had never felt fully accepted in US society. Rather, because he was a foreigner, he had felt the need to outperform his white colleagues. "We are not white. We are foreigners," he admonished. "We have to perform better than those Americans. We have to work harder. I remember I got a bad job evaluation one year. It's really unfair. I thought it was other team members that conspired to give me a bad evaluation for no good reason. I knew I was a foreigner, and Americans might think they could have an advantage over me. So I tolerated it back then, and I decided to work harder."

Many of the immigrants I interviewed had sought to use their class position to dissociate themselves from other ethnic Chinese populations. Phenotypically similar to other Chinese people, some had relied on class markers to distinguish themselves. Mr. Chiang, in his midsixties, maintained that as a younger man, he had sought to perform well, both academically and professionally, to prove that Taiwanese people are exceptional and not like the Chinese "trapped in Chinatown."

Like her husband, Mrs. Chiang had intentionally become an active member of her local community when her son was still in primary school. Her efforts had given her a sense of achievement and allowed her to feel capable of forging pathways into the mainstream United States and joining the respectable "social elite." "When my kids were still in school," she recounted, "I was a volunteer worker. My husband and I were helping Boy Scouts. We were both team leaders. School teachers and the principal knew me very well. I was the only Taiwanese and even the only Asian doing this back then. Of course, I was very proud of myself. I was an immigrant, but I could tutor American kids and help American teachers. Then people would know that people from Taiwan are outstanding."

These attempts to be socioeconomically incorporated into mainstream US society and escape the stereotype of Chinatown informed decisions about where to live. The respondents reported preferences for living in predominantly white areas, and most went to Chinatown only when necessary (e.g., when shopping in the Chinese supermarket or getting a haircut). Moreover, living in an upper-middle-class, predominantly white community facilitated their children's pursuit of education. Whereas many of the respondents did move up socioeconomically, they still lacked a sense of complete social membership in the United States. Despite taking on what they perceived to be middle-class American values, habits, and lifestyles, most of them felt like social and cultural outsiders. This sense of "outsider status" often focused on phenotypical features and was, in this sense, racialized. Emphasizing that they did not look and act "white" enough, they believed they had become only hyphenated, rather than authentic, Americans.

Mr. Chang retired from work and lived in Greater Boston with children holding high-status professional jobs. Yet even after living in the United States for many decades, he still wondered whether he could define himself as a "pure American." "I am a legal American citizen," he reported. "I speak their language, read their news, and interact with their people. However, if I look at my own face in the mirror, I know I am different. I look different. I don't look like one of them. I am still Taiwanese. . . . [In Taiwan] I never thought about that. Everyone's skin color in Taiwan is the same. Coming to the US made me realize, 'Oh, I am a racial minority.'" Like Mr. Chang, Mr. Tam—a businessperson who had relocated to Kaohsiung in 2005—saw his status as an immigrant of color limiting his incorporation into mainstream US society, even though he had lived in the United States for more than thirty years. He elaborated, "I felt like I was assimilated into US society in a lot of ways. But my head and my emotions are just not fully assimilated. I still feel like a foreigner. Of course, a lot of my American coworkers were very nice to me, and many of them were decent too. Yet they are white, and we are not. They are superior white people. They have clear senses of superiority. You can learn that by hearing them talk and interact with you. Even though their ancestors are immigrants from other countries, they still have a sense of superiority."

Encounters with the class structure and racial assumptions that pervade US society had not only challenged these Taiwanese immigrants' original perceptions of the United States but also transformed their understanding of Taiwan. Their experiences of dislocation and being a foreign-born racial minority in the United States provided the context for sustaining emotional and cultural connections to the homeland to which they felt close and to which they felt they belonged. The respondents reported missing Taiwanese food, family members, friends, and the familiarity of language, lifestyles, and popular culture. While they still regarded the United States as more socially and culturally advanced than Taiwan, they no longer framed Taiwan as a place they desired to leave but instead stressed their desire to see its improvement and progress. Once in the United States, therefore, these migrants developed and maintained diasporic ties to Taiwan.

Mr. Wu, an immigrant in his seventies at the time of our interview, reported that coming to the United States caused him to start appreciating the ways Taiwan had nurtured him in his young adulthood and set an important foundation for his life:

> MR. WU: I often make this comparison. Taiwan is like my mom. Yet after I grew up, I got married to my wife. Yet I am still concerned with the well-being of my mother. This analogy captures my relationship with Taiwan.
>
> KS: OK, but why mother rather than father?
>
> MR. WU: Because I think mothers are greater than fathers. . . . We were born out of our mothers' bodies. Mothers can be compared to our homeland that breeds us. It's more like what mothers do.

Mr. Wu's analogy softened the image of Taiwan. He framed Taiwan not as an island of problems and corruption but as a place of emotional warmth and connections. Even the respondents who criticized Taiwan as politically repressive and socially reactionary had ceased to see it as a society from which they wanted to escape. Instead, Taiwan had become the home and country that they would like to help, and their dissatisfaction had become the reason for continuing to care about its future. Mrs. Tsai, an immigrant woman in her sixties, described reading about the Kuomintang regime and wanting to work for political transformation in Taiwan. "I remember reading some information on Taiwan in the United States," she recalled. "This antigovernment information was forbidden in Taiwan then. I was crying when reading this information. I had not found a job back then. I read a lot of information about how the Kuomintang government killed people and censored speech. I feel like Taiwanese people were screwed for no reason. I told my husband we need to stage a war to liberate Taiwan; we need to stage revolution. My husband was like, 'Why don't you get a job soon to distract yourself a bit.'" Situations change people's views. Living somewhere foreign—together with new experiences accumulated overseas—had quickly prompted immigrants like Mrs. Tsai to look at their homeland in a different way. Taiwan quickly shifted from a place my respondents wished to escape to a place they missed. The sense of dislocation, coupled with the hostility that many immigrants encountered in new societies, contributes to the formation of racial, ethnic, and diasporic identities (Bashi 2007; Espiritu 1996; Kibria 1994). This phenomenon was evident in the accounts of Taiwanese immigrants I interviewed.

Transition to Later Life: Staying, Returning, and Uncertainties

The economy of belonging evolved again as the respondents transitioned to a later life stage, further shaping their perspectives on home and host societies. For many, entering later life was accompanied by changing needs, goals, and priorities and represented a new crossroad between temporalities and migration. Most respondents claimed that, to a significant extent, they had accomplished the goals they had set when deciding to migrate. Some even considered themselves and their families the embodiment of an American dream that makes class mobility possible through hard work and God-given talent. Many cited their assets, accomplishments, middle-class lifestyles, and children's academic and professional successes to illustrate why they believed they had fulfilled the American dream through their own efforts and hard work. Yet many were aware that, after decades of modernization, Taiwan was no longer the homeland they had left behind. As these aging migrants assessed their needs and desires, the constellation of resources, nationally and transnationally, profoundly shaped their sense of social membership, further influencing their decisions to stay (or ambivalence about staying) in their host society. Both immigrants in the United States and returnees in Taiwan positioned themselves in relation to the changing structural, cultural, and contextual features of sending communities as they considered where to settle in the later phase of life.

Remaining in the United States

For most immigrants in the United States, living in their adopted country for so many years had led them to establish a new sense of belonging and become accustomed to its way of life. For example, many immigrants—especially those who came initially as international students and later joined the professional class—preferred to live in suburban areas of the United States rather than in densely populated cities in Taiwan (such as Taipei). Their long-sustained familial and social ties in the United States—children, grandchildren, in-laws, and close friends—made them reject the possibility of moving back to Taiwan. To be sure, many of these immigrants regularly traveled to Taiwan to visit family and friends. Some took advantage of retirement and even stayed for a couple of months at a time. Few, however, thought that they would like to return to and settle in Taiwan. While Taiwan was the ancestral home that they missed and remembered, the United States was the new home they had struggled to establish. Returning to visit or even staying for an extended period might be fun and exciting, but returning permanently was both undesirable and unrealistic.

Some immigrants also no longer recognized the Taiwan that they remembered. Finding material life in Taiwan significantly improved since the economic take-off in the late 1980s, they felt that Taiwan had lost many important traditions and values they held dear. They were therefore no longer comfortable with the idea of living in their ancestral society, although they occasionally returned to visit family and friends. Mrs. Liang, in her midsixties, explained, "We lived on [a road] in Taipei where . . . there were farms and ditches beside our house. Now they have all become high-rise modern buildings standing beside the asphalt road. When we left Taipei, there was no Rapid Corporation Transit System [subway] either. The subway in Taipei is really convenient and well networked. It is so much cleaner and so much more comfortable than that in New York. Yet we also feel that Taiwan has become so chaotic. The air is so polluted. The traffic is terrible, and the drivers are crazy."

Living in the United States for many or most of their working years complicated my respondents' relationship with Taiwan. Many claimed that taking on what they perceived as US values and practices might cause trouble if they sought to resettle in contemporary Taiwan. Mr. Yang, in his sixties, described experiencing culture shock. Rather than feeling comfortable and excited when visiting Taiwan, he had found his home country too materialistic. "Well, I personally think I am so Americanized I cannot return to Taiwan," he elaborated. "As a matter of fact, every time I return to visit Taiwan now, I have a cultural shock. I can give you numerous examples of how I don't fit in the current Taiwanese society. . . . A lot of people [in Taiwan] were like frogs at the bottom of a well [*jing di zhi wa*] [referring to people who are narrow-minded and have limited worldviews]. There are so many rich people in the US, but they are just not as demonstrative as those newly rich Taiwanese people." This sense of superiority that many respondents expressed is influenced by both their migration trajectories and their class standing in the United States. Those who had achieved a middle-class lifestyle attributed their success to hard work and distinguished themselves from nonmigrants for having suffered and "finally made it" despite being a racial minority in another country. In contrast, the working-class immigrants I interviewed rarely criticized Taiwan in the same ways. Rather, they frequently mentioned their sense of inferiority when encountering older friends, classmates, colleagues, and family members who had managed to accumulate considerable wealth without emigrating. As Mr. Fong reflected,

> We came to the United States and thought that we could have a better future here. But now a lot of our old friends and classmates who did not migrate are also doing very well. Some of our friends started their own business. Some of our friends made a fortune by investing in stock or the housing market. Some of our friends own really fancy cars and apartments in downtown Taipei. And today the value of real estate in Taipei is also skyrocketing. It's no longer like the time when we still lived in Taiwan. Given our income, we could not afford to buy an apartment in Taipei City. We moved to the US when we were younger, and then we ended up living a life worse than people who did not migrate. What is the point of moving back to Taiwan?

Mr. Fong's reflections vividly illustrate the role of social class in immigrants' considerations about returning and settling in Taiwan. Unlike their middle-class or professional-class counterparts, working-class immigrants like Mr. Fong could not brag to their family and friends in Taiwan about their lives in the United States and instead worried that they might be considered "losers" if they returned. Like their better-off counterparts, working-class immigrants were also concerned about reintegrating into contemporary Taiwan. Spending many working years in the United States, in their view, had changed their cultural disposition and heightened their sense of outsider status in their homeland culture.

Returning to Taiwan

The return migrants I met had developed perspectives on the changing features of contemporary Taiwan that were different from the views of their counterparts who had stayed in the United States. For returnees, the resources and opportunities available in Taiwan helped to reactivate connections to their homeland, encouraging them to move back. Some had used changes in Taiwan to create an environment where they could construct the lifestyles they wanted. Some had used resources available in Taiwan to provide for the care they or their spouses would need in later life. Acknowledging the evolution of Taiwan, some sought to prompt further changes in their homeland. A few had moved back because they needed to care for older generations, usually living parents or parents-in-law. My respondents' different narratives all justified a decision to return home and constituted strategies to reincorporate into sending communities and secure their well-being at a later stage of life. Their decision making reveals a variety of trajectories through which returnees (re)confirm their membership through a distinctive time-space configuration, choosing to spend the last days of life in a changing homeland.

One group of respondents was motivated by a desire to pursue a lifestyle that they felt possible only in Taiwan. For them, contemporary Taiwan had become both modern and traditional, and many highlighted such developments as public transportation and efforts toward environment conservation, traditional elements of culture like food and language, and the relatively low cost of living. Taiwan, they maintained, had become safe, secure, and convenient. Much like postretirement "lifestyle migrants," who try to maximize their physical, psychological, and social well-being across borders (Bolzman, Fibbi, and Vial 2006; Gustafson 2001; Sunil, Rojas, and Bradley 2007), they also differed in their desired way of life.

Mr. Xia, in his seventies, reported that the decision to move back to Taiwan was mostly practical. He and his family had moved to the United States primarily because he disliked Taiwan's educational system, which he described as one-dimensional and oppressive, and he wanted his daughters educated in the United States, where the system could better develop their individuality and creativity. His relationship with Taiwan was social and cultural. He emphasized that life there was easier because he could enjoy the language, weather, and food that he preferred. Now home, he vividly described "easy access to so many traditional Taiwanese foods" and no need to "eat bread, salad, or pizza as I used to when I was still working" [in the United States]. Mr. Xia further talked of his emotional attachment to Taiwan. He had lived in the United States for more than two decades and was naturalized as a US citizen, yet he still identified himself as a Taiwanese citizen with a stronger sense of belonging to Taiwan. He used the Chinese idiom "falling leaves return to their roots," to describe why he thought an older person like him should eventually go home. He had returned after his youngest daughter graduated from college and had settled in a rural area because, he said, "the largely undeveloped landscape in [the town] reminds [him] of [his] childhood and youth in the preindustrialized Taiwan."

While Mr. Xia pursued what he perceived to be a traditional Taiwanese life, he also recognized that Taiwan had changed. At the time of our interview, he lived in a modern apartment in a rural area. This type of housing, according to Mr. Xia, was not available when he left for the United States and was drastically different from the shabby flat he had occupied during his young adulthood. Now he lived within a ten-minute walk of a major medical center with a staff of doctors, advanced equipment, and high-quality services. He also praised the convenience of public transportation that he used when visiting friends and relatives in metropolitan cities such as Taipei and Kaohsiung, even though public transportation was not well developed in the area where he lived. Thus, for Mr. Xia, returning to his homeland offered a combination of the traditional and the modern with which he could organize the life he desired.

Another group, comprising about three-fifths of the respondents, had sought myriad types of transnational support. These return migrants differed from lifestyle migrants in both their physical needs and the constellation of resources available to them. Whereas lifestyle migrants had returned to convert their economic capital into a comfortable lifestyle, care seekers were concerned primarily with using their financial resources most efficiently to meet their everyday needs. For them, the availability and affordability of aging-related facilities in Taiwan—the institutions and programs that serve the elderly—were attractive factors that motivated their return and resettlement. As many reported, aging-related facilities were uncommon when they left for the United States. Because of demographic aging, however, market-based elder care had become increasingly common and a popular lifestyle option among middle-class Taiwanese families since the 1990s.

For many of the respondents, the emergence of facilities to support aging in Taiwan provided a satisfactory solution to many of the problems of later life. Mrs. Chin, in her seventies, was widowed when her husband passed away about thirty years earlier and had relocated to Taiwan to settle in an assisted-living facility. At the time of our interview, she could not walk without a walker and sometimes relied on her wheelchair to move around. She told me that she had lost much of her mobility after unsuccessful spinal surgery in the United States and thus needed other people to help with her activities of daily living. Like many return migrants, she not only accepted but also embraced her independence from—rather than dependence on—the next generation. Instead of living with her children or moving into assisted living in the United States, Mrs. Chin had come to Taiwan as a strategy for better managing her everyday life. In this way, she resembled many older migrants who accept cultural differences between Taiwanese/Chinese communal culture and the US valorization of individuality. She thus welcomed the development of assisted-living facilities in Taiwan, which allowed her both community and self-sufficiency.

Mrs. Chin had clearly compared the differences between assisted living in the United States and Taiwan. She told me that, because of her savings and income, she was disqualified from living in government-funded nursing homes in the United States and would have had to spend more than eight thousand US dollars per month for an assisted-living facility in Chicago, where she used to live. In contrast, by choosing to move to Taiwan, she could live in a spacious, one-bedroom apartment in a high-end assisted-living facility that cost her only about one thousand US dollars per month. Beyond the services there, she spent approximately five hundred US dollars per month to hire a domestic worker to care for her. Assisted living in Taiwan was clearly financially advantageous, but for Mrs. Chin, it was also culturally desirable. In a nursing home in the United States, she explained, she would have had to "tolerate" American food, such as hamburgers, salads, and sandwiches, but in Taiwan she was offered a variety of traditional Taiwanese and Chinese meals.

Apart from hands-on physical care, Mrs. Chin praised the availability of public health care in Taiwan, which was established in 1996. By way of contrast, the marketization and privatization of health care in the United States had left her with a strong sense of economic and social insecurity. She was a naturalized US citizen and was qualified for Medicare, the public health insurance system for Americans aged sixty-five and over. But Mrs. Chin preferred Taiwan's National Health Insurance (NHI). In Taiwan, she explained, the fees were lower for the same services, such as physical therapy, and the NHI covered more services, including dental and eye care. Most important, for her, was the ease of communicating with medical professionals in Taiwan. Although she considered herself fluent in English, Mrs. Chin resembled other immigrant newcomers (Holmes 2013; Shim 2010) in her frustration approaching American doctors about her medical problems and had difficulty understanding some complex medical terminology. This sense of frustration reached a peak after her spinal surgery went badly. By contrast, she felt comfortable talking, even chatting, with her doctors, nurses, and physical therapists in Taiwan.

To be sure, the health conditions of return migrants who seek care in Taiwan vary widely. While some of the returnees I interviewed could barely sustain themselves, others could readily manage their daily lives. Mrs. Chin's situation, however, clearly illustrates the myriad, complex ways in which return migrants could acquire care and construct a safety net through both market forces and state support. While not all of the respondents sought as much help in Taiwan as Mrs. Chin, her experiences speak to the constellation of resources available for returnees who seek care and the comparative context in which they decide to return home.

About one-fifth of the respondents had decided to return because they wished to bring about change in Taiwan. As self-appointed "social reformers," they had particular agendas or sought to function as a bridge between Taiwan and the United States. Many were professionals seeking to use their accumulated knowledge, experiences, and overseas networks to help Taiwan. When younger, they had put a premium on hard work and establishing a career, to prove themselves socially and professionally in the United States. Once established, however, they had begun to reflect on their connections to Taiwan and wondered what they could do for the place that had raised them. Taiwan, in turn, has been eager to secure a global niche, and, as in other industrialized Asian societies, its institutions, such as hospitals, universities, and research centers, have sought to capitalize on the internationally recognized expertise of migrants willing to return. Expatriates who established themselves as experts in academically and intellectually oriented fields in the United States have thus been recruited as highly valuable resources by elite Taiwanese institutions.

Mr. Shen, in his sixties, had accepted a position as chief of the psychiatry department at a major hospital in Taiwan in the mid-2000s. In the 1970s, he had gone to the United States as an international student and stayed after acquiring his PhD. Mr. Shen maintained that during his twenties and thirties he had been mostly concerned with proving to his American colleagues—most of whom were native-born white men—that he, as a foreign-born member of a minority, was competent. Mr. Shen underscored his ongoing emotional attachment to Taiwan, even while he had lived living in the United States, and noted that he often thought about what he could do for his homeland. His sense of social belonging to Taiwan intensified as he entered his forties and grew even stronger as he grew older. In his fifties, therefore, he had decided to spend the remainder of his working years in Taiwan, in part because he had already "had a great career and accomplished things" in the United States and in part because he believed Taiwan was more in need of his expertise. Mr. Shen asserted that he had worked even harder after moving back to Taiwan because he strove to lessen the intellectual and technological gap between his professional communities there and in the United States. He had made this sense of duty manifest in the significant time he spent keeping up with recent research and practice in US medicine and advising younger colleagues, junior scholars, and students. After almost three decades in the United States, he felt a commitment and a responsibility to cultivate his professional community in Taiwan and to help his younger colleagues "succeed."

Of course, not all the return migrants I interviewed returned for new career opportunities. Some lacked formal positions in Taiwan but still found ways to contribute to their homeland by participating in various forms of civic engagement, such as social movements and charitable or educational activities. These returnees felt they had more to contribute to Taiwan than to the United States, and their contributions made them feel more empowered in later life. Mrs. Yeh had come to the United States with her husband in the 1970s and lived there for approximately forty years. After moving back to Taiwan with her husband in 2007, she dedicated her time to helping underprivileged children. When we met, Mrs. Yeh had been teaching English and math on a weekly basis at an orphanage for about five years. Articulating her feelings about deciding to return, she clearly believed she could contribute more to Taiwanese than to US society:

"In the US, we could probably only do things like donate money or help at a food bank. Yet in Taiwan, we could teach English and math in orphanages and elementary schools, helping those kids in need. Because we gave the prime of our lives to American society, we wanted to do something for Taiwan in our later life, too."

Unfinished caregiving responsibilities in the homeland could further complicate returnees' decisions. Among the respondents, a small group had relocated to Taiwan, at least in part, because they needed to care for older family members, usually parents or parents-in-law in their late nineties and early hundreds. One return migrant couple had moved back to provide care for the father on the wife's side, and two other couples had relocated to care for the mother on the husband's side. One divorced returnee had moved back to Taiwan to look after her mother. These women and men shared a similar commitment to supporting their parents or parents-in-law, but their household division of labor remained markedly gender based. Mrs. Bai is a case in point. She and her husband acknowledged that she performed most of the care for her mother-in-law, but Mrs. Bai also told me that she often felt exhausted from her workload. Especially frustrating was assuming responsibility for her mother-in-law's care after having cared for her children earlier in life. For returnees who had relocated to Taiwan to care for aging relatives, women, no matter their relation to the person in need of care, were typically the family's primary caregiver.

Ambivalence and Uncertainties

Most of the immigrants I interviewed spent most of their time in one country and traveled to visit their family members and friends in another. A few, however—both in the United States and in Taiwan—revealed ambivalence and, potentially, a future change of plan. Several respondents told me that, after they were finished with various commitments in their respective countries, they would begin to consider where they wanted to spend the rest of their lives. Commitments that, for the moment, delayed these decisions included helping their family and community members, caring for grandchildren, and serving in an organization.

Mrs. Yang, in her midsixties and living in the United States, was busy helping her daughter care for her children at the time of the interview. Against this backdrop, Mrs. Yang believed that it was infeasible for her to consider relocating to Taiwan before her grandchildren started school. Mr. Shen, a return migrant in his sixties, reported that he might consider moving back to the United States after he retired from his work in Taiwan. None of these respondents, however, was sure about whether and when they might relocate. As Mr. Shen told me, "One thing I learned as a lifetime migrant is 'never say never.'"

Changing health conditions were the primary rationale for considering another move. Some immigrants reported that the relatively affordable health care facilities and services available in Taiwan could be the motivation for relocating. Several return migrants, however, were concerned about their deteriorating health, and although they thought they could access affordable, quality health care in Taiwan, their children were pressuring them to return to the United States. Mr. Dai, a return migrant in his midseventies, had been diagnosed with motor neuron disease in Taiwan and reported that he received good care, with support provided by his wife and her siblings, public health insurance, and the Filipino domestic worker he hired to care for him and his wife. He did not think that he would want or need to move back to the United States and did not want to become a burden that his children would have to manage. Yet Mr. Dai told me that his children complained about having their parents halfway around the globe and worried that he might die alone there. Thus, he was under pressure to move closer to his children.

This chapter offers the concept of economy of belonging to analyze the processes through which older Taiwanese immigrants negotiate their sense of membership in sending and receiving communities. Central to this concept is the intersection of place and time—what I term temporalities of migration—which shaped the respondents' desires to move to and stay in a particular society at different points of life. The ways in which these migrants developed connections to changing structural realities in their home and host societies are indispensable to understanding their decisions and struggles about where to migrate and settle at different life stages. While this research focuses on migrants from Taiwan, similar experiences could be found in aging populations in different geographic regions, including Europe, Africa, and other parts of Asia (Coe 2017b; Hunter 2011; Toyota and Thang 2017; Zechner 2017).

This research highlights the ways in which the historical connections between the United States and Taiwan shaped my respondents' aspiration to emigrate. Most had constructed their image of the American dream long before setting foot on US soil. Many factors had provided material and symbolic resources through which they claimed US superiority over Taiwan, among them US support to Taiwan between the 1950s and 1970s, global media as sources of information, and prior contact with other Taiwanese immigrants. Before visiting the United States, many had believed that, compared to Taiwan in the 1960s and 1970s, the United States was both materially more abundant and socially more progressive. Thus, they believed that migrating to the United States would be better for them and, importantly, for their children.

Only after arriving in the United States did my respondents experience a clash between their dreams and their lived realities. The American dream that they had imagined was typically challenged by social currents of hostility toward newcomers of color. Many felt constrained by the structural reality of white domination and the constraining image of Chinatown, with its relative poverty and ethnic stereotypes. In this context, many Taiwanese immigrants aspired to class mobility as a form of resistance to perceived white superiority and Chinese stereotypes. Therefore, the narrative of "successful" struggle for upward social mobility—including hard work and the next generation's educational accomplishment—was central to my respondents' accounts of their experiences at an earlier life stage.

Later in life, my respondents started to assign new meanings to their home and host societies. Many no longer felt that they needed to prove themselves in US society, especially given their various accomplishments. Simultaneously, they found that decades of industrialization, modernization, and globalization had remade Taiwan, which was no longer the place they had left. Against this backdrop, many aging immigrants began to rethink their social membership in both the United States and Taiwan and grappled with deciding where to spend the rest of their lives.

Although they were long-term migrants that had lived in the United States for three to five decades and shared many demographic features, the respondents employed different strategies to pursue the ideal later life they desired. Those who stayed in the United States still considered Taiwan their home, even though they considered themselves and their families integrated into US society. Most possessed strong emotional attachments to their homeland, despite having rejected relocating to Taiwan permanently and believing they would have trouble adjusting to its contemporary environment. In contrast, most returnees in Taiwan cited their decision as the best use of the resources available to them there. For return migrants, changes that had occurred in Taiwan provided opportunities to combine both modern and traditional components of their homeland in later life. Nationally and transnationally, these Taiwanese immigrants evaluated their welfare, together with the welfare of their families, as they aged. Temporalities of migration are thus key to understanding the ways migrant populations of similar ages and similar ethnonational backgrounds make distinctive decisions about where to settle.

RECONFIGURING INTERGENERATIONAL RECIPROCITY

To date, scholars of migrant families have demonstrated that relationships within intergenerational households are changed and challenged in the processes of international migration and globalization (cf. Foner 2009; Foner and Dreby 2011; Lamb 2009). These scholars highlight the reconstruction of values and practices within migrant families across generations and social worlds (C. Chen 2006; Shih and Pyke 2010). Rather than empirically examining their relationships with younger generations, however, most studies still treat older people as family dependents (Treas 2008). At the same time, a few recent studies have challenged the underlying assumption that older migrants are guided mostly by ethnic traditions inherited from their home societies, however long they have stayed in the host societies (e.g., Coe 2017a; Lamb 2009; Purkayastha et al. 2012). This body of research cautions us to reconsider assumptions about the "unassimilability" of older generations, further suggesting that aging migrant populations actively fashion reciprocal relationships with younger generations, both transnationally and in host societies.

In this chapter, I trace the trajectories of older immigrants from Taiwan to the United States to analyze the processes through which these aging migrants reconstruct norms of intergenerational reciprocity. Manifestations of what I term temporalities of migration explain the ways they manage ethnic traditions governing intergenerational relations. While some try to sustain intergenerational reciprocity, most immigrants transform cultural ideals of aging and family in response to the changing contexts of their lives. Building on existing research on reciprocity (Hansen 2005; Nelson 2005), I offer the concept of *reconfigured reciprocity* to analyze the processes through which aging immigrants fashion logics of reciprocity—rationales that can be invoked to govern the ways group members perceive, give, and ask for support.

Like many nonmigrants (Cohen 1998; Lamb 2009; Lock 1993), the immigrants I interviewed grappled with adapting, negotiating, and changing intergenerational relations as they grew older. Their reconfigured practices of reciprocity, however, differed from norms of native-born Americans. Through the interplay among subjectivities, temporalities, and migration—the social, cultural, and psychological processes through which they learn to be legitimate members in different social and cultural contexts—respondents selectively learn and strategically address changing intergenerational relations across time and national borders.

Older immigrants' assessment of family relations is undoubtedly biased or selective, and their understanding of receiving and transnational contexts might be stereotypical or oversimplified. Complex factors (e.g., industrialization, economic restructuring, declining fertility rates, cultural globalization, emigration/immigration, women's participation in the labor market, and changing educational systems) account for shifting power dynamics in families around the globe (Klinenberg 2012; Lan 2018). Largely unaware of complex structural forces driving social changes, many immigrants exaggerate their partial observations of cross-cultural differences (e.g., Americanization or US culture of elder care) without noticing similarities between Chinese and American families. The accounts of my respondents, however, reveal views of elder care that guide their feelings, emotions, and decisions. Rather than debating whether or to what extent their claims are questionable, this chapter analyzes the construction of their subjective realities by delineating the cultural logics behind the narratives that older immigrants craft about themselves and their children. Their perceptions of changing intergenerational intimacy, I argue, are strategies used to anchor themselves emotionally and symbolically in the context of social and generational change.

The ways in which my respondents negotiate ethnic tradition regarding geriatric care need to be situated in relation to the Chinese concept of "filial piety" (*xiao dao*). For many scholars, Confucian notions of filial piety are the framework for intergenerational dynamics in Asian and Asian American families (Kibria 1993; Lan 2002; Sun 2012). In traditional Chinese culture, filial piety is both a system of reciprocal rules governing power and the exchange of resources within Chinese households (Greenhalgh 1988) and a culturally enforced norm of parental authority passed from one generation to another (Blieszner and Hamon 1992). According to the concept of filial piety, children—especially sons and daughters-in-law—are supposed to shoulder the physical and emotional care of aging parents. Daughters-in-law in Chinese families typically are the primary caregivers for elderly persons, but many daughters also feel culturally obligated to take care of their own aging parents (Lan 2006). Filial piety also requires respect and deference to parental authority (C. Chen 2006, 579). In traditional Taiwanese and Chinese families, aging parents have power over their children and over family affairs. Within immigrant families, however, the complex interaction between time and migratory experience can change the power dynamics between younger and older generations.

Two Tales from the Field

On an afternoon in late fall, I was conducting an interview with Mrs. Gao in her house, located in a middle-class, predominantly white neighborhood in a suburb near Boston. Mrs. Gao had moved to her current residence after her husband relocated to an assisted-living facility. Mrs. Gao told me that she and her husband had dreamed about traveling around the world after their children finished college, but she had never had the chance to fulfill this dream because her husband had developed Alzheimer's disease soon after their youngest child graduated from college. After trying to care for her husband at home for an extended period, Mrs. Gao felt exhausted, and her health had significantly deteriorated. Reluctantly, she carefully selected an assisted-living facility for her husband, sold her previous house, and purchased her new place close to her husband. She visited him as often as possible, even though he did not recognize her most of the time.

Mrs. Gao told me that when she began to live alone without her husband's company, she felt extremely insecure and was often anxious at night. To dispel the silence and lessen the darkness, she would turn on the TV and all of the lights. Despite the difficulties of living alone, Mrs. Gao was adamant that she did not want to cohabit with her children and their spouses. She was worried about her own health deteriorating to the point that she could no longer take care of herself, but she insisted that "every smart old person should learn how to care for themselves rather than depending on their children." For Mrs. Gao, anticipating or asking for care from her children, who had been born and raised in the United States, risked losing her own autonomy and making her children miserable.

On another afternoon during early summer, I was conducting an interview with Mrs. Chin—whom we met briefly in the previous chapter—in her room located in a high-end old-age home in Taipei, Taiwan. Mrs. Chin had moved with her husband to the United States in the 1970s and, like many Taiwanese immigrants of her generation, had dreamed of a better life. Unfortunately, her husband had been diagnosed with cancer and passed away several months after receiving his PhD, and Mrs. Chin had become a single mother striving to make ends meet. Mrs. Chin had then decided to stay in the United States rather than move back to Taiwan, so her children could receive what she believed would be a better education. She told me that, as the only breadwinner, she had been cautious about spending money and sacrificed certain pleasures, such as visiting her friends in California, whom she had not seen over her more than thirty years in the United States. Despite economic hardship, Mrs. Chin was proud that, with her support, all of her children had graduated from elite universities. But she had believed that her life would become easier once her children finished college and that she would finally have the time and money to explore the United States. Once again, however, misfortune came unexpectedly. After unsuccessful back surgery, she had lost most of her mobility, and although a lawsuit later provided a significant settlement, she had paid her attorney, given money to her children, and relocated to Taiwan. Mrs. Chin considered herself supportive of her children and did not want to "become a selfish mother who burdened the children" at a later life stage.

To address the difficulties of biological aging, Mrs. Gao and Mrs. Chin had made fundamentally different decisions: Mrs. Gao to age in the host society, Mrs. Chin to move back to the homeland. Yet they shared a resolution to remake intergenerational reciprocity. Instead of viewing their children as default caregivers, they fostered new ways of thinking and new strategies to find the support they needed to sustain themselves and protect their loved ones.

Transforming Ethnic Tradition

Unlike Mrs. Gao and Mrs. Chin, few of the immigrants I interviewed were widowed, and many, together with their spouses, enjoyed good health at the time of the interview. Most neither expected nor required their children to be their primary caregivers. Even if, like Mrs. Gao and Mrs. Chin, they had concrete needs that their children might meet, they were highly reluctant to turn to younger generations. The respondents thus changed and challenged the reciprocal norms of aging and geriatric care within traditional Chinese families. Instead of anticipating support from their children, they expressed strong desires to be self-sufficient, independent "American parents" or "parents for American(ized) children."

The experiences of these immigrants challenge the notion that elderly persons are the keepers of ethnic culture. Rather, these accounts underscore their efforts to negotiate and contest norms of aging and geriatric care across social worlds. Studies of international migration tend to focus on later generations— often described as "the new second generation" in the immigration literature— grappling with the tension between mainstream US society and expectations from ethnic communities (Kibria 2002; Lee and Zhou 2015). In contrast, older migrants, even those who had relocated at an earlier life stage, are often assumed to be oriented toward their ancestral cultures, functioning as self-appointed guardians of cultural heritage in their destination countries (cf. Gardner 2002; Treas and Batalova 2007). Scholars of international migration thus tend to downplay, if not completely overlook, the possibility that aging migrants might transform ethnic traditions.

This oversight is particularly salient in research on intergenerational relations in migrant families, which typically highlights the worldviews of aging migrants that shape their relationships with later generations (Shih and Pyke 2010). For instance, in their studies of the living arrangements of Chinese and Japanese elders, Yoshinori Kamo and Min Zhou (1994, 556) have emphasized that "[many elderly migrants] are still holding on to their own cultural traditions regarding extended family, filial responsibility, and kinship support for elderly family members, even if they have lived in the United States for a long time or even if they were born in the United States." In her review article on aging and intergenerational relationships, Tamara Hareven (1994, 440) has similarly asserted that "ethnic values rooted in various premigration cultures call for a more exclusive dependence on filial and kin assistance than the more contemporary attitudes, which advocate reliance on supports available from government programs and community agencies." These pioneering studies do shed light on the influence of ethnic tradition on migrants' perception of family and kin support, yet scholars rarely pay equal attention to the changing structural contexts that might lead aging migrants to reconstitute their expectations. The assumption that older generations lack agency to fashion social practices and cultural expectations can then limit scholarly understanding of changing subjectivities across social worlds (Lamb 2009).

Only a few studies have hinted at transformative experiences across borders. Judith Treas (2009) has found that many older immigrants to the United States disavowed their roles as authority figures in their families. Yuri Jang and her colleagues (2008) have found that, whereas 19 percent of seniors in Korea expressed willingness to enter a long-term care facility, 44.7 percent of older Korean immigrants to the United States were willing to do so. As Katherine Newman (2003, 205) has astutely observed, being exposed or even acculturated into the mainstream United States shapes the ways in which aging Hispanic newcomers in the inner city rethink the cultural norms of intergenerational reciprocity: "Reciprocity across generations, particularly in the more traditional Latino communities, implies that the favor will be returned. When parents grow old, the children they have 'raised right' will care for them in exchange. Yet this expectation is complicated by the influences of modernism, the intergenerational autonomy that is normative in the American middle class."

These studies point toward the concept of reconfigured reciprocity to explain new ways of thinking that (re)orient feelings and expectations of geriatric care across generations and social worlds. Reconfigured reciprocity represents a practical attitude in response to what Vern Bengtson and his colleagues (2002, 568) call ambivalence: "the contradictions we experience in our intimate social relationships." Like many American-born parents heavily influenced by individualism, older immigrants may no longer expect the hands-on care provided by their children at the expense of their own autonomy and dignity (Pyke 1999; Rosenmayr 1968). Among the respondents, a few older Taiwanese immigrants did wish to depend on their children, and some accepted and even embraced the intergenerational reciprocity embedded in traditional Chinese culture. But most had transformed their ethnic tradition of elder care and sought instead to sustain self-sufficiency without becoming a burden to the next generation. Three distinct dimensions reflect the effects of myriad temporalities on views of reciprocity among these immigrants: (1) relationships with prior generations, (2) assessment of the next generation's situation, and (3) perceived acculturation into receiving and sending societies.

These older migrants' connections to their own parents influenced the ways they position themselves within a cultural ideal of family caregiving. Not having looked after their own parents, many of my respondents had undermined their own sense of entitlement to receive care from younger generations. Furthermore, they assessed their children's resources and constraints—time, money, and physical as well as emotional capacity—to rethink the feasibility of maintaining ethnic traditions, and they had applied their understanding of US society to adopt different modes of aging. Long-term residents in the United States had thus relearned parenting for their "American" children. Although their interpretation of US culture was partial, they evoked Americanization as a new cultural schema to interpret changes and challenges—such as the erosion of elder-care traditions and the loss of parental authority—they encountered in later life. Grappling with the tension between modernity and ethnic traditions, they reconstructed norms of intergenerational reciprocity to pursue a dignified later life and sustain connections with their children and their children's families.

Minority Perspectives: Maintaining Reciprocity

Only eight of the migrants I interviewed, among them three returnees, cohabited with their children's families and received hands-on care and material support from them. These respondents claimed that living in the United States for decades had not changed their views of intergenerational relations. Rather, they embraced the ethnic tradition of intergenerational reciprocity and expected their children and their children's spouses to be their primary caregivers in later life. This interpretation of the ways American families operate—adult children leaving home at age eighteen, becoming independent, and feeling little obligation to care for aging parents—is problematic. In fact, many older people in the United States receive various forms of care—money, information, driving, company, and hands-on care during a parental health crisis—from their children and grandchildren when they are in need (Lamb 2017). Immigrants like Mr. Fang, however, still contended that children's caregiving responsibility for older parents differentiated the Chinese from the American family. Chinese families, he believed, should operate differently. Because Mr. Fang and his wife had devoted much of their time, money, and attention to their children and because they had endured many difficulties to raise their children in the United States, he felt he could expect gratitude and care at later stages of life.

To Mr. Fang, relationships among Chinese family members were far more interdependent than in most American families, and Chinese parents tended to do more for their children's families than most American parents he knew. At the time of the interview, Mr. Fang and his wife lived in his house with his son, daughter-in-law, and their grandchildren. This arrangement, he believed, not only saved his son from paying rent or a mortgage but also enabled him and his wife to provide "free" childcare and domestic services for his children's family. Mr. Fang also planned to have his son inherit his house and most of his money. He commented, "After we've done so much for our son, what is wrong with expecting him to care for us one day when we are not mobile? This is what Chinese families do for each other." Given his contribution to his son's family, Mr. Fang felt it reasonable for his son to provide physical care for his aging parents.

Mr. Ruan, in his seventies, faced a slightly different situation, living with his two daughters after a car accident had left his wife severely injured, with multiple fractures and deteriorating health. Mr. Ruan and his daughters agreed that living together would be the best option because taking care of his frail wife would be beyond his capacity. His wife had passed away, however, by the time of the interview. Nonetheless, because he too had lost much of his mobility, Mr. Ruan remained with his daughters and relied on them for various forms of assistance (e.g., cooking, driving, cleaning, and helping to get around). He appreciated their efforts and enjoyed the time he spent with them, walking in the neighborhood or watching Taiwanese television over the internet. Yet he also emphasized that an elderly Chinese person relying on children was "natural." He had "filial daughters," he explained, stressing that his daughters had inherited filial piety from his homeland.

Majority Perspectives: Reconfiguring Reciprocity

Overall, most of the respondents I interviewed had transformed ethnic traditions regarding intergenerational reciprocity. They did so by critically reflecting on the interplay between long-term migration and various intimate relationships. These relationships include respondents' changing connections to their own parents, their offspring, and their home and host societies.

Relationships with the Previous Generation: Unfulfilled Responsibilities

First, that most had not provided hands-on care for their parents tended to undermine any sense of entitlement and pushed them to adapt alternative expectations of their children's caregiving responsibilities. Even those who hoped their children would be able to provide some form of support when they were no longer able to sustain themselves remained ambivalent about any moral right to care. For about four-fifths of respondents, the experience of migrating to the United States had caused them to rethink their children's obligations.

For example, Mrs. Huang, an immigrant in her sixties, maintained that she very much regretted not taking care of her parents in Taiwan. As she recounted, her parents had become very ill about thirty years earlier, just as she and her husband had settled in the United States. To care for her aging parents, therefore, she had been forced to rely on her siblings and her siblings' spouses, especially her sister-in-law, in Taiwan. Although Mrs. Huang reported that her siblings were understanding and supportive, she still felt sorry, even guilty, for contributing little to the caregiving that her parents had needed. She thus had no moral right to expect her children to look after her later in life, as she contended.

> Fortunately, I had a lot of siblings [in Taiwan]. They took care of my parents back then. My brothers and sisters took turns taking care of my parents. My parents lived with my younger brother. My sister-in-law is especially great; she took good care of my parents. The only thing I could do is fly back and visit them. . . . [*Sigh*] After we settled . . . after we became permanent residents, my mother was already pretty ill. She had serious diabetes, which caused multiple strokes. She was in bed for most of her later life. So I felt really sorry that I was not there for her. My parents actually never saw my house in [this city]. It is one of my biggest regrets. . . . A lot of times, I think that if I didn't even take care of my own parents, then how can I expect my children to take care of me?

Like Mrs. Huang, many older immigrants who had provided little to no hands-on care for their own parents in Taiwan had profoundly changed their expectations for their children in the United States. Similarly, the return migrants I interviewed highlighted the challenge that spatial separation posed for Taiwanese and Chinese traditions of parental care. Many could not provide hands-on care and had counted on their siblings in Taiwan. As a result, they explained they had a reduced sense of entitlement for themselves. Mr. Sun, a returnee in his seventies, had migrated to the United States so that his children could receive a Western education, which he perceived as better than an education in Taiwan, and he believed that a good education had been central to their success. But he had left his father in Taiwan in the care of his brother and sister. His father had expressed no interest in moving to the United States, and his siblings never accused him of abandonment. Yet he felt that he made a choice between his father and his children. "My mother passed away when I was little. I did not take care of my father either," he elaborated.

> He retired from [teaching] when he was seventy-five years old. Then he continued to teach part-time until he turned eighty-eight. He got a stroke at the age of eighty-eight and passed away at the age of ninety. . . . Many immigrants like me left our parents in Taiwan. When my father was sick and needed people to take care of him, I was in the US. . . . My sister and my brother took turns taking care of my father. My father's students even cared for him more than I did. I think I should not expect or ask my children to look after me.

From Mr. Sun's perspective, he had transferred the burden of caring not only to his siblings but also to his father's students, and even these nonfamily members had contributed to his father's later life more than he had. Reflecting on his absence—which kept him from fulfilling his familial duties—he had concluded that he had no right to ask his children to look after him.

To be sure, some of the immigrants in this study regularly sent economic remittances home when their parents were still alive and so supported their parents financially. To some degree, then, they compensated for the care that they were unable to provide. Research has shown that economic remittances sent by emigrating family members constitute an important way to express loyalty, devotion, and affection and can be viewed as a form of care from afar (Coe 2011; Mazzucato 2007; Thai 2014). With this money, stay-behind parents, siblings, and other relatives are able to secure housing, purchase food, and cover medical procedures. Despite the instrumental and symbolic value of economic remittances, some transnational family members still express ambivalence or regret about being far away from their loved ones, especially during family crises (King and Vullnetari

2006; Sun 2017). The older immigrants I interviewed similarly expressed the view that money failed to offset their moral debts to parents and siblings. Mrs. Fong, at sixty-six, reported that before her father passed away from cancer, she had regularly sent checks to her siblings in Taiwan to alleviate her father's and siblings' financial burden. But she recognized that money was an incomplete substitute for the physical care performed by her siblings and their spouses. Mrs. Fong's sense of unrealized responsibility had then influenced her expectations for her own children, as she explained.

> When I learned that my father got cancer, I knew that he would not live much longer. And back then I could not fly back to Taiwan regularly. My kids were little; I had to work; and my financial situation was not stable yet. Making one trip home was not that easy. Yet I did try my best to send checks home as much as I could. I still felt really bad about not being there with my father. You know it's exhausting to take care of sick old people. You need to go to the hospital a lot. You need to be constantly on call. You need to pay attention to sick people's diets and other minor things. I could not do much because I was so far away. . . . So you asked me whether I expected my children to look after me. I didn't even take care of my own father. What can I say to my children?

Like Mrs. Fong, return migrants who had sent economic remittances to Taiwan from the United States described a sense of regret for their physical absence in their parents' twilight years. Money could symbolize their indebtedness (Fomby 2005; Mazzucato 2007) but never fully compensated for the care they were supposed to provide. As Mr. Lu, a returnee in his early seventies, recounted, the money he regularly sent to his parents before they passed away not only reimbursed his siblings for some of his parents' expenses but also conveyed his appreciation for his upbringing. Yet the money fulfilled only some of his responsibilities. As a child living thousands of miles away, he had been unable to address his mother's physical and emotional needs in a timely manner, especially when his mother suffered a stroke several years before she passed away. His siblings had used the money he sent to hire an *obasan* (older Taiwanese woman) to help look after their mother, but his brothers and sisters had spent much time, attention, and energy caring for her. To show his appreciation, Mr. Lu had given up the right to inherit his parents' assets. "I sent money, but the only thing I did was give money," he explained. "I did not really do anything for my mother other than that. Since I am not a filial son myself, I do not expect my children to take care of me in my own later life." Geographically separated and having contributed only economically, Mr. Lu had developed a new understanding of intergenerational reciprocity.

Assessment of the Next Generation: Thinking about Children

Their children's well-being offered my respondents another rationale for rethinking reciprocity. This emphasis on the needs of their children was heavily influenced by their previous experiences with both elder care and childcare. Seventeen respondents, eight of them returnees, had brought their parents to the United States to stay with them but emphasized that they did not want their children to be "sandwiched," as they had been, by caring for young and old generations at the same time. Most notably, perhaps because women are the conventional caregivers in Taiwanese migrant households, these older women emphasized the overwhelming task of simultaneously caring for elders and children, recollections that their husbands echoed. Even immigrants who had cared for their own parents in the United States stressed that they preferred to be self-sufficient rather than become a burden on the next generation.

Mrs. Gu, in her late sixties, described caring for her mother-in-law at the expense of her own mental and physical health. She and her husband had insisted that her mother-in-law migrate and live with them so that they could provide the care she needed. As Mrs. Gu explained, however, although she loved her mother-in-law, she resented the "round-the-clock" caregiving. She had felt exhausted and overwhelmed over the last few years of her mother-in-law's life. Her mother-in-law's health had deteriorated after a fall in the bathroom, and Mrs. Gu blamed herself for allowing this incident to happen. She then quit her job, only to have her mother-in-law again fall and then pass away six months later. Although no one in her family blamed her for the accident, Mrs. Gu felt responsible. She had suffered from severe depression, which she believed led to early-onset menopause. Because of this experience, she stressed, she and her husband wanted to spare the next generation a struggle with simultaneous childcare and elder care.

Mrs. Jiang, a return migrant in her late sixties, reported that the responsibilities of simultaneously caring for children and parents led not only to stress but also to marital discord. Lacking English fluency, driving skills, and social networks in the United States, Mrs. Jiang's parents-in-law had become completely reliant on her. Mrs. Jiang's parents-in-law had been far less familiar with US culture than she and her husband had become, yet she still felt that counting on their children for support would bring them additional stress and would inevitably cause conflicts across generations or between her children and their spouses. "My children do not have much time for me," Mrs. Jiang asserted. "They have their own family to take care of. If I counted on my children, I would bring a lot of inconveniences to their life and become a needy mom to them."

In addition to their concern for the structural squeeze between childcare and elder care, many respondents believed that the time bind with which their children struggled made the prospect of their caregiving even more unrealistic. Arlie Hochschild (1997) analyzed a time bind through which paid work increasingly encroaches on people's lives, creating tension between job requirements and familial responsibilities. My respondents typically attributed the limited amount of time their children had available for visiting, communication, and assistance in everyday tasks to the next generation's career goals and child-rearing duties. Expecting the next generation to have sufficient time to attend to their needs, these immigrants observed, would be unrealistic, given that both their children and their children's spouses spent most of their time at work.

These evaluations of their children's situations are closely related to the migration experience. Respondents emphasized that the time bind was exacerbated by the lack of kin support in the United States, as most of their family members were in Taiwan. Many emphasized their children's academic and professional opportunities as reasons for migration. Therefore, they reasoned that expecting the next generation to care for them would defeat their purpose for migrating and distract their children from focusing on their careers. Many respondents further recalled unfair treatment in the workplace and worried that their children, marked as Asian, would have to overcome enough obstacles without navigating the demands of elder care. Indeed, more than two-thirds of respondents reported that expecting their children to attend to their needs would likely either compromise their children's success, leading to their own disappointment, or frustrate their children's lives with additional demands.

Lack of geographic proximity and the quality of family relationships further informed these considerations. Those with children living far away were more skeptical about expecting their children and their children's spouses to be their primary caregivers. Separated from their children by an ocean, most returnees were steadfast about their choices. So were those with strained intergenerational relations. Mrs. Sun, a return migrant in her seventies, expressed both rationales. Lack of physical proximity was a major barrier, she explained: "My son lives in San Francisco, my daughter lives in Seattle, and I used to live in [a metropolitan city on the East Coast]. How can they take care of me?" But intergenerational conflict also discouraged her from seeking support, as her children and their spouses wanted to maintain distance: "If I move somewhere closer to my children, I am sure they will prefer to move back to the East Coast themselves," she emphasized. Physical distance and clashing intergenerational relations thus constituted structural conditions that could shape expectations.

These concerns about the feasibility of intergenerational care and the effects of elder dependence were particularly evident among the women I interviewed.

Given the highly gendered nature of caregiving, aging migrant women tend better than men to understand the impact of additional demands for hands-on care. Many stressed that, as mothers, they were more accustomed than their spouses to thinking about the needs of their children. Mrs. Chin told me that her decision to relocate to Taiwan was in part an effort to relieve her children of the competing demands of paid work and elder care. Having lost much of her mobility after her unsuccessful surgery in the United States, she "chose" to move back to Taiwan, where she could afford to hire domestic workers and live in a well-equipped assisted-living facility. Using the rhetoric of maternal responsibility to frame her decision, Mrs. Chin cited consideration of her children:

> As a mother, I don't want to see our children stressed out because of me. We should think about our children rather than just ourselves. Especially given my health condition, I really don't want to become a burden in my children's life. My children are stressed out enough because of work. How can I see them become more stressed out because of me? So I always told my children not to worry about me. I live in Taiwan well. The lady I hired from Indonesia is very nice. I have lots of friends. I never feel lonely. Don't worry about me.

Perceived Acculturation: The Lens of Americanization

In October 2011, I was invited to give a talk to a Taiwanese immigrant organization on changing intergenerational relations within migrant families. The person who invited me (an immigrant in his sixties) was particularly interested to hear about my research, and most of the audience was also composed of older Taiwanese people with children born and/or raised in the United States. Indeed, approximately one hundred fifty Taiwanese immigrants, many of them retired, attended my talk. During the Q&A section and the dinner party afterward, audience members were eager to share the ways US society had shaped their children's views of filial piety and required them to adjust their expectations. Some complained that US culture made their children "selfish" and willing to challenge parental authority. Some blamed themselves for bringing their children to the United States, where they had learned a different set of norms. Some, however, praised "American" parents for democratic parenting and thought that Taiwanese parents should treat their adult children as equals rather than subordinates. Migration, many emphasized, meant learning an American mode of aging.

Despite their differences, these views point to a central theme: many aging immigrants are determined to stay independent rather than depend on their children, even though this dominant, "American" mode of aging is fundamentally different from the norms they had learned in Taiwan. For them, a longitudinal stay in the United States had consequences and required adjustments of their connections to children who had become what they consider American. As my respondents' accounts revealed, Americanization refers to three structural and cultural changes: (1) changing culture of elder care, (2) declining parental authority, and (3) commercialization of geriatric care.

ARTICULATING THE CULTURE OF ELDER CARE

What the respondents understood as "US culture" or "Americanization" is central to understanding their changing attitudes toward their children's caregiving obligations. Given the larger social and cultural contexts of the United States, most had found it impractical to expect their US-raised children to care for them. These immigrants actively invoked the concept of Americanization to rationalize the impracticality of anticipating hands-on care and financial assistance from their children. US individualism, their accounts illustrate, encourages children's individuality and parents' independence, whereas Taiwanese and Chinese culture values aging parents' dependence on their children. Mr. Chao, contended that his children will not care for him and his wife in ways mandated by filial piety, which would burden them and induce conflict: "It is just impossible to expect the younger generation in the US to care for their parents," he mused.

> Respecting older people is necessary, but expecting your children to look after you is just too much. We first-generation immigrants need to adjust our expectations too. Since we came here, we have learned the larger social context here. Children have their own family and career to be busy with. . . . Asking your children to give you money? Don't be silly. They don't even have enough money for themselves and their own children. If we keep expecting our children to care for us in traditional Chinese ways, we would only end up being disappointed and upset. Taking care of aging parents is just not part of the American culture. We have to realize that.

Like Mr. Chao, most return migrants I interviewed noted the low priority afforded the needs of aging parents in US culture. Many emphasized that US culture encouraged aging parents to remain independent of their children's support, and oriented by this view, they emphasized self-care. As a seventy-five-year-old return migrant, Mr. Dai, maintained,

> The US is a society that encourages people to become independent. Everyone should be self-sufficient and be responsible for their own business. In the US, someone who is above eighteen will be required to be independent and will be kicked out of his or her parents' house. . . .

Growing up in such an environment, our children become very independent too. They don't want to rely on parents, and they don't want the parents to rely on them either. This is the US culture. We have to accept it. We never dreamed about having our children take care of us.

My respondents' articulation of the American ideal of aging mirrors the prevalent discourse of "successful aging" in the United States and transnationally. This discourse—which encourages older people to stay independent, energetic, and, to some degree, eternally youthful—points to a biomedical paradigm that transforms biological aging from a process of normal human development to a set of symptoms that requires scientific intervention (Conrad 2007). More importantly, the idea of successful aging reinforces the larger cultural narrative about independence and self-sufficiency. Even the people who "successfully" age need support from family and community members at some point (Lamb 2017; Loe 2011).

The class privilege of the respondents is also important for understanding their accounts. While aging immigrants who had experienced economic insecurity during their adulthood are likely to suffer "premature aging" and have early-onset health problems (Hunter 2018), most of my respondents were middle-class, many of them professionals and in reasonably good health. At the time of the interview, therefore, they neither needed nor expected their children to provide economic support or physical care. Indeed, many of these immigrants—like lots of other aging people—deliberately budgeted their finances and sought to maintain their health so they could prevent becoming a "burden" to their children. In contrast, my working-class respondents were less confident about their finances and more worried about having sufficient resources to handle the "worst-case scenario" that could come with deteriorating health. Even these respondents, however, maintained that they did not anticipate receiving money or hands-on care from their children and their children's spouses.

Working-class immigrants whose children had college educations typically cited hefty student loans and debts that would interfere with the tradition of filial piety. Those whose children had limited educations or blue-collar jobs cited long hours or inadequate pay as reasons to limit any expectations for intergenerational care. My working-class respondents thus resembled their more middle-class coethnics. Mr. Fong, who lived with his wife in a rented apartment in a large eastern US city, relied on her savings and pension but ruled out the possibility of support from his children. Unlike his generation of Taiwanese, he argued, this younger generation was "polluted" by mainstream US culture. Rather than thinking of their parents, he lamented, his son and daughter "wasted" money on concert and theater performances, movies, electronic appliances, and social activities. Mr. Fong blamed Americanization for such priorities but reasoned that, if necessary, moving to a government-funded nursing home or assisted-living facility in the United States or Taiwan would be more realistic than asking for his children's support.

Many respondents simultaneously asserted that they too were Americanized and no longer inclined to expect their children to adhere to traditional ways. Maintaining that they were Americanized by choice, they reported reluctance to impose the burden of elder care on their children and their children's spouses. As Mrs. Chen, in her sixties, asserted, "As immigrants, we have to learn and adjust to US society. . . . Children who grow up in the US will not prioritize your needs over theirs. We need to take care of ourselves rather than bother our kids. We know that we have to be independent. We need to take care of our own business. If we don't set up our expectations right, we will put a lot of pressure on our children and end up having lots of intergenerational conflicts." Similarly, Mrs. Wei, a returnee who had just turned seventy at the time of interview, had been inspired by her American neighbor, whom she described as a white American determined to be self-sufficient. Mrs. Wei's neighbor had been widowed and lived alone until she passed away, and for Mrs. Wei, the neighbor represented the spirit of American independence, a model for adjusting her expectations and learning from the aging Americans around her. "When we lived in [our previous neighborhood], one of my neighbors was named Mrs. Spring. She lived alone until she passed away at the age of ninety-nine," Mrs. Wei explained. "Her children were in Boston and came to see her once or twice per year. She told us that she definitely did not want to rely on her children, because she wanted to maintain her independence. You know . . . I feel so inspired by her, and I definitely want to learn from her. I prefer to take care of myself like these elderly Americans. We don't want to intrude on our children's lives or become a burden for them."

Agreeing with his wife, Mr. Wei anticipated remaining independent of his children's support. For him, relocation to Taiwan was a way of conforming to American ideology, as the move underscored their lack of expectation of care from their children. In the United States, Mr. and Mrs. Wei had lived on the East Coast, while their children lived in the South and West. Geographical distance had thus minimized the effect of moving back to Taiwan, which he considered just farther away. Settled in Taiwan, Mr. Wei likened his independent life and occasional visits with his children to an American norm. Strategically mobilizing the notion of the American family, he downplayed the effects of spatial distance and highlighted his cultural assimilation. "We don't expect to count on anyone, especially our children," he explained.

> Some people in Taiwan asked me why I don't want to live closer to my children, because then my children can take care of me when I need them. I totally disagree with them. I don't think my life has to be entangled with my children's, and my children would not like to organize their life around my schedule. . . . When I was in the US, my children were all over the place. And we typically saw each other only on holidays. Now I live in Taiwan. Yes, it is farther away from my children, but I can still manage to see my children several times a year. It is not so different from most American families.

Whereas most of the respondents focused primarily on differences between cultures of elder care in Taiwan and the United States, some observed changes to the values and practices of elder care in Taiwan. To be sure, most believed that their children would have acquired a stronger sense of moral duty for taking care of aging parents if they had grown up in Taiwan. Yet several mentioned that Taiwanese society has also undergone what they perceived as Westernization or Americanization. Even in Taiwan, they noted, traditions of filial piety have eroded. Those who saw increased Americanization or Westernization in Taiwan were most insistent about revising intergenerational reciprocity.

Mr. Tseng, at age seventy, reported that in the 1960s or 1970s, a child placing parents in a nursing home in Taiwan would have been subject to charges of abandonment and severe criticism from neighbors, relatives, colleagues, and friends. But visiting Taiwan several years earlier, he had been surprised to learn that some of his friends had voluntarily moved to a nursing home in Taipei. Moreover, the perception that, even in Taiwan, members of the younger generation were increasingly eschewing responsibility for elder care had led him to conclude that he should not insist on support from the next generation. "When we left Taiwan, people of our generation typically would live with our own parents. Back then, how could we even imagine sending our parents to a nursing home?" he recalled.

> When we just arrived in the US, we felt so sympathetic for elderly Americans who were abandoned by their children and had to live in a nursing home. I don't think younger people in Taiwan today will live with or care for their parents. It's a tendency. It's a process of Westernization and modernization. Taiwan today is becoming more and more similar to the US in terms of how the younger generations treat old people in the family. . . . So why do we insist on having our children [in the United States] take care of us?

Compared with immigrants in the United States, return migrants in Taiwan more often noted that many elderly people in Taiwan no longer rely on their children to attend to their everyday needs. Many of these returnees had found not only an increasing number of nursing homes and assisted-living facilities but also a growing number of migrant domestic workers engaged in elder care. For these return migrants, such changes represented modernization, Westernization, or Americanization. Even those nostalgic about the tradition of filial piety believed that expecting care from the next generation was nearly impossible in contemporary Taiwan. For the respondents, this observation reconfirmed a determination to live without receiving support from their children.

Mr. Peng, an immigrant in his late seventies, reported seeing more and more domestic workers of Southeast Asian origin responsible for elder care in Taiwan. In his neighborhood, he often saw younger migrant women pushing wheelchairs or helping elderly Taiwanese walk with crutches. Mr. Peng had initially thought of these female migrant workers as daughters or daughters-in-law, but he had found many unable to speak Mandarin or Taiwanese. The increasing number of migrant workers caring for an aging Taiwanese population, Mr. Peng believed, mirrored changing norms of elder care. For him, Taiwan was becoming similar to the United States in that children were no longer primary caregivers for aging parents. Like many returnees I interviewed, Mr. Peng reported that expecting his children to provide care was unrealistic in contemporary Taiwan.

REASSESSING PARENTAL AUTHORITY

Immigrants' perceptions of the defining characteristics of US culture—or Americanization—not only reoriented their sense of entitlement to intergenerational care but also challenged their power over their children. Beliefs about changing intergenerational relationships inspired these aging immigrants to be practical about reciprocity. Most emphasized that, under the influence of US culture, they could no longer subordinate their children's will to theirs. Not every immigrant I interviewed whole-heartedly embraced the softening effects of Americanization on parental authority. Some, especially parents who had relocated to the United States for the benefit of the next generation, thought that they might have compromised their well-being. Virtually all, however, asserted that US culture—which they believed emphasized adult children's individuality rather than deference to parental authority—is a social trend that they could not realistically resist.

Mrs. Tseng asserted that parents with children growing up in the United States should refashion their expectations of parental authority by interacting with their children on an equal footing. Aging parents, she believed, could no longer "boss" their Americanized children around in traditional Chinese ways. As a result, she had become alert to the ways in which she talked to her children and their spouses, concerned that she might risk ruining her relationships. "I sometimes give advice to my children," she elaborated.

But I am very careful about how I talk to them. They grew up in the US and have very strong opinions about how things should be done. And I am a mother. My children might think, "Oh, it's Mom. We have to show respect for her opinion." Yet at the same time, they want to do things in their own way and don't feel comfortable about me telling them what to do. So I always emphasized to my children, "I just gave you a suggestion. You can take it or leave it. It's up to you to make the final decision." . . . As a mother, I just cannot help but give advice to my children. I am older, and I hope that my experience can be helpful for my children. But I know these American children, so I always preface my advice and let my children know that they have the final say in their life. Otherwise, my children might avoid me altogether.

Mr. Lee, a returnee in his sixties, similarly described limited power over his Americanized children and reported trouble asking them do things according to his will. Under such circumstances, Mr. Lee thought that cohabiting with and expecting care from his children would not only take a lot of negotiation but also require him to compromise the life he truly wanted. Against this background, he had preferred to remain self-sufficient. "I think social values make a big difference," Mr. Lee reflected. "You know, we cannot expect our children growing up in the American society to listen to us. They are very opinionated about what they want. As for us, we have to find what works best for us. They don't want to compromise their life, and we don't want to compromise our lifestyle. Inevitably, relying on children would cause lots of problems."

Admitting, even accepting, a loss of power over their children, many of the respondents worried that care provided by their children and their children's spouses would come at the expense of their own autonomy and dignity. This concern arose most clearly when respondents addressed questions about living with their children or receiving physical care in their children's homes. Far from a guarantee of care, cohabiting with their children might require them to compromise and adapt their lifestyles. In her late eighties, Mrs. Lai pointed to a short-term experience living with her son and daughter-in-law, both of whom she described as Americanized, to explain her reluctance to cohabit. Wanting not to exchange her autonomy for their care, Mrs. Lai explained,

Our children will not care for us in the ways we like. They do things and think about things in American ways. Elderly parents are no longer their primary concern. . . . Living with our children will cause unnecessary conflicts. My daughter-in-law is one example. . . . I remember that when we went to the supermarket together, I put a bottle of KimLan [a Taiwanese brand] soy sauce in the basket. Then I left and got something else. After I came back, the soy sauce I had picked was already gone! My daughter-in-law said, "KimLan is too expensive. Let's buy another brand." This is an example of the problems coming from living with your children. . . . When I live alone, I can make decisions about my own life.

Mrs. Lai's comments also reveal the hidden tension between many older immigrant women and their daughters-in-law, which has been chronicled in recent scholarship on immigrant families. Kristy Shih and Karen Pyke (2010), for instance, found that immigrant women with married sons were more forthcoming than their male counterparts about the potential conflicts of caregiving. Probably for this reason, the immigrant women I interviewed expressed more hesitancy than their spouses about depending on their sons' families.

Expressing a similar sentiment, Mrs. Lam—one of the returnees I interviewed in Taiwan—explained her choice to move back rather than live with her children in the United States. She had been a mother who took care of the needs of her family members and opposed becoming a responsibility that her children had to manage. Taking care of her family members had made Mrs. Lam feel empowered, but anticipating care from her children made her feel vulnerable. Oriented by the perception that receiving hands-on care from children was far from a norm in American culture, Mrs. Lam thought dependence would force her to rationalize her needs and exchange her dignity for support. "My children are very Americanized," she asserted.

If I need anything from them, I have to give them a reason. It's not like children always listen to elderly parents in traditional Chinese culture. This is why I hate bothering my children. I definitely don't want to live with my children. I like to decide my own life. Because I live alone, I can do things I want. If I want to hang out with friends, I can hang out with friends. And I don't have to tell my children where I go. I don't have to wait for my children for dinner, and they don't have to wait for me. . . . I just don't like relying on my children for things. If I have my children pay my bills, I might have to tell them how I spent the money. For example, when I use the phone to talk with friends, I might have to worry about the bill that my children have to pay. Because I pay everything myself, I don't have to worry about how my children think about it.

Among the respondents, returnees were more likely to highlight the distance between the United States and Taiwan as a mechanism for preventing or resolving conflicts with their "Americanized" children. A returnee in her sixties, Mrs. Gui attributed her return to Taiwan to her sustained relationship with her sons and daughters-in-law, all of whom were native-born Americans. Considering herself a strong-minded person, Mrs. Gui speculated about likely disagreements, had she relied on her US family for care. Instead, she explained, the distance between Taiwan and the United States allowed her to avoid complex issues involved in receiving care from her children's families. "I am close to my children," she reflected.

> But our children are all Americanized and have strong opinions on things. So are their spouses. At the same time, we also have our ideas about our lives. In the long term, we and our children will inevitably have arguments and misunderstandings. . . . If it is just between us and our children, things might be easier. But now our children have their own families. They have their spouses. Things become very complicated. Even if our children trust us and want to have open communication with us, their spouses might not want to do so. So these conflicts become hard to resolve. I feel like living in Taiwan makes things so much easier. We don't expect our children to take care of us. We live our own lives, and they live theirs. Distance ended up creating better relationships between me and my sons' families.

What these immigrants perceived as Americanization enabled them to blame larger sociocultural contexts rather than criticize their children. In this way, many respondents used Americanization as an emotional shield to avoid or resist disappointment, frustration, or anger. By reminding themselves of cultural differences, they sought to neutralize conflicts and reassure themselves that their children did not intentionally hurt their feelings. Mrs. Chou reported sometimes feeling disappointed by the ways in which her son and daughter-in-law treated her, but she convinced herself that they were well intentioned and just heavily influenced by US culture, which led them to interact in ways she felt inconsiderate. By highlighting the difference between the United States and Taiwan, Mrs. Chou used a vaguely defined notion of Americanization to reconstruct her expectations of parental authority and so marked the boundary between what she felt and what she thought she should feel. "I remember that one day I called my son and told him that I was going to see him and my grandchildren," she recalled.

> I called him in advance, but he and my daughter-in-law did not pick up the phone, so I left a message. They were probably busy all day and did not listen to the message carefully. When I arrived, they were on the way out to dinner, and they did not ask me and my husband if we wanted to join. I was a bit disappointed. In traditional Taiwanese families, we would assume that our children would ask if we wanted to go together. In traditional Taiwanese culture, I would expect them to ask,

"Do you want to come?" or at least explain the situation to me. However, my son and my daughter-in-law are both very Americanized, so they did not ask us. I was disappointed that day. Yet I kept telling myself it's a cultural difference. So I tried to let it go.

Like Mrs. Chou, many of the Taiwanese returnees I interviewed mobilized the concept of Americanization to manage their emotions when their children failed to respond in ways they wanted. A return migrant in her seventies, Mrs. Xia, highlighted the influence of US culture on her children, claiming that she had reconstructed her expectations for a younger generation that had grown up in the United States. This rationale allowed her to avoid negative feelings and intergenerational conflicts, as she elaborated.

If we set up high expectations that our children cannot live up to, we end up being disappointed. We know some of our Chinese friends in the US feel very disappointed about their children who do not listen to them. I think expecting too much from my children will end up making me emotional. It's not good for you, and it's not good for your children. Children growing up in American culture will not act as you want them to. If they want to do it, they will do it. If they don't, asking too much will only hurt your own feelings and your relationships with kids.

Blaming Americanization was thus a strategy through which respondents sought to avoid negative, emotionally charged interactions with their children and their children's spouses. This rationale is central to understanding the stress they placed on remaking cultural norms. These immigrants foresaw conflicts in negotiating care with children and their spouses and had concluded that independence would better enable them to sustain affective connections with the next generation. Given the larger sociocultural processes that they described as Americanization, they could maintain this view with reference to broader norms among American families.

PURCHASING CARE AND PRACTICING AMERICAN WAYS OF AGING

The availability of programs and institutions that serve the elderly, nationally and transnationally, reassured my respondents about the feasibility of choosing independent sources of care. They anticipated needing care, despite their desire to be self-sufficient. Although most were in reasonably good physical condition at the time of interview, they were uncertain about their future health. Among the respondents, ninety-one (forty-five of whom were returnees) planned to resort to what Carroll Estes (1979, 2) has termed aging enterprises—"the programs, organizations, bureaucracies, interest groups, trade associations, providers, industries, professionals that serve the aged in one capacity or another." Aging enterprises, both public and private, include long-term residential facilities and employment of domestic workers, both strategies cited by the respondents. To be clear, some might have exaggerated the prospect of abandonment by their offspring and overemphasized the possibility of life in a nursing home. Their narratives of receiving care through market mechanisms, however, vividly illustrate the effect of institutional support provided by aging enterprises on the cultural schemas of aging immigrants.

Moving to facilities. Many of the immigrants I interviewed were open to the possibility of moving to nursing homes or assisted-living facilities "like many American elderly." Mrs. Gao, who had cared for her husband for an extended period after he was diagnosed with Alzheimer's disease, had ultimately placed him in assisted living, and she recounted the overwhelming physical and emotional work involved in caring for him at home. The experience had led her to tell her children that she would be willing to enter a care facility if she were to suffer from some serious illness. Cohabiting with her children, she believed, would be far from ideal for everyone, given the time, energy, and resources required for someone seriously ill, and she was unsure that her Americanized children would be willing to provide such care over time. Using the Chinese idiom "If you are bedridden for a long time, your filial son is sure to disappear" (*jiu bing chuang qian wu xiao zi*) to explain her thinking, Mrs. Gao noted that even children brought up in Chinese culture would become tired of looking after ailing parents, and even if her children were willing, she would not want to become a burden. Instead, she would relocate to a care facility, as she thought most American elderly people do.

In Taiwan, the return migrants I interviewed also noted the rise of what they viewed as US-inspired aging enterprises. Indeed, the establishment of these facilities in Taiwan had motivated them to move back. Highlighting changes in their homeland, these return migrants saw aging enterprises as indicators of a Westernizing culture of elder care. In Taiwan, however, such facilities were more affordable than those in the States and maintained important components of Taiwanese and Chinese life. Mr. Yen, a returnee in his seventies who lived with his wife in a newly built old-age apartment, told me that the needs of an aging population in Taiwan had spurred the development of old-age facilities much like those in the United States. Just like children in the United States, he explained, those in contemporary Taiwan no longer had sufficient time to care for their aging parents. Taiwanese old-age homes, however, better satisfied his needs. First, Mr. Yen explained, he could spend much less in Taiwan, where fifteen hundred US dollars per month covered rent, electricity, air-conditioning, cleaning services, and three meals per day, seven days a week—all for an amount that would buy only a shabby nursing home in the United States. Moreover, an old-age home in Taiwan enabled him to fit in culturally with other Taiwanese elders who shared familiar ethnic foods and language. As Mr. Yen elaborated,

> I was thinking about moving to an old-age home in Taipei. Taiwan has changed so much since I left. Like the US, old-age apartments, nursing homes, and assisted-living facilities have been introduced to Taiwan. The old-age home I live in has a good reputation, and I really enjoy living here. . . . I've made lots of friends here. And I knew if I moved here, I could talk with staff in my own language. And the most important thing is that these new old-age apartments in Taiwan provide you with meals. They prepare Taiwanese food for their residents. If I want a porridge, rice noodles, or beef noodles, it will be so much easier. I cannot live in the nursing home in the US because I don't want to eat pizza or a sandwich every day. I can handle American food for one meal, but I cannot have American food every day. No way!

To be sure, many of the returnees I interviewed did not live in these types of facilities. Most, however, agreed with Mr. Yen that the development of aging enterprises in Taiwan is evidence of the erosion of family-based elder care in the wake of Westernization. At the same time, though, these returnees also agreed that the rise of Western-style aging enterprises promotes the independence valued in US culture while allowing residents to maintain a Taiwanese lifestyle. Language was a particular concern. Although returnees with whom I talked considered themselves fluent in English, most felt that they could more precisely communicate their needs in either Taiwanese/Ho-lo or Mandarin Chinese. They also preferred Taiwanese food.

The rise of old-age homes in Taiwan was attractive not only to older returnees but also to respondents in the United States who echoed returnees' concerns and considered relocating to Taiwan. When asked about elder care, Mr. Lai, age eighty-seven, suddenly walked to his desk and took out a brochure for an old-age home in Taipei with apartments for both independent and assisted living. Mr. Lai told me that he had received this brochure from a Taiwanese return migrant who lived in the facility and, given his deteriorating health, was considering a move. Living with his children and their spouses, he believed, was not a good way to satisfy his needs, especially in a US context, where his children and their spouses spent most of their time at work and caring for aging parents is unappreciated. Relocating to a nursing home or to assisted living, he thought, would be a better option for him and for his children's families. Flipping through the brochure,

Mr. Lai excitedly delineated the advantages of this old-age home in Taiwan. Implicit in his account was that these Western-style aging enterprises there were reconfigured to meet the expectations of Taiwanese and Han Chinese populations.

Recruiting helping hands at home. Some of the older immigrants I interviewed mentioned in-home services, available in the public or the private sector, to attend to their needs. For these immigrants, in-home services for seniors were another American, or Western, way of managing later life and seemed preferable to old-age or assisted-living facilities. Mrs. Ma, in her sixties, considered assisted living acceptable if her health deteriorated to the extent that she required daily medical care, but she preferred to maintain her independence by purchasing in-home services. To her, these were "American inventions" designed to address the basic needs of the elderly in a country where the needs of aging parents are a low priority in their children's lives. Mrs. Ma had learned about in-home senior services from her neighbors and had asked herself,

> If elderly Americans can take care of themselves in this way, why can't I? I think smart parents should live on their own and not rely on their children. . . . You know, in the US, they have in-home services for seniors because their children are not going to take care of them. I don't know if Taiwan has similar services. But in the US, you could use home services for elderly people. Then some workers can come and clean your place. They could also send meals to you. One of my neighbors, who I think is Irish American, was using in-home services for seniors. . . . I can take care of myself like those American elderly people.

Unlike the respondents in the United States, those in Taiwan did not mention in-home services for seniors. Rather, they considered hiring full-time female migrant workers from Southeast Asian countries, such as the Philippines, Cambodia, and Indonesia. Many returnees in this study believed that the growing number of migrant workers hired to care for aging parents reflected the Westernization of elder care in Taiwan. Aging returnees typically viewed migrant workers as a resource that they could use to accomplish the self-sufficiency that US culture encouraged. Mr. Yeh, a returnee in his seventies, maintained that employing a migrant woman to look after him would be more realistic than expecting care from his children. "I saw a lot of migrant workers take care of old people in Taiwan," he noted.

> In the neighborhood where I live, I see a lot of migrant women who push old people in their wheelchair on the street. . . . Taking care of old people is very overwhelming. We cannot rely on our children to take care of us if we became really ill. For example, if we were sick and laid on the bed eternally, we might need someone to clean us regularly. We might also need

someone to turn us over regularly and massage our back in order not get a skin ulcer. How can we expect our children or our children's spouses to do that for us? How can they have time? So if one day something happens to me, I will hire a woman from Indonesia or Vietnam to take care of myself.

For return migrants like Mr. Yeh, the decision to hire migrant workers in Taiwan involved complex gender-, class-, and race-based micropolitics in a transnational context. Like other Taiwanese employers who hire migrant workers, these returnees preferred women to take care of their everyday needs. Their choice points to the gendered nature of care work. Their thinking also renders visible the economic disparities among the United States, Taiwan, and Southeast Asian countries. Most return migrants, who had worked in the United States at a younger life stage, could readily use their resources to afford a migrant domestic worker, whose services would cost much more in the United States. The respondents in Taiwan reported needing only about eight hundred dollars per month at the time of interview (between 2011 and 2016) to pay a live-in domestic worker of South Asian origin who would attend to their needs around the clock. The same amount in the United States, some noted, would barely cover a part-time caregiver. The returnees I interviewed were less worried about the physical, psychological, and social well-being of the domestic workers they hired or considered hiring than they were with their own children and their children's spouses. As several explicitly indicated, hired migrant women were not a part of the family.

Mrs. Gui was a case in point. She had hired a migrant woman from Indonesia to care for her and for her mother, who had celebrated her hundredth birthday just before the interview. Mrs. Gui had fired two other migrant workers, and although she occasionally mentioned her gratitude to her employees, she knew she could dismiss them if they failed to meet her expectations. This tendency to hire "market proxies" to perform care work that is traditionally allocated to women (especially daughters-in-law) has become common in many late-developed societies, such as Singapore, Taiwan, and Hong Kong. The demand for care workers also fuels the emigration of many women from the global south, such places as the Philippines, Indonesia, and Sri Lanka (Ehrenreich and Hochschild 2004; Hondagneu-Sotelo 2007). For my respondents, these migrant caregivers became "disposable labor" with whom they saw no need to sustain a permanent connection (Lan 2006). Rather than consider these workers' needs, Mrs. Gui expected the migrant women she hired to follow her instructions and to do their jobs well. "I fired a Filipina before. I don't like the ways in which she interacted with me," Mrs. Gui reported. "She was not that deferential to my will. Another migrant worker I hired was from Vietnam. She was in a bad health condition. When we drove somewhere else, she always felt car sick. She got sick quite often. I just felt that I hired her to take care of me and my mother, so why would I hire someone that I had to spend time taking care of? They were not my children or grandchildren. . . . I like the one I have better. She is good and always follows what I tell her."

Both the possibility and the practice of purchasing care enabled respondents to highlight their affective, rather than instrumental, ties with family. With the support of aging enterprises, the immigrants I studied carved out what they considered noncommercial space in their family lives, sustaining emotional connections with their children, children's spouses, and grandchildren. Some viewed intergenerational gatherings as the embodiment of positive relationships with younger generations. Others thought of their children's regular visits and welcoming attitudes as evidence of their children's efforts to maintain emotional connections to them. Still others believed that their children and their children's spouses cared about them because they regularly checked in by phone, email, or some other communication technology. Although these immigrants expected their children to display affection, virtually all believed that, far from a blessing, relying on their children in a US context could become a curse to the family. Reconfiguring rather than maintaining cultural norms of aging and geriatric care thus allowed these immigrants to sustain more positive intergenerational relationships.

Temporalities of migration explain relationships between aging migrants and their children. Whereas a small portion of my respondents embraced ethnic traditions regarding elder care, most reconfigured reciprocal relationships with their children and their children's families. These aging immigrants' interpretations of social, cultural, and generational changes across time and social worlds transformed logics of aging and intergenerational reciprocity. The concept of reconfigured reciprocity thus reveals a web of intersecting relationships influencing the ways these immigrants develop temporal reflexivity and reconstruct reciprocal rules of geriatric care.

Temporalities of migration manifest in older immigrants' relationships with the previous generation, with the next generation, and with receiving and sending societies. These three temporal-structural-cultural dimensions explain the processes through which older immigrants change their attitudes toward norms of intergenerational reciprocity. This study documents the experiences of Taiwanese immigrants, but the concept of reconfigured reciprocity offers a framework for understanding other migrant populations as they move across boundaries and encounter different ethnic traditions regarding family and caregiving.

Immigrants' relationships with the previous generation reveal the ways these migrants consider intergenerational reciprocity with their own parents. Having left their parents behind when they moved to the United States, most believed they had undermined their own entitlement to receive care from the next generation. This assessment led them to reflect on their expectations for their children, and they questioned whether their children were financially and socially equipped to satisfy the needs and desires of aging parents. Competing demands of paid work and family care, with which respondents had also struggled, motivated them to rethink cultural norms and seek to minimize stress in their children's lives. Incorporated into a receiving society, they had come to accept what they called the "American" mode of aging. Their perceptions of this phenomenon fundamentally transformed their worldviews, encouraging cultural flexibility in enacting intergenerational norms.

Here I make no causal link between what US society "really" is and my respondents' changing attitudes about family relations. Rather, I contend that their *perception* of US individualism—especially its impact on parental authority—pushes them to rethink their connections to children who have grown up in the United States. The elderly who never migrate or live abroad might express the same fears or anxieties about their own declining status and decision-making power in the family; many also attribute such familial and societal changes to the "negative" influence of the West (Cohen 1998; Lamb 2009). The aging immigrants I interviewed, however, differ from these nonmigrant elderly in that they voluntarily moved to the United States and their children grew up in a society where Western sensibility prevails. My respondents also had to face the fact that linguistically, socially, and culturally, their children were better incorporated than themselves. Against this backdrop, applying an internalized, Americanized version of successful aging becomes a likely response to the consequences of their choices.

The respondents attached layers of meaning to the notion of Americanization. To them, Americanization referred first to the processes whereby younger generations adopt the US value of individualism rather than family collectivism and parental authority, thereby prioritizing their own needs and desires over those of the older generations. This notion of Americanization reversed the hierarchy within traditional Chinese households, motivating these older immigrants to adjust their expectations of children's obligation. Oriented by this thinking, most respondents believed that they had little influence over the ways their children and their children's spouses organized their lives (e.g., where to live), distributed resources (e.g., how to spend time and money), and cared for them (e.g., how to solve the disagreements over caregiving). Their assumptions about their Americanized children informed decision making about any number of concrete issues arising from dependence in later life. These immigrants, my findings illustrate, had adopted a dynamic approach to rethinking intergenerational reciprocity, emphasizing their efforts to stay self-sufficient. For them, Americanization was an imposed reality, whether they embraced or criticized it.

Americanization explains the efforts of many aging immigrants to assimilate into the cultural landscape by staying independent. Staking claims about their assimilation to larger US cultural settings enabled these older immigrants to modernize and Westernize themselves. They believe that, compared with other traditional Chinese populations, they had become more progressive and open to social, cultural, and generational changes. In this sense, many long-term migrants—including those who stayed abroad and those who returned—thought of assimilation and acculturation as empowerment. For them, embracing US cultural norms of independence and self-sufficiency could offer a modicum of power as they aged and required geriatric care.

Some respondents regretted the loss of ethnic traditions. Yet even these parents believed that, because mainstream US culture discourages younger people from caring for their frail parents, anticipating care from their children was next to impossible. Instead of criticizing their children and their children's spouses, however, the respondents strategically deployed the concept of Americanization to rationalize this loss of children's filial responsibilities and their own parental authority. To claim "It's all about Americanization" could offer older immigrants an emotional shield, which protected them from disappointment, frustration, and anger that might be caused by culturally specific expectations that their children could not readily fulfill.

For these aging immigrants, the Americanization of intergenerational reciprocity focused more intensely on affective, rather than instrumental, connections to younger generations. The commercialization of elder care reveals this focus, as respondents interpreted access to hands-on care outside the family as an American or Western cultural product. Institutional support (e.g., assisted-living facilities) and programs (e.g., in-home services) could replace hands-on elder care that ethnic traditions demanded of family members. Accessing formal support services, many asserted, could reduce family conflict. Americanization could thus prompt these immigrants not only to rethink the sources of care they could mobilize but also to improve relationships with their children and other family members.

Respondents' accounts of Americanization are often oversimplified and fail to represent the complexities of US society. Studies have shown, for example, that aging Americans are not as independent or self-sufficient as my respondents imagined (Lamb 2017). Many American elderly need or have support from kin in their later life (Hareven 1994). Furthermore, assistance from family members is still important for American elderly living in nursing homes or assisted-living facilities. Research has found that among assisted-living residents, those with assistance from kin reported significantly higher life satisfaction than those without it (Street et al. 2007). The effects of Americanization on younger generations are also multidimensional. Many children of Asian immigrants want to fulfill their filial duties of caring for their aging parents (Kibria 2002; Pyke 2000), and even though Taiwan has changed radically over the past forty years, failure to achieve filial piety still induces social blame (Lan 2006). In many respects, then, the respondents overlooked the complex variation within what they depicted as American, Taiwanese, and Chinese. Highlighting Americanization, however, had become an important rationale for actively assessing and managing their expectations of intergenerational reciprocity.

The perception of Americanization or an "American way of aging," which seemed valid to respondents, also obscures the search for autonomy in later life that is becoming a global phenomenon. As Eric Klinenberg (2012, 17) has found, "from Japan to Germany, Italy to Australia, aging alone has become common, even among ethnic groups that have long exhibited a clear preference for keeping multigenerational homes." Myriad social forces—including urbanization, industrialization, the availability of public benefits, the rise of aging enterprises, the development of medical and communication technologies, women's paid labor, and a general cultural shift toward individualism—encourage older people around the globe to value and pursue self-sufficiency rather than depend on the next generation. This global restructuring of norms regarding aging and geriatric care is often cast as the invasion of American or Western culture (Cohen 1998; Lamb 2009). In this broader context, the narrative of Americanization as a causal force overemphasizes the cultural influence of the United States by overlooking structural forces driving a transformation in different corners of the world.

Notably, even though most of the respondents stressed the impact of American individualism on intergenerational relations, their children might think otherwise. The children of immigrants with whom I talked informally during fieldwork—the second generation—felt responsible for parental health crises. Most children agreed with their parents about differences in intergenerational relations between American and Taiwanese families. In the eyes of their parents, and in their own view, they were deeply "Americanized." Many did, however, express a willingness to care for their parents, despite some ambivalence about the degree of their involvement. Their decisions had much to do with the availability of sibling support (i.e., having brothers or sisters who could also look after their parents), relationships with parents (e.g., feeling close enough to step in and provide care), and attitudes of spouses (e.g., whether their spouses would support a decision to care for or even live with a sick parent).

The children I met, particularly those with connections to extended families in Taiwan, also agreed that parental authority is challenged in the United States.

They recognized that they were not as deferential to their parents as their cousins and friends growing up in Taiwan, and they were sometimes labeled "self-centered" or "rebellious" in their ancestral homeland. In this regard, aging immigrants accurately depicted US individualism as a challenge to the power that older people in Chinese families can exert over younger generations. Nonetheless, children who confront their parents may still very much want to help their parents in need. During my fieldwork, I never heard a child of immigrants speak of abdicating responsibility for older parents. Instead, most of the second generation considered provision of care for older parents a major duty. Future research should address the ways immigrant parents in need negotiate care arrangements with their children during family crises.

The perspectives of older Taiwanese immigrants thus reveal only one manifestation of change in family and caregiving practices. The children of these immigrants might reveal others. For example, some of the younger people I encountered over the course of this research expressed a willingness to provide "hands-off" forms of care—visiting, supervision of care, communication with caregivers, and so on—despite the difficulty of residing with their parents. Nonetheless, the respondents' insistence on independence and self-sufficiency points to their changing subjectivities informed by the temporalities of migration.

REMAKING CONJUGALITY

For older Taiwanese immigrants, settling in the United States for decades had shaped perspectives on relationships, not only with children but also with spouses. Over the past three decades, scholars have attended to the impact of migration on gender and spousal relationships within migrant families (Friedman 2015; Friedman and Mahdavi 2015; Hirsch 2003; Lui 2016; Pedraza 1991; Pessar 1999; Zinn, Hondagneu-Sotelo, and Messner 2011). To advance this scholarship, this chapter demonstrates the ways aging, life transition, and their intersection with migration affect intimate connections between spouses (cf. King et al. 2006). Specifically, I pay close attention to the operation of gender in the intimate lives of migrant spouses as they encounter opportunities and constraints at a later life stage.

Some pioneering studies have shown that migration—mostly international but in some cases internal—empowers women, giving them additional leverage to negotiate with their spouses (Choi and Peng 2016; Espiritu 1996; Hondagneu-Sotelo 1994). As these studies of relocation reveal, several factors—women's differing employability and wage-earning abilities, legal regulation against domestic violence, changing connections to kinship networks, and modern discourses about love, intimacy, and conjugality—all contribute to the emancipation of women from patriarchal constraints (Espiritu 1996; Hondagneu-Sotelo 1994; Kibria 1994). While many migrant men feel that dislocation has compromised their masculinities by challenging their position in an ethnic patriarchy, quite a few migrant women have devised new strategies to bargain with their spouses in their respective receiving communities (Choi and Peng 2016).

At the same time, scholars of migration caution that the effects of migration on gender and conjugality are multilayered, situational, and relational (Dreby and Schmalzbauer 2013; Mahler and Pessar 2006; Pessar 1999). Many migrants become protective and even militant about what they perceive as traditional family values and practices (Espiritu 1996). In the larger context of racism and xenophobia, immigrant women and men construct a sense of ethnic pride and self-respect. Some defend gendered double standards (e.g., regulating women's sexuality and an unequal division of labor at home) to differentiate themselves from what they see as the individualistic and chaotic "American" family (Espiritu 2003). These studies point to the variation, multidimensionality, and complexities of conjugal relationships in the contexts of international migration. Adding temporal dimensions to analyze migratory experiences, I uncover ways in which long-term immigration complicates gender and spousal relationships among couples.

Drawing on the concept of temporalities of migration, this chapter delineates the ways older Taiwanese immigrant women and men negotiate ethnic patriarchy over time and space. Bandana Purkayastha and her colleagues (2012) use the concept "cumulative disadvantages" to highlight the processes through which difficulties experienced by Asian Americans at earlier life stages can have long-standing implications for their psychological, physical, and social well-being later in life. Along a similar line, I argue that the impact of long-term migration on spousal relations is not only cumulative but also path dependent (i.e., shaped by the decisions made across different life phases).

The intersection between time and migration is notably evident through four life experiences: (1) leaving kinship behind on departure, (2) receiving education and working in the United States, (3) negotiating the cultural ideal of Western intimacy, and (4) undergoing aging and life transitions transnationally. All significantly influence intimate relations between older migrant spouses. Migration to the United States shapes both connections to homeland kin and socioeconomic standing in the host society, promoting a perception of Americanization, which can, in turn, soften gender hierarchies after retirement. As my respondents used newly acquired cultural schemas to evaluate their situations, they changed how "they feel—emotionally, viscerally, sometimes violently—about" (Ortner 2006, 18) gender norms at home.

Some female respondents insisted on the husband's authoritative roles, but most stressed gender flexibility and found ways to reconstruct masculinities and femininities. Identifying egalitarianism as the dominant cultural feature of spousal relations in the United States, many emphasized harmonious relationships maintained not through coercion but through mutual communication, coordination, and respect. Yet while they acknowledged mutuality, these Taiwanese immigrant couples also evidenced gender inequalities. Many were deeply concerned about the man's image as an authority figure, both at home and in public, and they engaged in face-saving practices that reveal persistent symbolic inequality. Guided by "perceptual, interactional, and micropolitical activities that cast particular pursuits as expressions of masculine and feminine 'natures'" (West and Zimmerman 1987, 126), these older immigrant women would "do" gender differently across public and private spheres.

Conjugality in Chinese Societies

Married life in traditional Chinese culture is marked by four features: gender specialization, male domination, multigenerational relations, and lack of mutuality. Consistent with the literature on gender and families in Western contexts, research on conjugality in Chinese families points to a persistent gendered division of labor between husbands and wives (Lui 2013; Man 1997). Husbands are economic providers and wives, homemakers. This gendered arrangement is related not only to men's economic resources but also to dominant gender ideologies in Chinese societies (Zuo 2008). Wives—even when participating in the labor force and, in some cases, earning paychecks larger than their spouses—still shoulder more familial responsibilities than their husbands (Qian and Sayer 2016). In addition, as in Western industrial societies, husbands in Chinese families act as authority figures. In traditional Chinese societies, "while a wife has ritual rights in relation to her husband's ancestors, her interests are not with this family and its male members as a whole but are only aligned with her husband's interests and his portion of the joint family wealth which shall eventually become available to her sons" (Barbalet 2014, 197). Decades of modernization have significantly improved women's status, but many Chinese husbands remain the symbolic centers of their families, with significant control over their wives (Li 2015; Shih and Pyke 2016).

The discursive construction of conjugality in Chinese and other Asian societies differs from conjugal norms typical in Western contexts. As Mark Lewinsohn and Paul Werner (1997, 44) write, "Chinese marriage has been viewed as the continuation of the parent's family, rather than as the beginning of a new and separate family." Unlike wives in North America and Western Europe, wives in Chinese societies typically understand, assess, and perform their responsibilities in a multigenerational context (Y. Li 2015; Zuo 2009). Women not only marry into their husbands' families but also need to manage connections to their husbands' kin (Greenhalgh 1988; Gu 2006). This expectation creates complex dynamics for many Chinese couples, especially for women (Shih and Pyke 2010).

Moreover, couples in Chinese families assess their marriages with criteria that differ from Western norms. Mutuality, in particular, is not an important indicator of successful married life. Whereas Western couples value open communication and self-disclosure, Chinese couples "are socialized to be more restrained, more reserved in their interactions, and to frown upon verbal expression" (Fitzpatrick et al. 2006, 114). Intimacy in a Western sense is often discouraged in traditional Chinese families; husbands and wives are expected or even encouraged to maintain psychological distance from each other (Barbalet 2014). Compared with Western couples, many Chinese spouses are more accepting of a marital life that lacks mutuality, reciprocity, and emotional closeness (Li and Wickrama 2014). These varying cultural tendencies mediate the evaluation of marital life and foster responses to love and intimacy distinctly different from expectations in the West (Lewinsohn and Werner 1997).

Ideas about gender and marriage can "travel" with Chinese people who cross national borders. In her recent book on gender and Taiwanese Americans, Chienjuh Gu (2017) argues that migration exacerbates the patriarchal constraints with which immigrant women struggle. These women, who used to do paid work in the homeland, compromise or sacrifice their careers so that their husbands can land better job opportunities in the United States. Despite their employment status, most of Gu's respondents also shouldered domestic responsibilities—such as cooking, cleaning, raising children, planning family social activities, managing household finances, and, in some cases, performing elder care—without much help from their husbands. These responsibilities, as Gu vividly describes, take an emotional toll on immigrant women, but their pains are often invisible to their family members.

Although I witnessed some of the phenomena that Gu (2017) describes, this chapter highlights the transformation rather than perpetuation of gendered conjugality. The respondents had experienced long-term settlement in the United States, and my findings differ from Gu's in five ways: (1) the outcome examined, (2) the migration paths, (3) the age of respondents, (4) the research design, and (5) the positionality of the investigator. Gu focuses on the gendered division of labor between husbands and wives. By contrast, I concentrate on immigrant couples' assessment of their status as spouses across life phases. As Gu (72) emphasizes, "regardless of such unequal division of labor, it would be wrong to assume that Taiwanese immigrant wives are powerless in the family. . . . The power issues in spousal relations is far more complicated than a single sphere of family life can fully portray." Echoing Gu's observation, this chapter shifts the focus from the division of labor at home to the ways older immigrant couples consider mutuality and male domination in their marital relations at different life stages.

Second, while most of the women Gu (2017) studied came to the United States initially as the spouses of international students, about half of my respondents migrated through family sponsorship. As I described in chapter 1, immigrant families that migrate through kinship networks typically experience downward mobility during their early years in the United States because their educational credentials in Taiwan lose value in the new society. To make ends meet, therefore, both husbands and wives have to work outside the home, and the gendered divide between public and private life that I observed is not as clear-cut as Gu describes. Because of long working hours, respondents who arrived to the United States through family reunification typically shared both financial and domestic responsibilities. Such changes facilitate the equalization of spousal relations at a later stage of life.

Third, in contrast to Gu (2017), this chapter considers the voices not only of immigrant wives but also of their husbands. Many immigrant husbands I interviewed, while acknowledging their wives' indispensable role in domestic responsibilities, also talked at length about the ways relocating to the United States had changed the dynamics of relationships at home. Furthermore, interviewing both husbands and wives—in most cases separately and in some cases together—might also have influenced respondents' stories about their marriage. Knowing that I would be talking with their spouses might also have prompted them to downplay marital conflicts and instead stress the compromises both they and their spouses have made.

Fourth, the immigrant couples I studied were significantly older than those in Gu's (2017) research. The ages of her respondents ranged from thirty to sixty-two, whereas mine ranged from their early sixties to their early nineties. This age difference is important because aging and life transitions had pushed my respondents to reconsider status in their respective families. For example, they discussed biological aging, especially declining health and physical mobility, that pushed them to become flexible about a gendered division of labor at home, and they recounted the ways their "Americanized" children shaped their assessment of spousal relations (see chapter 2). These findings testify to the centrality of aging and life transition in understanding the experiences of older immigrants who are long-term residents in receiving contexts.

Fifth, my position as a younger Taiwanese man likely influenced the respondents' answers to my questions. For example, few of my respondents talked about the sexual dimensions of spousal intimacies in front of me, and I avoided actively pursuing this line of questioning because I knew it would violate community norms and make my respondents uncomfortable. As Russell King reminded me when we took a walk together in Hong Kong in 2017, if I were closer to my respondents' age, some might have been willing to talk about intimacy and spousal relations in different ways. The age difference probably also informed my respondents' concerns about my marital status. They often used their own experiences to "instruct" me on finding a good wife, interacting with her, and the reasons marriage would be important as I grew older in the United States (see appendix A). To highlight the "benefits" of a sustained, healthy marriage, they focused on the transforming rather than constraining dimensions of their own intimate lives across time and borders.

Most importantly, cultural ideals of gendered conjugality in Chinese families are neither static nor monolithic. Exposure to US society may not have a direct impact on the gendered division of labor in immigrant households as Gu (2017) suggests, but as this chapter shows, it has unintended consequences on couples' consideration of spousal relations, including communication, decision making, and sense of status. Heavily influenced by the cultural ideal of the American family, immigrants' children could also intervene and propel their parents to re-evaluate marital life. As prior research has shown, many Chinese couples adopt what they perceive as Western modes of love and intimacy and remake intimate relations accordingly.

For instance, Karen Quek and her colleagues (2010) demonstrate that the dominant US culture motivates Chinese immigrant couples to soften gender hierarchies, thereby promoting more egalitarian relationships. Jacki Fitzpatrick and her colleagues (2006, 122) found that Chinese immigrants in the United States are more willing than their nonmigrant counterparts in mainland China to disclose their emotional struggles to their spouses. Of course, the perceived democratic nature of intimate relations among Western couples overlooks the persistence of gender inequalities in North American families (see Garey and Hansen 2011; Hochschild 1997; Nelson 2005). This perception, however, points to the cultural ideal of Western intimacy and "may reflect [immigrants'] changes in marital communication congruent with more 'North Americanization'" (Fitzpatrick et al. 2006, 122). Building on these insights, this chapter examines conjugality among immigrants who are long-term US residents by analyzing the ways time, migration, and their intersection shape perspectives on love, intimacy, and marriage.

I identify two patterns that explain the respondents' perspectives on their conjugal connections: reproducing conjugality and remaking conjugality. The few who reproduced conjugality evinced a clear gender hierarchy. They sought to maintain lives congruent with their understanding of traditional Chinese culture. For them, the worlds of wives and husbands should be interconnected but separate. Respect was important, but wives, they believed, should defer to their husbands in disagreements and major family decisions. Those who sought to remake conjugality instead negotiated and, to some degree, transformed their intimate relationships. Changing structural, cultural, and contextual factors across time and space motivated these migrants to value mutuality and flexibility over hierarchy. This transformation occurs slowly and is profoundly affected by decisions made at different stages of life. Long-term migration had altered my respondents' sense of duty and responsibility, as temporalities of migration led to accumulated changes, reinforced across the life span.

For migrant families, moving to the United States challenges control exerted by extended family and so alters decision making. Adapting to the United States also forces women to "toughen" themselves, sometimes to the point of challenging their husbands' authority over family welfare. The experience of cultural change thus prompts negotiation, as Western ideals render gender hierarchies more flexible. Many of the respondents invoked the rhetoric of "Americanization" to explain the need for more democratic and egalitarian relationships with their spouses. The experiences of aging and expected or perceived declining health could, in turn, require greater flexibility in the division of domestic labor. Temporalities of migration thus challenge the ethnic patriarchy, often in surprising ways.

Reproducing Conjugality: Sustaining Gender Hierarchies

A small subset of the respondents (four couples, two of them returnees) insisted that their spousal relations continued to conform to Taiwanese or Chinese traditions. For them, neither time nor migration had altered beliefs or behavior patterns. These couples typically emphasized gendered obligations between spouses and hierarchical relationships between husbands and wives. Mr. and Mrs. Fang were one such couple. Mr. Fang perceived himself as traditional, stating that he and his wife shouldered different responsibilities and that his status in the family depended on successfully fulfilling his role as economic provider. Although retired from work by the time of our interview, Mr. Fang had purchased apartments in Boston and, with the rents he collected, continued to contribute approximately seven thousand dollars to the household each month. With this money he paid his children's college tuition and lived comfortably, but he relied on his wife as homemaker and caregiver. Having cared for her children, Mrs. Fang had become the primary caregiver for her parents-in-law, who had also moved to the United States. Mr. Fang appreciated the work his wife performed for his family, but he maintained a clear, even rigid division of labor with his wife.

For Mr. Fang, living in the United States had changed little in the ways he thought about his relationship with his wife, and they lived separate but interconnected lives. He had been the manager of a Chinese restaurant, which had been his focus, and after retiring, he fostered a new community with a group of older Chinese immigrant men with whom he golfed and hiked. His wife, he asserted, had her own friends (an assertion that his wife confirmed). Home almost every day at dinner, Mr. Fang was usually silent and listened to his wife talk. He claimed that he respected her opinions but considered himself the authority figure to whom his wife deferred, even though he rarely expressed his own views. Mr. Fang was clearly aware of the power he exercised. Interviewing his wife separately, I heard Mrs. Fang admit that he could be stubborn and quick-tempered. At times, Mrs. Fang told me, she struggled to reconcile conflicts between her husband and her children and found both sides hard to convince.

Mr. and Mrs. Fang were not alone in their efforts to reproduce the conjugality of traditional Chinese/Taiwanese culture. In Taiwan, Mr. and Mrs. Wei—two professional-class returnees—described similar dynamics. Mrs. Wei identified them as "a very traditional Chinese couple" in both their divided duties and their adherence to male authority. Mrs. Wei told me that her husband had been a lawyer in the United States and had accumulated considerable wealth there, which provided her with material privileges and no worries about money. For example, she had owned four different cars in the United States (in Taiwan, she had never driven), all of them Mercedes-Benz. "I don't even know how to drive other types of cars because I only drive Mercedes-Benz," she jokingly told me.

Yet Mrs. Wei had shouldered all the homemaking and childcare because paid work had occupied most of her husband's time, and now in a later stage of life, she continued to defer to her husband. Her "decision," in 2006, to return to Taiwan and care for her mother-in-law vividly illustrated her understanding of her duties as a wife and daughter-in-law. The decision was not a preference. She knew that caring for an ailing person was overwhelming, especially at her age, but she wanted to avoid upsetting her husband and felt unable to object to her default role as caregiver. (She also reminded me not to reveal her feelings about caring for her mother-in-law when I interviewed her husband.) Mrs. Wei reported never thinking about challenging her husband's decision. Noting that the gods (*shang tian*) created men and women, she saw the responsibilities of husbands and wives as different but complementary and even encouraged me to find a wife who would prioritize my career over hers.

Remaking Conjugality: Transforming Gendered Relationships

For most respondents, conjugality had undergone profound changes, not only across borders but also over time. These gendered changes are intimately tied to the decisions long-term immigrants make at different life stages and the various ways in which they adapt to new life in the United States. How respondents address opportunities and constraints transnationally and transtemporally paves the way for the transformation of conjugality later in life.

Living in a Nuclear Family by Leaving Kin Behind

The decision to migrate to the United States changed spousal relations in profound ways. Women, in particular, reported that migration to the United States marked a transition in gender relations (Hondagneu-Sotelo 1994). The confrontations between daughters-in-laws and parents-in-law (especially mothers-in-law) have been widely documented in academic research as a major source of conflicts in Asian and Asian American families (Chong 2006; Gu 2017; Shih and Pyke 2016). Less often surrounded by extended family, immigrant women and men could center their attention on their own nuclear households. For most of the women I interviewed, relocation had meant escape from the domestic politics of kinship networks in Taiwan and fewer worries about the views and expectations of extended family members, especially parents-in-law. Communicating with their husbands, these women could concentrate more often on their own needs and desires, and once in the United States, both women and men reported greater control over their lives.

For example, Mrs. Chang, in her late sixties, reported that, after moving to the United States, she and her husband usually consulted with each other about all the important family decisions. When they were younger, Mrs. Chang recalled, they had talked about educating the next generation and saving money for their children's education. As they grew older, they discussed whether to stay in the same neighborhood, move closer to their children, or relocate to Taiwan. Mrs. Chang described an established pattern of respecting and listening to each other because, in the United States, "it [was] only two of [them]." "If we lived in Taiwan," Mrs. Chang explained, "we would have a lot of relatives on my or my husband's side that we would need to deal with almost on an everyday basis. I might have to live with my parents-in-law if I lived in Taiwan. In this situation, when I educated my own kids, my father-in-law might say something, and my mother-in-law might say something, too. My own parents might give me a lot of suggestions as well. In the United States, our family only consists of my husband, my children, and me. In Taiwan, it's just so complicated."

Like his wife, Mr. Chang, in his midseventies, recognized a transition in gender norms, and like most of my male respondents, he reported listening to his wife without interference by parents-in-law. In Taiwan, Mr. Chang asserted, he needed to consider the feelings, emotions, and perspectives of both his wife and his own parents and had felt stressed by occasional conflicts. Now in the United States, he no longer worried about these disagreements. With his parents on the other side of the Pacific Ocean, he had come to consult mainly with his wife over important decisions, and this communication pattern had persisted into later life. Rather than imposing his will, Mr. Chang claimed that he often deferred to his spouse. For example, he and his wife negotiated about when to retire and where to live after his retirement, and he had given up the idea of moving closer to his children. "In the United States," he recounted,

> I am used to talking to my wife about almost every important decision, because it's just two of us. My company offered me a really attractive package for early retirement a few years ago, and I talked with my wife about whether I should take it. Then, we ended up retiring together. . . . I thought about moving to Illinois to be closer to my son after retiring, but my wife was reluctant to do so. She prefers to stay in Massachusetts and has her own friends and social life. And I respect her opinion. When I was in Taiwan, we [my wife and I] lived with my parents. I felt very stressed out. My parents and my wife often have conflicts over minor things. Both my mother and my wife are very strong-willed. They often have fights, and they always came to me when they had disagreement. But after moving to the United States, it is just me and my wife. We talk about and solve things between us.

Like their coethnics in the United States, the return migrants I interviewed, especially the women, stressed that moving to the United States had transformed their conjugal relationships. Mrs. Shen emphasized that if she had never left Taiwan, she would have had to organize her life around a large kinship network. After she and her husband received master's degrees in the United States, they had returned and worked in Taiwan for about a year, but the experience of cohabiting with her mother-in-law and interacting with her sister-in-law had made her determined to encourage her husband to apply for a PhD program in the United States. Mrs. Shen described both her mother-in-law and her sister-in-law as "savvy" and "controlling" people, who had specifically directed the distribution of her household income. She spoke bitterly of their objections as she helped her birth family purchase an apartment in Taipei, a conflict that was three decades old, exclaiming "my mother-in-law and my sister-in-law thought that since I was already married into the Shen family, I should not use my own money to benefit my own parents and siblings, and I should prioritize the Shen family over my birth family. But it is my money, and my parents are the ones who raised me."

These accounts illustrate not only patriarchal practices that govern married women but also tense relationships that can ensue within extended families. For Mrs. Shen, even more difficult was that her husband could not relate to her feelings. This lack of empathy, she maintained, stemmed from her husband's view that his mother was "the most wonderful and caring person in the world" so that he failed to understand why she "misinterpreted" her in-laws' well-intentioned advice. After these unpleasant experiences, Mrs. Shen had been determined to convince her husband to establish his career in the United States. She had emphasized the benefits of a US education for their children, but as she admitted to me, she had secretly hoped to distance herself from her in-laws and establish a "simple" nuclear family life in the United States. Settling in the United States, Mrs. Shen reported, did indeed transform her relationship with her husband, and their nuclear family structure reinforced their mutual dependence, especially after their children moved out of the household.

More importantly, returning to Taiwan later in life made Mrs. Shen acutely aware of her changing status among her kin; she was no longer the daughter-in-law who was expected to defer to the will of members of older generations. During their fifties, her husband mentioned the possibility of moving back to Taiwan, but she had remained strongly opposed, largely because she was wanted to avoid sharing the caregiving for her mother-in-law. Returning in her sixties, after her mother-in-law had passed away, however, she had assumed the role of matriarch, with the status of grandmother, aunt, and great-aunt. This role meant authority among her kin, and she rarely had to subordinate her will to an older generation. Mrs. Shen admitted that she felt relieved because, as she explained, "I no longer had to serve anyone but my husband." Disembedded and then reembedded in a large kinship network, she could now negotiate within her marriage.

How Long-Term Migration Empowers Women

Migration transformed the ways in which my respondents evaluated their status in conjugal relationships. To overcome obstacles in a foreign society, many women I interviewed claimed that they were forced to become tough. These women also believed that they were much tougher than the nonmigrant women they encountered during their return visits or after they moved back and settled in Taiwan. For them, being a homemaker in a foreign context was more difficult than doing so in their homeland because they had to learn to be wives and mothers from scratch. This experience pushed them to become stronger willed than the Taiwanese women who lacked experience living abroad. Toughness sometimes meant that they questioned or challenged their husbands' authority, especially when a decision seemed important for the welfare of the entire family. Most migrant women learned techniques for bargaining with their spouses. Their strategies, however, depended on their economic circumstances.

Migrants who came for lower-wage labor or through family sponsors typically lacked educational credentials recognized in the United States and thus encountered economic obstacles and even downward mobility. These men often relied on their wives' paychecks, and some lower-middle-class and working-class women even became primary earners in their households. This reversal in norms led many working-class men to share some domestic responsibilities (e.g., housework or childcare) as their wives spent much of their time working outside the home. A changing division of labor might then promote new power dynamics between spouses so that women with lower-class origins could gain significant leverage in family decision making.

Mrs. Ma, in her sixties, had gained economic muscle in the United States but attributed the profound changes in marriage to her persuading her husband to adapt more US gender norms. Mrs. Ma had been a homemaker in Taiwan, and her husband had worked as a high-level manager in a government-run company, but they had decided to move to the United States for their children's education and future. As she recounted, her husband had faced trouble finding a job and was unemployed for about a year, largely because he lacked a degree recognized in the United States and could not speak English well. To support the family, Mrs. Ma had taken several jobs—as a tailor by day and a janitor by night—while her husband took on childcare at home. According to Mrs. Ma, her husband was unhappy about the changing division of labor and wanted to move back to Taiwan, but she had objected. A good wife and mother in the United States sometimes had to give her husband "wake-up calls," she explained.

> My husband thought about moving back to Taiwan. He was a manager in a government-owned enterprise in Taiwan, but here he could not find any decent job. He was unemployed for almost a year, and I had to work several jobs at the same time. . . . He ended up finding a job at a Japanese supermarket and was not happy. He wanted to move back to Taiwan. I actually said no to him, "If you want to go back, you can go back yourself. I am not leaving. I will be here with my children. If you want to go, you will probably be alone facing walls and ceilings. It's up to you, but the children and I will not be moving with you." I am a homemaker. My job is to hold this family together. I need to tell my husband what is the right thing to do.

Lower-wage women who had returned to Taiwan similarly emphasized the new gender norms they had encountered in the United States. Mrs. Deng, in her seventies, cited an expanded understanding of homemaking, which for her had come to include both financial and domestic responsibilities. Because the cost of living in the United States was much higher than in Taiwan, she had taken on paid work to supplement her husband's income. In the United States, she explained, homemaking also required her to interact with US institutions (such as schools and real estate agents), which pushed her to develop new linguistic and social skills. She had learned to drive, to approach teachers who spoke only English, to gather information about public school districts, to arrange extracurricular activities for children, and to deal with a landlord whom she suspected was racist. "When we left Taiwan," she asserted, "we also left our comfort zone and were forced to grow up." Many migrant women, Mrs. Deng believed, had to become stronger and more independent than the women back home, and these women gained power not only through their economic contributions to the household economy but also through their interactions with other social institutions in the United States.

From Mrs. Deng's perspective, the "toughness" she learned as a newcomer had profoundly shaped her relationship with her husband. Becoming a tough, rather than a deferential, wife was important because she could help her husband think clearly about difficult issues, including the decision to move back to Taiwan. Learning of her husband's cancer, Mrs. Deng maintained that she felt upset but spent little time crying and instead took the initiative to return. She carefully researched old-age homes and paid caregiving and consulted with her friends about facilities for medical treatment. Her husband was initially ambivalent about physical separation from their children, Mrs. Deng explained, but she had been determined and eventually "strong-armed" her husband to return. As a wife and default caregiver, she believed that her firm position had prevented much suffering. "If my husband became really sick and immobile," she speculated, "who are we going to rely on? In the US, there was no way we can afford to hire a full-time caretaker or moving into a private nursing home. I don't want to overwhelm my children. I insist on moving back because this is the best way for everyone in the family."

Many lower-middle-class and working-class men who arrived in the United States through family sponsorship or as labor migrants spoke in similar ways about changing gender dynamics. Some lamented their loss of power. Mr. Long, in his sixties, had migrated for better economic prospects and a better future for his children. Working in a restaurant in Chinatown, he had hoped to save enough to open his own restaurant. Having hurt his back at work, however, he then hurt his spine after falling on black ice and had trouble working long hours. He thus came to rely on his wife to be the major economic contributor to the household. For Mr. Long, his wife's work outside the household had transformed their relationship, not only because of her financial contribution but also because of the worldview she had developed. As his wife had become vocal about her needs and desires, Mr. Long often felt as if he had lost power in his family, and he suspected that his wife no longer cared about his opinion. Yet he also realized that his wife's newfound independence was necessary. "Increasingly, my wife made more money than me, and she made more and more friends outside of the household." He elaborated,

> She had changed since then. She started to compare me with other Chinese men. How come I cannot speak English well? How come I cannot

make money and help her buy our own house? My wife was probably not happy with me, and I am sure she has a lot of complaints. Since we moved to the US, she has changed a lot. She began to have her own dreams, and she began to have different ideas. I often have to make concession. But I am glad that she is autonomous. She makes money and takes care of me. I feel sorry and fortunate. Especially now, as we grow older, I realize that she is becoming more important for me, because I become more and more reliant upon her.

For professional-class women who had arrived in the United States as international students, academic training supported negotiation over deference in relation to their husbands. These respondents typically talked of educational and professional experiences in the United States that had offered insights for surviving and maximizing the well-being of their families. They also emphasized challenging husbands who might require their expertise. Mrs. Yang considered her US education and work experience the basis for the advice she gave her husband. Contradicting the idea that married women should defer, she believed in offering her perspective. "I got an advanced degree from [the school name] in the US," she explained.

My education does not prepare me for being a housewife. I was trained to have my own ideas. . . . I worked as a real estate agent, and my husband is a computer scientist. I work with lots of clients and make a lot of friends, including Americans, Chinese, and Taiwanese. I can see things my husbands as an engineer cannot see. If my husband and I have different opinions, we will talk. It's always like this since there are only two of us here [in the United States]. Sometimes I listen to him, and sometimes he thinks I am more correct.

Mrs. Yang's independence and newly cultivated confidence had helped her organize her later life. To be closer to their daughter and granddaughter, she had convinced her husband to leave New Jersey for Boston. Evoking her status as an immigrant, she emphasized the difficulties that had prepared her later-life changes. According to Mrs. Yang, her husband was initially reluctant to leave their neighborhood, but she had urged him to be more flexible. "Moving to the US really changed my lifestyle," she noted.

If I stayed in Taiwan, I probably did not have much chance to explore different societies. But after so many years in the US, I am so used to different cultures and lifestyles. . . . [For example,] my son-in-law lives in Massachusetts. So I convinced my husband to move to be closer to my daughter and her family. Americans are not very mobile, but we are migrants. We have been mobile since we were younger. We are like rootless people and are probably more cosmopolitan than most Americans. We have been to different societies and experienced different things than ordinary Americans.

Return migrant women similarly cited education as the basis for greater agency. Mrs. Lee reported that her work at an elite US research institution had come to "equalize" her spousal relationship. As a scientist trained in the United States during the 1970s, she had encountered much gender discrimination and even sexual harassment. As she recalled, one of her male colleagues once said to her, "If you wore pants, I might listen to you." For Mrs. Lee, such misogyny, coupled with the common notion that a woman should be primarily a homemaker, had prevented many female scientists from "making it." Mrs. Lee had also witnessed the effects of affirmative action policies, and although she claimed she had never benefited from them, her experiences had led her to challenge women's subordination and support racial minorities. Drawing on these perspectives, she preferred to confer with her husband, believing that rational discussion rather than deference brought about the most sensible decision.

Echoing their wives, professional-class men who had come to the United States as international students also maintained that their authoritative status at home was now weaker. Those with stay-at-home or minimally employed wives described relying on their wives to handle the household, but many emphasized mutual respect and communication through which a homemaker could offer insights or expertise. Interdependence, they explained, now sustained their later lives. Mr. Yang clearly stated that he relied on his wife to "run his life" because, as homemaker, she had gained a working knowledge of US society that he lacked. In the United States, he had moved several times for his work and relied on his wife to pack, transfer children to different schools, and communicate with the moving companies while he had concentrated on his work:

> I have relied on my wife for many things since we moved to the US. There are only two of us in the US. She handled many things in my family. She organized everything every time we moved. She figured out which neighborhoods have better schools for our children. She dealt with movers, and I basically did nothing. Now I retired. She spends a lot of time volunteering for [a community organization]. She knows a lot of people and knows where we can get the services we want. . . . She has always been caring and thoughtful. I respected her thought and often listen to her.

Some of the professional-class men I interviewed had wives who initially came to the United States on student visas and had then secured white-collar jobs in such settings as hospitals, financial firms, and universities. These men used their wives' accomplishments to explain changing spousal dynamics. Mr. Lee, a return migrant, commented on the ways studying and working in the United States had transformed his marriage. "Many women's mentality has changed after coming to the United States," he noted, "because they have seen more of the world." Mr. Lee claimed that he had no desire for authority over his wife because she "outperformed" him. He had served in the military in Taiwan after graduating from college, and his wife (then girlfriend) had come to the United States two years before him, received her PhD degree, and negotiated a spousal hire for him. Mr. Lee described his wife as an "introvert" in Taiwan but felt that many years of working in the United States had "toughened" her. Now a strong-willed person, he noted, his wife had worked as a scientist in a male-dominated field since the 1970s, and the experience had broadened her horizons and increased her confidence. They were now equal partners, and he consulted with her about family and career matters, including whether to accept a job offer and return to Taiwan. "My wife is literally the head of the house," Mr. Lee jokingly commented. "I cannot force my wife do anything. If my wife said no, I cannot move back."

Perceived Acculturation: Learning from "Egalitarian" American Families

Many of my respondents discussed the softening effects of Americanization on gender hierarchies. As Karen Pyke (2000, 241) points out, the dominant cultural ideal of family in the United States emphasizes "sensitivity, open honest communication, flexibility, and forgiveness," and these traits are less valued "in many cultures that stress duty, responsibility, obedience, and a commitment to the family collective that supersedes self-interests." By contrast, some of my female respondents emphasized the importance of learning cultural practices common to the American nuclear family. Their understanding of American families influenced their assessments of their own conjugal relationships. Research has shown that many Asians and Asian Americans associate white American masculinity with the image of a gender-egalitarian "new man" (Kim 2006; Kim and Pyke 2015) and link white American femininity to gender liberation (Pyke and Johnson 2003). In this way, a few of the women I interviewed suggested that their husbands should learn from "American" men of similar age about communicating and conveying their emotions, and they pushed their husbands to do so.

Claiming that American men were more expressive than most Asian men— and Chinese men in particular—these women contended that communicating feelings and thoughts maintained a "healthy" spousal relationship, especially when problems needed solving. Some respondents envied the ways in which American couples interacted. For them, American men were in general more emotionally expressive than Taiwanese/Han Chinese men, and American women were more willing to demand a genuine conversation with their husbands than Taiwanese/Han Chinese women. Mrs. Guo maintained that she did not expect her husband to be as frank with his feelings as other American men, and she would not push her husband as hard to communicate as would American women. Yet as he sat beside her during our interview, she seized opportunities to lecture him about open communication. "American men are more forthcoming about their feelings," she lamented. "Even older American men are very sweet and very willing to convey their feelings and thoughts. In our neighborhood, you can often see older couples call each other 'honey,' 'sweetheart,' and 'darling.' And they are often having coffee and exchange ideas about things happening to them. Most Taiwanese men are not really like that. And I think they need to change and become more compassionate."

Unlike their wives, the men I interviewed rarely talked of learning US norms about conjugality, but some recognized that US society valued mutuality between spouses and encouraged couples to communicate sincerely and honestly. Practicing Christians most often made this point. Mr. Ou Yang, a return migrant in his early seventies, used the Bible to illustrate the cultural ideal of conjugal relations in the United States. Having converted to Christianity while in the United States, Mr. Ou Yang equated US culture with Christian values. For him, becoming American had also been a process of learning Christian attitudes and practices (C. Chen 2008), and he thought he saw much commonality between Confucianism and Protestantism. Spousal relations, however, were an exception. The Bible made the husband head of the family, but it also stressed that men should love their wives as they love their own bodies. As Mr. Ou Yang maintained, "If you love your wife as much as you love yourself, how can you not try to understand each other's needs?" Mutual understanding and communication were thus keys to an American cultural ideal.

Most notably, the respondents spoke of the impact of their "Americanized" children on their relationships. Because most did not expect their Americanized children to care for them in later life, migrant men had become increasingly aware of their wives as companions and caregivers. Consequently, many couples I talked with stressed the importance of cooperation, as Mrs. Ro, in her sixties, asserted: "In the US, your children will move out after they turn eighteen and go to college. Then, the only companion you have is your spouse. This is the very typical American nuclear family, and this is why American couples very much stress the importance of communicating. I think since we are in the US, we should also learn this cultural practice by listening to and communicating with our spouses." Mr. Liang, in his midsixties, described his relationship with his wife as a collaborative partnership, citing equality and mutuality rather than hierarchy and authority. His children, born and raised in the United States, were adamant about their own space and unwilling to submit to their parents, and even though their relationships remained positive, he expected his wife rather than his children to be with him as he aged. Reflecting on his American children, Mr. Liang explained,

> They are not like our generation, who has some responsibility and commitment to caring for parents. American children grow up and start looking for their own lives. They have their own career, family, and friends. We had better not bother them too much or too often. The most intimate company for me at this life stage is my wife. My relationships are becoming more and more like companionship, and we discussed about lots of possible situations. We had our financial plans and discussed about the possibility of moving to an assisted-living facility if we could no longer sustain ourselves. It is not that I said something, and my wife follows the order. My wife and I learn new things and broaden our horizons as we get older. We depend on each other.

Return migrants like Mr. Yeh made similar comments about changing conjugal relationships in the United States. At the time of interview, Mr. Yeh and his wife lived in an old-age home in a suburban neighborhood about forty minutes' drive from Taipei. He maintained that, with US culture encouraging the elderly to remain self-sufficient, he and his wife had been reluctant to burden their children. They "only had each other" at this life stage, Mr. Yeh explained, so their relationship needed to be mutual and reciprocal. Understanding each other's needs was important because each spouse would be the only person to "be there" until the end of life.

For some of the women I interviewed, rejecting hierarchy for mutuality meant pushing their husbands to be less paternalistic and less authoritarian, and concern for their husbands' bonds with their children could offer a strategy for softening male authority more broadly. For many of these women, narratives of Americanization challenged overtly masculine practices. Mrs. Chou, at age seventy, described using intergenerational tension between her husband and children to convince her husband to change his communication style. He had been heavily influenced by Japanese culture, she explained, and had the tendency to be "chauvinist," but their children, growing up in the United States, had been influenced by the individual freedom, equality, and open communication emphasized in US culture.[1] Concerned that her husband would alienate their children, Mrs. Chou had encouraged her husband to reconsider such practices as giving them orders. She had encouraged more reciprocal communication, which had altered her husband's mode of interaction with her as well. "Many Taiwanese men of my generation were influenced by Japanese culture when they were younger. Thus, they were very chauvinist." She elaborated,

> But in the United States, you cannot act like that, especially when your children are Americanized. Americanized children aspire to individual autonomy and demand your respect. I always told my husband that our children are already adults. You have to respect their opinions. You cannot impose your will on them. You will be pushing them away if you keep forcing them to do things. He knows I am right although he never said so. But I noticed that he increasingly changes the ways he interacts with us [Mrs. Chou and her children]. He now hesitates about yelling or raising his voice when we disagree with each. He became more willing to communicate with me in an egalitarian way.

Some women who had returned to Taiwan similarly spoke of Americanized children who had inspired their husbands to rethink conjugal intimacy. Mrs. Jiang indicated that her children often reminded her husband to be gentler and considerate with her. She believed that growing up in Taiwan and working as a medical doctor in the United States had inclined her husband to "order" family members to do his bidding. As Mrs. Jiang explained, her adult children had fought for her since their adolescence, telling her husband, "Mom was not your patient or supervisee; you cannot talk to her like that." And they would remind him not to interrupt her. Her children's assertions, answering back and challenging parental authority, were for Mrs. Jiang evidence of US culture. While her husband was not always happy about their children's behavior, Mrs. Jiang perceived a softer tone and more respectful approach. For example, her husband had consulted her about moving back to Taiwan.

Many of the men I interviewed explicitly or implicitly reported reflecting on their status in the family in response to their Americanized children, often with prodding from their wives about interacting with adult children as equals. Mr. Hsieh, in his late sixties, reported hearing frequent warnings from his wife about his authoritative stance, and to sustain close relationships with his adult children, he had tried to treat them as peers or friends rather than subordinates. Mr. Hsieh appreciated his wife's reminders and had developed more democratic practices with her as well. "My wife is basically responsible for educating our children," he related.

> She always told me that I cannot be stubborn and cannot be unreasonable; since this is the US I should not impose my will on them. They will compare me with the parents of their friends and become alienated from me. . . . Now my children grow up, and my wife keeps reminding me that

I should stop giving orders to my children. This will lead to a lot of unnecessary clashes and conflicts. They are all adults and have their own family and lives. I am aware of my problems and try to be less authoritative and more reasonable with my children and my wife. Often, my wife will correct me or communicate with me about how I should approach our family members or friends.

In several cases, the male respondents, in both the United States and Taiwan, described their wives as strong-willed and controlling and their family problems a result of their wives' exercise of authority. These were the men who used their "Americanized children" as a rationale to push their wives to change. Mr. Sun, a seventy-six-year-old return migrant, described his wife as a "control freak" (*kong zhi kuang*) who "planned and organized everything"—including his diet, his clothes, and his daily activities. Overall, he claimed, he was fine with his wife making decisions for him, but he sometimes reminded her to "democratize" her communication style with their children. Describing his wife as a typical "Asian tiger mom," he had been concerned about her micromanaging their children's academic performance, which he believed had strained intergenerational relationships. While all had entered elite colleges and landed well-paid professional jobs, the children kept their parents at arm's length. Reflecting on family life, Mr. Sun reported advising his wife to become more relaxed. "I often said to her, 'The children are adults now,'" he recounted. "If you continue to boss them around, you will push them away."

Not all respondents had been pushed to adapt less authoritative roles. A few claimed to have gladly embraced the Americanization of their conjugal relationships. Mr. Shen, who had returned to Taiwan, emphasized the impact of American individualism—with respect for personal space and individual autonomy—on connections with his wife. He had witnessed his children become increasingly Americanized and had begun to reflect on how he could treat his wife differently. "The US is a completely different context, and we are also in a different era," he began.

According to Taiwanese tradition, we expected our children to listen to us. But the US values individual growth and freedom. Our kids feel like they are responsible for their own decision and lives, and parents should not interfere too much. I think it's a healthy relationship, and it's also applicable to my relationship with my wife. My wife and I should be responsible for ourselves. This is necessary to maintain a harmonious relationship. If you don't respect individual freedom and will, you cannot develop your ideas and cannot communicate well with each other. If my wife limited me, I cannot do the volunteering work I am currently doing. If I impose a lot of constraints for my wife, she cannot pursue other goals in her life, such as to learn painting and realize her artistic potentials. American individualism is actually very good for the relationship between me and my wife.

How Aging Promotes Gender Flexibility

Aging reinforced mutuality between spouses as they enacted greater gender flexibility in their domestic responsibilities. Expectations of each other changed to accommodate equality over long-standing gendered norms. As Quek and her colleagues (2010, 371) argue, flexible familial roles show that "both husbands and wives feel free to modify their roles within the family structure as needed, rather than determine them by gender or tradition." For the respondents, gender flexibility could arise under unfortunate circumstances. Mrs. Fong's husband developed mobility issues after a car accident and needed frequent medical attention. The accident, Mrs. Fong claimed, had made her both sad and strong. She had considered retiring earlier, but her husband now relied on the insurance provided by her job. Mrs. Fong saw her circumstances as evidence that migrant women should not depend solely on their husbands and needed to be independent both financially and socially, especially as they grew older. For her, gender flexibility was a way to deal with concrete problems, as she elaborated.

> My husband and I had a pretty equal relationship. He could not work a few years ago. I am the primary economic pillar for my family. . . . I thought about retiring, but if I retire before turning sixty-five, I will not have medical insurance. If we were in Taiwan, we would be more relaxed since we would have access to National Health Insurance. But in the US, I will not qualify for Medicare until I turn sixty-five. My current job gave me good insurance coverage. And my husband relied on my insurance. Otherwise, I have to buy medical insurance myself. It is very expensive. I continue to work until we both qualify for Medicare.

For Mrs. Liao, in her seventies, gender flexibility had become necessary after the sudden death of her husband seven years before our interview. Together with her husband, Mrs. Liao had run a small business in a suburban area near Boston, where her husband had managed the finances, along with finances for their household. With his death, however, she had "forced herself to learn financing and account keeping." Mrs. Liao described her initial panic followed by a "rough period of time," which had led her to urge her coethnics to learn to be more independent from their spouses. "We never know what will happen to us as time goes by, so we should expect the best and prepare for the worst," she told me.

Some respondents had indeed seen the consequences of inflexibility. In Taiwan, Mrs. Bai, a return migrant in her midsixties, described a heartbreaking story of her birth family. Her father had been a "very traditional Chinese man who works hard but knows little about how to take care of himself," and her mother had been responsible for arranging and managing her father's life. After her mother passed away, however, her father was not only deeply upset but also completely lost, requiring help even to join his daughter and her husband at lunch. Arriving at her father's apartment in Taipei, she recalled, he sobbed and said to her, "Your mom left me as a lonely elderly man in this world, and I do not even know how to pick up the clothes I should wear now." Startled, Mrs. Bai considered what might happen to her husband if she passed away first. She had happily assumed the role of homemaker for most of her adult life, she said, but now encouraged her husband to learn basic domestic skills, like shopping and cooking, and to establish a broader network of relatives and friends. Later life, she felt, was unpredictable and potentially marked by disease, illness, and death. Greater gender flexibility could help her husband manage the unknown.

Many of the men I met were less articulate than their wives about gender flexibility, and most had begun rethinking their responsibilities only as they retired and their focus shifted. Their accounts present three distinctive responses: voluntarily sharing domestic responsibilities, taking on greater responsibility because of the health conditions of their spouses, and becoming more dependent because of their own deteriorating health. A subset of the men I interviewed had, like Mr. Chao, begun to see housework as a new and interesting experience. For him, domestic responsibilities, which he had once considered an exclusively feminine domain, had offered a new focus in life. Now he cooked, cleaned, and did yard work, spending ever more time on these tasks to avoid feeling bored. To his surprise, they were "a lot of fun," as he explained.

> After I retired, I started to shift my attention from the workplace to family. I started learning to cook. I started helping with housework. It used to be my wife's responsibility. I never did these things before, primarily because I didn't have time. Now I have more time [after retirement]. It is actually quite fun. Yesterday, I discussed with my wife about how to make roast beef: Why do I have to roast the beef first and then slice it? Why cannot I slice the meat before putting it into the oven? Is the latter approach faster? Would the beef taste as good as before?

Other men cited a wife's deteriorating health as the cause of greater flexibility in the household division of labor. Mr. Chou stressed the necessity of sharing domestic responsibilities with his wife after Mrs. Chou broke her arm a few weeks before our interview and required physical therapy that would probably last for months. This scenario had led Mr. Chou to reflect on his relationship with his wife and to conclude that gender flexibility would be an effective strategy for handling the family's needs, especially as he could not be certain whether or when she would again function normally. At his age, he could no longer be a "traditional" husband waiting to be served by his wife. "Both my wife and I are getting old," he emphasized. "We are taking care of each other at this life stage. I cook and clean when my wife is not doing well. And she cooks and cleans when I am not doing well. How can I continue to expect my wife to take care of me as when she was younger? This is not practical. Tradition needs to be changed according to practical situations rather than vice versa."

Mr. Yen, a return migrant in his seventies, also felt strongly about loosening the gendered division of labor. He and his wife had returned to Taiwan and moved into an old-age apartment after he was diagnosed with cancer. His cancer treatment had gone well, and he told me that he was cancer-free and healthier than most people his age. But two years earlier, his wife had suffered several accidents, one of which had caused a neck injury and several rib fractures. Then, while recovering, she had spilled a glass of hot water and caused a second-degree burn. As his wife was healing from these injuries, Mr. Yen had been in charge of cooking, cleaning, and shopping for groceries, all tasks that he had once deemed trivial. He had also shouldered caregiving responsibilities for his wife, such as feeding and bathing her. Only after these experiences had he come to understand that his wife was "really getting old," and he could no longer depend on her to attend to his needs and desires. Two older people living alone, Mr. Yen now believed, should have fluid and flexible responsibilities.

Some migrant men did, however, become more dependent on their wives. Worsening health could diminish their authority or control, especially if they experienced a loss of power or status in the household. Men who relied on their wives as their primary care providers often claimed that they now had to respect, even defer to, their wives. Mr. Lai, in his late eighties, reported losing his eyesight and ability to walk stably while also suffering from diabetes and high blood pressure. With difficulty sustaining himself, he was relying heavily on his wife and had come increasingly to value her presence, sometimes prioritizing her opinion. "Now I am completely dependent upon my wife for everything," he told me.

> Now I am not doing well and have a lot of dietary concerns and need to take different medicine per day. My wife is taking care of me. She had to bring food to the table, but I cannot drive. She needs to drive to get things we need, and she is close to her nineties too. My wife also has to remind me to take different kinds of medication and pay attention to my diet. It's a lot of responsibilities, and I don't know how to

live my life without her. I completely respect her idea. If she does not want me to do anything, I will listen. . . . For example, I was invited to attend a book-releasing conference in Taiwan, but I did not go since my wife did not want to fly the long distance. I don't want her to worry.

Mr. Chuan, a return migrant in his seventies, pointed to changing power dynamics. When younger, he reported, he had made all decisions, including the return to Taiwan in the mid-2000s and his decision to become an active member in political campaigns and protests. His wife had disapproved, citing concern for his safety, but he had ignored her until he had a heart attack while exercising and was hospitalized for about two weeks. His wife slept beside his bed four to five nights per week and had then become "stricter," micromanaging his daily life. His condition, Mr. Chuan asserted, had seriously affected his wife's everyday life, so he had reduced his participation in politics, both because of his health and because of his wife's worries. "We don't have children around," he stated. "If anything happened to me, my wife suffered. She was no longer young either. So sometimes I want to volunteer [for a candidate], but I listen to my wife and give up."

Gender Uncompromised: Performing Loyalty and Obedience

Despite softening familiar gender hierarchies, both women and men I interviewed set strict boundaries that marked the limits of acceptable behavior, and often, expectations from members of their ethnic communities exercised a discipline that affected their choices. Women's chastity—or more precisely, their coethnics' perceptions of wives' sexual fidelity to their husbands—especially oriented the behavior of the "young old" (those between fifty-five and their late sixties). Mrs. Gao, who had struggled with the decision to send her husband, who had Alzheimer's disease, to an assisted-living facility, continued to maintain a home-based business and work as a tailor. But she had stopped accepting orders from male customers unless they were accompanied by their wives. Living alone, Mrs. Gao did not want her neighbors and coethnics to see "male strangers" coming in and out of her apartment. Her personal policy both protected her reputation and "saved face" for her husband. Already sorry that she could not care for him at home, she sought to avoid embarrassment and remained deferential, a "chaste and loyal wife."

Mrs. Chin, a return migrant who had lost her husband in midlife, reported never thinking about remarriage, partly because she was busy earning money to pay bills and partly because she worried about her appearance to her coethnics and its effects on her reputation and her children. She avoided going out with men alone or meeting them in private settings, and to avoid fueling rumors and their ramifications, she had decided to stay single. For her, sex required marriage, but to marry again, she needed to go out and meet men, and if she were seen to "bring men back home," she would invite gossip. She thus eliminated the possibility by keeping her distance from male friends until she lost her mobility after failed spine surgery. Only then did she ease her caution, considering herself "old and disabled," so that no one would suspect she had personal relationships with men.

Mrs. Gao and Mrs. Chin were not entirely paranoid. Although I never formally asked respondents about sexuality, I often heard them talk about the personal lives of their coethnics. During my fieldwork, a couple in the United States, the husband in his early seventies and the wife in her midsixties, divorced. I never interviewed either husband or wife, but among my respondents I heard dinner-table conversations about this divorce and claims that it followed a long-term sex scandal in which the wife had engaged in an extramarital affair with another Taiwanese immigrant. This story spread quickly within the Taiwanese immigrant community. Some immigrants claimed that the cheating wife had often made eye contact with the man; some claimed to have witnessed inappropriate body contact or felt weird sexual dynamics. These coethnics expressed great contempt for the wife and much sympathy for the husband. (He was also undergoing chemotherapy for liver cancer.) They also criticized "the third person," who had, presumably, also wrecked his own family, but their views of the wife were harsher. This gossip supports the worries of single/widowed migrant women I interviewed, especially the "young old." Their coethnics were indeed watching and talking about them. The effect, their accounts reveal, was social control exerted through community norms and reinforced through social networks in which they were embedded (Dreby 2009; Kibria 1994).

Many of the women I interviewed also sought to protect their husbands' image as "the head of household" in the eyes of their coethnics. To me, migrant men may have privately acknowledged a shift in gender norms, but publicly they also enacted gender conventions. Mr. Chou told me that he and his wife took turns cooking and that he had assumed responsibility for housework after his wife hurt her arm. After the interview, however, he invited me to stay for dinner, which Mrs. Chou alone prepared. During dinner, I watched her monitor our rice bowls and apologize for failing to notice earlier that his rice bowl was empty. After adding rice to our bowls, she offered us ice cream and apple pie and returned to the kitchen to prepare dessert. Because of Mrs. Chou's injury, I expressed surprise, but Mr. Chou joking replied, "My wife is cooking because we have a guest here. She tried to save face for me."

Here, the presence of a coethnic mediated the performance of gender between spouses. During my fieldwork, I witnessed similar scenarios at social events, where older migrant women prepared food in the kitchen while their husbands sat outside, chatting about politics or other communal affairs. Many of the respondents, both women and men, described this division of labor as routine, and while most acknowledged change in their own intimate relationships, they were loath to challenge gender norms in public spaces, especially where other Taiwanese immigrants were present.

This chapter has examined the ways aging migrant individuals negotiate spousal relations through what I called temporalities of migration. Scholars to date have examined the effects of internal and international migration on the intimate relationships between husbands and wives (Choi and Peng 2016; Hirsch 2003; Schmalzbauer 2014). Adding to this research, I have detailed the temporalities of migration through myriad social processes that affect immigrants' relations with their spouses at different points in their lives. Indeed, gender relations in the family may vary over the course of modernization, but my respondents had transformed intimacies with their spouses in response to their experiences as long-term immigrants in a new social and cultural context.

More specifically, the interplay among time, migratory experiences, and gendered conjugality can be observed through four analytical dimensions: (1) the experience of leaving multigenerational families, (2) the impact of relocation on male domination, (3) migrants' and their children's adaption to what they perceived as the American family ideal, and (4) the impact of aging and life stage on gendered divisions between husbands and wives. This analytical framework, while developing from the experiences of older immigrants from Taiwan, could be applied to aging migrant populations of other racial and ethnonational origins.

For the respondents in this study, the effects of migration on gendered conjugality had accumulated over time rather than overnight. Emigration from Taiwan had marked a gendered transition at an earlier life stage, and settling in the United States had brought challenges to the domestic patriarchal order. Moving to the United States, the respondents had escaped the patriarchal constraints often exercised through kinship networks in traditional Taiwanese and Chinese societies and had gained new social standing in the United States. There, women had assumed more power over the organization of their lives and had become better able to negotiate with their spouses about family decisions.

Long-term immigration promoted what the respondents perceived as sociocultural acculturation into US society. As I elaborated in chapter 2, their conceptualization of cultural norms in the United States could be partial and illusionary. Their narratives of Americanization, however, vividly demonstrated their perception of ideal spousal relations in the United States and were activated to challenge masculine domination at home and to explain the importance of mutuality, equality, and gender flexibility. Several social theorists have written about the ways equality, open communication, and mutual respect are viewed as defining features of spousal intimacy in many "modernized" Western societies (Giddens 1992; Gross 2005). For the respondents, the democratization of spousal relations was closely linked to cultural assimilation into a receiving context. Both women and men actively applied the rhetoric of Americanization to transform masculine identities and practices. Valorizing mutuality, they also sought to alter intergenerational dynamics.

As aging brought new needs and increased frailty, these migrants came to value flexibility in the division of domestic responsibility and the exercise of male authority. More flexible gender norms became a formula for managing the uncertainties of later life. Life transitions further motivated them to reconstruct their connections as life partners. Having spent many of their working years in the United States, the aging Taiwanese immigrants I interviewed had, to a significant degree, refashioned their sense of responsibility and commitment to their spouses. Negotiating gendered conjugality was not easy but was instead full of adaption, tension, and at least occasional conflict. Few of my respondents, however, considered divorcing, not only because divorce was uncommon among their coethnics but also because they depended on each other even more after migrating and needed their spouses to anchor life in a foreign land. Perhaps some of the married couples I interviewed might have been worried about revealing conflicts to me, especially knowing that I interviewed both spouses, but I found no salient differences between respondents whose spouses were interviewed and those who were not. Notably, staying married required most respondents to adapt. Their adaptation, as I have shown, needs to be understood in the context of time and migration.

4

DOING GRANDPARENTHOOD

Becoming grandparents constitutes a significant life transition. Given the changing demographic features of aging populations, scholars have demonstrated that older people today not only witness their grandchildren grow up but also play an important role in their grandchildren's lives (Arber and Timonen 2012; Mason, May, and Clarke 2007; Spitze and Ward 1998). This research challenges the assumption that elderly people are mostly recipients of care, and it underscores ways in which grandparents contribute to their children's families by providing care, money, information, and moral support. Becoming grandparents also motivates older people to reflect on relationships with their children's families (Cherlin and Furstenberg 1986; May, Mason, and Clarke 2012). In later life, they rethink the roles that they wish to play and assess their hopes for their children's families.

The ways in which older people make sense of grandparenthood are highly influenced by their ethnoracial and cultural backgrounds (Chen, Liu, and Mair 2011; King et al. 2014; Stack 1997; Xie and Xia 2011). Most notably, the literature on Chinese and Chinese immigrant families has demonstrated that grandparents commonly care for their grandchildren and even become primary care providers (Zhou 2012). To rear their grandchildren, Chinese grandparents may travel long distances or even emigrate. Much of this research presumes a division between the "modern" or "Western" and the "traditional" or "non-Western." In "American" and "Western" families, grandparents are assumed not to interfere in their children's lives and to respect their children's parental authority. In "non-Western" (particularly Asian) families, grandparents are considered more likely to be involved in rearing their grandchildren.

To be sure, this assumed division of grandparenting styles in Western and non-Western families is oversimplified. Many grandparents in North America and Britain—especially those who are "young old" and remain healthy—have helped raise their grandchildren. This practice is particularly salient during family crises (e.g., divorce) and common in working-class and minority communities (Arber and Timonen 2012; Hansen 2005; Nelson 2006; Roy and Burton 2007; Stack 1997). At the same time, older people may care for their grandchildren because they believe in a cultural ideal, because they wish to help their children, or because they expect their children to provide for them in their twilight years (Chen, Liu, and Mair 2011).

This chapter examines the ways temporal aspects of international migration prompt older immigrants to develop cultural reflexivity in connections to their children, grandchildren, and a transnational social field. Here, temporalities of migration exert deep influence, and my respondents' experiences with long-term migration led them to reflect on intergenerational relations in the United States. The interplay between time and migration generated new perspectives on their positionality as racialized immigrants, the cultural ideal of family, the meanings of modern intimacy, and the changing structural contexts that their grandchildren might face. Many scholars have highlighted the contributions of grandparents to networks of support in both migrant and nonmigrant families (Brijnath 2009; Dreby 2010; Hansen 2005; Moon 2003; Parreñas 2005). Building on this research, I analyze the effects of variation across time and national borders that propel immigrants to reconsider their obligations and commitments to their children's families.

The concept of *doing grandparenthood* explains this interplay between the time my respondents spent in the United States and their reflections on changing national and transnational contexts. Doing grandparenthood delineates the ways these older immigrants define their relationships with children and grandchildren and orient their participation in caregiving. The notion of doing grandparenthood extends the concept of "doing family" (Nelson 2006; Sarkisian 2006). From this perspective, family is a social construct that requires its members to accomplish tasks and negotiate duties. Doing family involves a process of "assigning rights, privileges, and responsibilities within the nexus of the web of the relationships of those we call 'family'" (Nelson 2006, 783). Along these lines, I contend that grandparenthood, like other forms of family caregiving, is not predetermined. Rather, becoming a grandparent motivates an active (re)interpretation of relationships with children, children's spouses, and grandchildren. Much as doing family encompasses the enactment of a wide range of beliefs and practices, doing grandparenthood connotes a range of processes for articulating relationships with grandchildren.

Grandparenting, I argue, varies in the degree and style of a grandparent's participation. Grandparents might minimize their involvement. They might actively participate in raising their grandchildren. Or they might grandparent from afar, operating transnationally. While some of my respondents did have a minimal presence in their children's families, most in the United States grappled with constructing a place in their grandchildren's daily routines. As they welcomed their grandchildren to this world, they assumed new rights, responsibilities, and entitlements. The return migrants I met in Taiwan similarly struggled to overcome spatial and temporal distance. In both the United States and Taiwan, therefore, respondents sought to construct an ideal role in the social worlds of their offspring, with an emerging sense of duty that profoundly shaped everyday practices. Notably, gender organized the division of labor between grandfathers and grandmothers. Women and men might value grandparenting equally, but they realized their responsibilities in gender-specific ways.

Minimal Grandparenting: Opting Out, Pushed Out, Crowded Out

Several temporal, structural, and relational factors precluded older immigrants from active grandparenting. Among the respondents who participated only minimally in raising their grandchildren, reasons centered on health conditions, geographical proximity, and prior relationships with children and their families. Mrs. Tan, in her eighties, recounted that, to help raise her daughter's children, she and her husband had relocated to Boston when they were in their sixties. She decided, however, not to move to Los Angeles to be near her son and help raise her grandsons. By then, Mrs. Tan explained, she was in her seventies and was losing too much physical strength. Together with her husband, she had already settled in an old-age home and had no interest in moving again.

Mrs. Tan told me that she had always been close to her daughter and her son-in-law respected her. She also cared about her son, but she was ambivalent about her relationship with her daughter-in-law, whom she described as strong-willed. She had therefore refused her son's request to migrate to Los Angeles, despite her son's complaints. "My son used to live in New York and moved to LA for work," she said.

> I did not want to go to look after his children. I am getting old and cannot care for kids in the ways I used to. The quality of air [in Los Angeles] is really bad. There is always traffic [in Los Angeles]. And I have no connections there. Instead, I was heavily involved in taking care of all of

my daughters' children. And my son did complain to me for not helping look after his children. He was like, 'Why do you only take care of the grandchildren who are not even under our family name? Why don't you take care of the kids who wear our own family name?'

In Taiwan, returnees often emphasized age and health conditions, spatial distance, and potential conflicts with children and in-laws as reasons for opting out of grandchild care. Mrs. Yen, in her seventies, felt sorry that she could not provide hands-on care for her grandchildren, but spatial distance gave her a legitimate reason. Even if she lived close to her children's families, Mrs. Yen explained, she would hesitate to play an active part in her grandchildren's lives. Given her health, she believed, this would be too much. As she reflected, "It would be very stressful to take care of my grandsons. I need to hold them in my arms when going upstairs and downstairs. If they run all over the place, I will have to follow them in order to prevent them from hitting something. And I still remembered I felt neurotic when taking care of my own children. I always felt like they were crying. It was very physically and emotionally demanding. I did not want to go through it again." Mrs. Yen and her husband maintained that, ultimately, it was their children's responsibility to raise their grandchildren. Their ideas and styles might differ from their children's, so they found giving advice difficult. As Mr. Yen maintained, their "suggestions" might be ineffective and could also negatively affect their relationships with their children and children's spouses. They had therefore decided to opt out.

Several of the respondents in the United States reported being pushed out of involvement with their grandchildren, as their children's families made them unwelcome. None of the returnees I interviewed described prohibitions against spending time with grandchildren, but these respondents were in Taiwan and already had limited in-person contact. Mrs. Sun, an immigrant in her seventies, described a strained relationship with children who had pushed her away from her grandchildren's lives. Though she was willing to help, preexisting tensions with her children—perhaps because she had been a "tiger mom," who had disciplined harshly and strictly supervised academic performance—had led to strong reactions to her unsolicited advice about paid work, housework, and child rearing, especially from her daughter. As Mrs. Sun vividly described, "Whenever I said something to my daughter, her reaction was 'What do you mean? You think you are smarter than me?'" Mrs. Sun blamed herself for having been too harsh with her children, leading them to want to avoid arguments with her.

Less confrontational were accounts of having been "crowded out" of caring for grandchildren by the other side of a grandchild's family. Four respondents (two couples, one in the United States and one in Taiwan) described children who had secured sufficient support and had neither asked nor needed them to step in. Mr. Lin, an immigrant man in his early seventies, saw no need to care for his daughter's children, because their paternal grandparents had become their full-time caregivers. Mr. Lin and his wife both claimed that they would like to spend more time with their grandchildren but avoided competing, or appearing to be competing, with their daughter's in-laws.

As returnees, Mr. and Mrs. Hung similarly cited their son's in-laws, who had retired and were committed to helping care for their grandchildren. Their son did not need them, Mr. and Mrs. Hung explained, because their daughter-in-law's parents had become full-time caregivers for their son's children, who even lived with their other set of grandparents on weekdays. Mrs. Hung jokingly commented, "My husband and I were *hao ming ren* [blessed people]," unconstrained by having to provide care for grandchildren. With more time to pursue other goals, they had relocated to Taiwan and enjoyed their lifestyle there.

Active Grandparenting in Place

Most of my respondents in the United States were involved in their grandchildren's lives. Overall, approximately three-fifths provided hands-on care for their grandchildren, especially those younger than five. From their perspective, hands-on care relieved their children of the tension between paid work and family. Many had reorganized their lives around their children's and grandchildren's schedules, and some had given up social activities that they really enjoyed, such as Bible study, golf, dancing, music classes, and time with friends. Some had traveled long distances or even relocated to look after their grandchildren. Prior experience as racialized others in the United States often motivated them to help their children. Explicitly or implicitly they told me that race—or, more specifically, skin color—might be an obstacle to their children's career success. By providing care for their grandchildren, they explained, they might minimize the burden of race for their children.

Noninterference of "American" Grandparents

Temporalities of migration oriented the ways in which these immigrants constructed grandparenthood, for which they drew on their perception of American family culture. As most of my respondents emphasized, grandparenting in a culture of American individualism means noninterference. According to Andrew J. Cherlin and Frank F. Furstenberg Jr. (1986, 57), the norm of noninterference refers to "the widely held belief that grandparents ought not to interfere in the ways their children are raising the grandchildren." The respondents thus cared for their grandchildren because their children asked them to do so, and they respected their children's ultimate authority as parents. For them, this boundary marked both a generational shift and a cultural difference between the United States and Asia. By stressing their children's needs and wants, they represented themselves as altruistic and respectful helpers rather than uninvited intruders. In the United States, grandparent involvement could be neither assumed nor given cultural primacy. Rather, it required consent. Otherwise, these grandparents risked ruining relationships and losing access to their grandchildren.

Many made sure their children were "on board" with their participation in their grandchildren's care. Mrs. Liang talked of soliciting the consent of her daughter's family before she offered help. She traveled from Boston to New York every week to help her daughter and son-in-law look after three of her grandchildren from Monday to Thursday and then returned to Boston to serve as a deacon in her church, where she was present on Sundays. Her daughter, Mrs. Liang reported, had facilitated this arrangement, and her son-in-law—who was white—was happy to accept her help. As Mrs. Liang vividly described, "Of course he [her son-in-law] loves this arrangement. Why wouldn't he? It is so nice to have a Taiwanese maid [tai yong] cooking and cleaning for free." She would not "dare to" step in and offer help, Mrs. Liang emphasized, as "these American-born children [her children] are very opinionated. We have to learn to respect their will; otherwise, they think we are invasive and try[ing] to control them."

Such noninterference became particularly clear when some respondents discussed their decisions to move closer to their children. Mr. and Mrs. Yang, both in their midsixties, had decided to move from Los Angeles to Boston to help their daughter care for their newborn grandson. When her daughter was about to give birth, they had lived in Los Angeles, where Mrs. Yang still had a full-time job. Nevertheless, Mrs. Yang had decided to resign and instead provide care for her grandson. This decision, they emphasized, was in large part a response to their daughter's request. As Mrs. Yang explained, "This is the US. After children get married, they had their own nuclear family [xiao jia ting], and they have their own ideas about how to lead their family life. If my daughter and my son-in-law disagree with us on moving to Boston and caring for our grandson, we will not do it." Although the ideal nuclear family fails to capture the complexities of family life in the United States (Hansen 2005), its cultural influence "remains overwhelmingly dominant" in North America (Gross 2005, 298). For immigrants like Mrs. Liang and Mrs. Yang, Americanization had diluted parental authority, and they had to respect the boundaries set by their children's families.

Noninterference was also manifested as grandparents deferred to their children's parenting styles. As older immigrants took care of grandchildren, they and their children might not always agree about raising their grandchildren. This issue constitutes a major source of conflict in many Chinese societies (Shih and Pyke 2016; Zuo 2009). As my respondents understood, however, the nuclear household is the cultural ideal in the United States and differs from the extended-family norm in Asian societies. Grandparents who disagreed with their children about childcare had therefore learned not to defy their children and their children's spouses. Mrs. Gao had sometimes disagreed with her daughter-in-law about such issues as child discipline and sugar consumption, but she felt the need to suppress herself, to avoid telling her daughter-in-law what to do. "I remembered that one time my grandson was misbehaving," she recounted. "My daughter-in-law put him on 'time out.' I heard my grandson crying over the phone and felt my heart break. I tried to say something to my daughter-in-law and let her know that this might be enough for the kid, but she was definitely not happy about it. I know that parents' love and grandparents' love for the kids are different. This is their family. I, as a grandmother, could not say too much." For Mrs. Gao, participation in rearing her grandchildren required her children's cooperation. Otherwise, she could be deprived of opportunities to participate in her grandchildren's lives. This narrative illustrates the depth of the US cultural ideal of nuclear family, which can erase the power of older generations in Chinese families. Like Mrs. Gao, many older immigrants cautiously maintained a line between parenthood and grandparenthood, to prevent disruption in their relationships with their children's families.

Considering Modern Intimacy

Temporalities of migration oriented these immigrants to rethink the meaning of intimacy. In the United States, establishing intimacy with their grandchildren was a process of learning to be a "modern" grandparent. Memories of their own grandparents in Taiwan informed their reflections, as did their observations of family norms and intimacy in mainstream US society. In their classic and groundbreaking work, *The New American Grandparents*, Andrew J. Cherlin and Frank F. Furstenberg Jr. (1986) demonstrate that older people's memories of their own grandparents inspire their participation in their grandchildren's lives. Many of the grandparents in their study desired close relationships with their grandchildren because they wished to avoid the emotional distance they had experienced with their own grandparents.

Many of the respondents similarly emphasized their histories as grandchildren, which they characterized as distant or ritualistic, as a reason for active involvement in their grandchildren's lives. Some recalled grandparents who had been authority figures and demanded deference. By contrast, they sought closer relationships with their own grandchildren. While physically demanding, they explained, caring for grandchildren was emotionally rewarding. Its intimacy gave them a sense of satisfaction. With declining fertility, they also had fewer grandchildren than their own grandparents had known and so might more closely focus their attention.

Becoming a compassionate grandparent often meant refashioning grandparenthood over time and across borders. Mrs. Ma, who had been the primary caregiver for her paralyzed husband at the time of interview, insisted on babysitting her grandchildren twice a week at her own place. She characterized her grandparenting style as completely different from that of her own grandmother. (Her grandfather had passed away before she was born.) She recalled her grandmother as a traditional woman who had received a Japanese education when Taiwan was a colony of Japan. Mrs. Ma had lived with her grandmother during her childhood, but she could recall no chatting, singing, or playing, through which she now interacted with her own grandchildren.

Mrs. Ma described her grandmother as an extremely "proper" lady in mannerisms, hairstyle, and dress, an authority figure who demanded respect and subordination. By comparison, Mrs. Ma maintained, her relationship with her own grandchildren was compassionate, and their presence brought her a lot of joy, allowing her temporarily to leave behind the stress of caring for her ailing husband. More importantly, she hoped her grandchildren would remember their intimate moments. Her daughter-in-law was a part-time piano teacher, and Mrs. Ma had volunteered to look after the grandchildren twice a week, seizing an opportunity to secure long-term intergenerational intimacy. "My daughter-in-law thought about hiring a babysitter, because she did not want me to feel overwhelmed," she explained.

> My daughter-in-law said to me, "Mom, but you already have so much to do." Yes, it's true. But I told her that I would be fine and that I wanted to take care of the grandchildren when she works. . . . Taking care of my grandchildren is exhausting, but it is also fun. I can talk with them, play with them, drive them around, and watch them grow up. This is how I want my grandchildren to remember me. And you can only do these things when they are little. After they start going to middle school, they want to spend time with their peers.

The ways in which the respondents conceptualized changing intergenerational relations in US society influenced their perspectives about connecting to their grandchildren. Because they saw the nuclear family as the social norm in the United States, they believed they needed to justify their involvement in their grandchildren's lives. Living with their children was usually out of the question, but becoming a caregiver guaranteed their presence in their grandchildren's lives and could establish a solid intergenerational relationship. Mrs. Yang clearly expressed this rationale:

> We wanted to see our grandchildren every day. [*Laughs*] My daughter said to us, "Why don't you move to Boston? If you were around, you would be much closer to your grandson." Back then, my daughter also planned to be pregnant again soon. So we decided to move to Boston and bought a house here. Because my daughter and her husband were both very busy with their work, we came to try our best to help take care of the kids. We love to be close to our grandchildren and have them grow up with grandparents around. This is a great arrangement for both us [Mrs. Yang and her husband] and my daughter. They have people who can help, and we get to see our grandchildren often.

Some immigrant grandparents stressed the practical value of intergenerational intimacy, contending that intimate understanding of their grandchildren—a particular knowledge and exclusive attention to (Zelizer 2005)—made them better able than paid caregivers to provide quality care. Here, the contrast between "love" and "money" became central. For many respondents, blood ties meant they could provide care with more authentic love than a nanny or day-care worker, and they tended to depict paid caregivers as motivated by money. These assumptions about the marketization of care are problematic because research shows that many paid caregivers do develop deep attachments to children under their watch (Ehrenreich and Hochschild 2004; Hondagneu-Sotelo 2007; MacDonald 2011). Oblivious of the genuine connections between paid caregivers and children they looked after, many older immigrants articulated a biological definition of intimacy and maintained that love for grandchildren was an innate part of human nature. Because the care they provided stemmed from "natural" love for their grandchildren, they could be more perceptive about their grandchildren's needs.

Becoming Cultural Mediators

Temporalities of migration are also manifest in the ways many of the older immigrants I met sought to operate as cultural liaisons. They retained attachment to their homeland, which they sought to pass on, but they also assessed their grandchildren's future and anticipated their needs for multicultural competence. Approximately half of the respondents in the United States who had grandchildren were motivated to become cultural mediators for their grandchildren, bridging the disjuncture between their ancestral and adopted homes (also see Lamb 2009). As cultural mediators, these immigrant grandparents consistently deliberated over the linguistic and cultural resources that they wanted to pass on to their grandchildren. Just like physical care, cultural mediation constituted an important component of grandparenthood, not only serving practical needs but also providing solutions to problems that their grandchildren might later encounter.

Language use was a key concern. Many immigrants who provided hands-on care reported frequent opportunities to familiarize their grandchildren with their mother tongue, typically Mandarin Chinese but sometimes Taiwanese/Fujianese or, in one case, Hakka. Furthermore, these immigrants were in general more fluent in Chinese than their children, and so, they reported, their children and their children's spouses had asked them to teach their grandchildren to read, write, and speak in Chinese. Mrs. Wu, who regularly assisted her children, reported that her children had asked her and her husband to spend a summer teaching her grandsons Chinese, as she related.

> My son and daughter-in-law sent their children to stay with us last summer. They intentionally didn't arrange other activities such as summer camping. They let our grandchildren stay with us for about a month. We taught my grandchildren to speak Taiwanese every morning last summer. Then we had lunch together. In the afternoon, we took turns teaching them to read Chinese characters. And at the end of last summer, my husband asked them to write an essay as the assignment at the end of the summer. And we also asked them to give lectures in Taiwanese and Mandarin at the end of that summer. They talked about what their names are, where their family is from, how many people there are in their family, what they want to do in the future. . . . My husband and I both enjoyed that summer. It was such a great experience.

Mrs. Wu and other immigrants I interviewed wished to teach their grandchildren Mandarin Chinese not only to reproduce ethnic traditions in the United States but also to ease their grandchildren's way. They often emphasized Mandarin Chinese over Taiwanese/Fujianese or Hakka because their grandchildren would be perceived as Chinese in the United States and could thus construct racial and ethnic identities. Some suggested that Mandarin Chinese was a practical decision because it is more common among people of Chinese descent, both in the United States and in Taiwan. Their grandchildren would thus have more opportunities to use Mandarin than other Chinese dialects and, in an English-speaking environment, were more likely to become bilingual. Some preferred that their children learn Mandarin Chinese because it is the national language of mainland China and thus a linguistic resource in a global age. In language, pragmatic concerns could thus trump symbolic identity.

Mrs. Luo strongly identified herself as Taiwanese and refused to be called Chinese, yet she made the strategic decision to teach her grandchildren Mandarin rather than Taiwanese. With Mandarin promoted in Taiwan since 1945, Mrs. Luo was fluent in both Taiwanese and Mandarin Chinese. Taiwanese/Fujianese had been the language used at home in Taiwan, while Mandarin was the language she spoke at school and in the workplace. Mrs. Luo struggled over the language to speak to her grandchildren but chose Mandarin because of its instrumental value. "We look Chinese, and people think we are Chinese in the United States," she reflected.

> I disagree and always told other people that I am from Taiwan and I am a Taiwanese. But then what? People regard us as Chinese here. Most Americans still think we are Chinese and don't get the nuanced and subtle differences between Chinese and Taiwanese. If you cannot speak your mother tongue, isn't that strange? You cannot forget who you are and where you are from. And I think, given the development of China, Mandarin is and will become an important international language. So even if my own native language is Taiwanese, I will let the grandchildren learn and speak Mandarin. It makes no difference. People in Taiwan speak Mandarin too. And more and more Chinese immigrants in the US speak Mandarin too. It is more practical for the kids to learn Mandarin rather than Taiwanese. I am a Taiwanese, and my mother tongue is Taiwanese. Ideally, I want my grandchildren to learn to speak both Taiwanese and Mandarin. However, it's very unlikely to ask the kids to keep using Taiwanese, especially when most of their Chinese peers speak Mandarin. I gave up and usually communicate with them in Mandarin.

The respondents' concerns about how the world might evolve over time (i.e., their considerations about varying time-migration configurations in the future) shaped interactions with their grandchildren. China's growth as a global superpower, for example, complicated the motivations for immigrants teaching Chinese to their grandchildren. As the anthropologist Aihwa Ong (1999) argues, many newly rich Chinese parents send their children to study in Western countries because they believe mastering an international language like English can facilitate their children's career success. Many of the respondents attached similar meaning to their grandchildren's command of Mandarin Chinese. With China's rapid economic development and political influence, many thought China might offer their grandchildren opportunities in the twenty-first century. China's rise had been inconceivable to many when they first left Taiwan, but because their grandchildren "looked Chinese," they might benefit from the ability to read and speak the dominant Chinese language.

Mr. Chao, an immigrant in his early seventies, contended that, nowadays, even many white Americans traveled to China for work, and he was thus convinced that, in twenty or thirty years, when China had become even more affluent and more developed, his grandchildren might have a more promising future in China than in the United States. Mr. Liu similarly reported that even his son-in-law, a Chinese American with limited understanding of the Chinese language, entirely agreed about the importance of learning Chinese. A retired professor of Chinese philosophy and literature, Mr. Liu had been asked by his daughter and son-in-law to teach his grandchildren to read and speak Mandarin Chinese, which he did every morning that his daughter and son-in-law were at work.

In Mr. Liu's living room, I noticed Chinese books for children, such as *300 Tang Poems*, *Chinese Folk Tales*, and a Chinese translation of *Andersen's Fairy Tales*, which Mr. Liu told me he used to teach his grandchildren. Believing that childhood is the key life stage for mastering a language, he took responsibility, mockingly noting the terrible accents with which his American-born son-in-law and his daughter, who had moved to the United States at age five, spoke Mandarin Chinese. He considered them semi-illiterate and wanted his grandchildren to be fluent in the language of a rising global superpower. "We are witnessing the rise of China in the twenty-first century," he emphasized.

> China is becoming a political and economic superpower globally. And I believe China will become more and more important in the future. Our grandchildren's future might be in China. They might have to look for jobs in China, and their company might send them off to work in China. Speaking Chinese can be an important niche for them. And children learn languages really fast. They are like a sponge. They absorb things quickly and easily. If our grandchildren can pick up Chinese now and keep it up, they can benefit from it in the future.

For some immigrant grandparents, learning certain Taiwanese and/or Chinese cultural values could prepare their grandchildren for the challenges of US society. While considering the United States a wealthy, liberal society, these respondents also associated the United States with such values as "wastefulness" and "lack of self-restraint" (C. Chen 2006). Therefore, they emphasized the Chinese virtue of "thriftiness" by telling their grandchildren about their own economic hardships, both in Taiwan and after arriving in the United States. These immigrant grandparents thus sought to protect their grandchildren from the negative influence of US materialism. Mr. Tan, in his eighties, reported that when his grandchildren were little, he seized every opportunity to teach them to cherish what they had and to develop the virtue of industriousness, which he associated with Taiwanese and Chinese immigrants of his generation. "One time when I took my grandchildren to a mall for dinner, they really wanted to buy toys," he recalled.

Sometimes I would buy some toys they wanted, but sometimes I would tell them that they were only allowed to see and play with the toys in the store. The kids at times would cry because I did not buy the toys that they wanted. Then I would tell them how lucky they already are! When we were kids, we could not afford these fancy toys at all. Even when my kids were little, we could barely afford these toys. I would let my grandchildren know how difficult our childhood was and how difficult it is to come to the US as immigrants. Many younger people are really spoiled by their parents and lacked discipline. And they can get whatever they want from their parents. I don't want to see my grandchildren become like that. They will run out of money very soon if they always waste money like Americans.

Mr. Tan's instructions formed an immigrant narrative: a story that immigrants tell about coming to the United States and managing the difficulties and hardships of dislocation (M. Waters 1999). Noting "how difficult it is to come to the United States as immigrants," Mr. Tan vividly highlighted the immigrant experience, which informed the education he gave his grandchildren. For the respondents, success never came easily. Rather, they believed success stemmed from the cultural virtue of their homeland (Kasinitz et al. 2008; M. Waters 1999). Seeking to pass on such virtues as industriousness, they recounted immigrant narratives that stressed the "right" cultural values. In this sense, the temporalities of migration shape grandparenting styles as older immigrants sought to prepare their grandchildren for the future by selectively passing certain knowledge, values, and experiences on to their descendants.

Grandparenting from Afar

Temporalities of migration were also manifest in the ways the return migrants I met did grandparenthood from afar. Most had grandchildren living in the United States and reflected on grandparenting in ways similar to their coethnics across the Pacific. The interplay between migratory experience and temporal factors—especially their experiences as racial minorities in the United States and their attempts to adapt to its cultural ideal of family—influenced their thinking. These returnees related to the challenges their children faced. Many invoked memories of an earlier life stage to emphasize the difficulty of balancing work and family in a context of racial hierarchy and xenophobia. Return migrants, however, differed from immigrants in the United States in the strategies they fostered. Rather than proximity, they sought to manage geographical distance.

Compensating for Lack of Hands-On Care

Some returnees talked about taking care of their grandchildren before moving back to Taiwan. Like their coethnics in the United States, they stressed the importance of respecting their children's parenting philosophy through noninterference and asserted that they had stepped in to look after their grandchildren only after their children asked or even "begged" for assistance. This group of returnees had typically moved back to Taiwan when their grandchildren were preteens or teenagers, old enough not to need intense physical care. They had thus fulfilled their responsibilities, not only to raise their children but also to care for their grandchildren, and they felt unconstrained to pursue life in Taiwan.

Physical distance prevented other returnees from providing hands-on care. Having relocated to Taiwan, they had no concerns about invading their children's families. Yet these migrants had developed strategies to compensate for the care they could not provide. Money was one way to help a child's family, and returnees with means reported offering money to relieve some of the financial burdens associated with childcare. With the cost of living in Taiwan much lower than that in the United States, many returnees had money at their disposal and saw it as compensation for direct care. They emphasized, however, that money also symbolized love and concern and might therefore sustain emotional attachments with their children's families. Mr. Deng, who had been a lawyer before retiring, explained substituting money for hands-on care:

> We are so far away. They grew up in the US. They know the American society better than us. They speak better English than us. I think they know better than us about how to raise kids in the US. Yet if they need money, we will try our best to help. We can do little to help take care of our grandchildren. However, if the kids need money or have financial problems, we will definitely step in or at least try our best to help. And we are very clear to our children about this. Even though we are not around, we are still parents and grandparents.

Several of my respondents viewed money as compensation when they had assisted some of their children but not others. Money could thus show that they did not "play favorites." Mr. Xia maintained that because he and his wife had already moved back to Taiwan, his wife could not physically care for their daughter's children, located in the United States, as she had for the children of their son's family. As a result, Mr. Xia and his wife augmented the tuition he paid for all of his grandchildren with an extra check to make up for the childcare they could not provide. Attempting to compensate their daughter for their absence, they sought also to reassure her and her son-in-law that they did not favor their son's family, thereby avoiding an older Taiwanese norm in which families blatantly favored the son. Money thus represented impartial love, as Mr. Xia elaborated: "My wife took care of my son's children for three years. In order to be fair, we decided to write my daughter another check every month to let her hire a nanny. It's completely up to my daughter in terms of how she wants to use this money. If she did not want to hire a nanny, she can still keep the money and use it at her will. . . . It is a matter of fairness. We don't want my daughter to think that we only care more about my son's family." Mr. Xia refused to reveal the amount of money he sent his second son but suggested that it was a generous contribution to the household economy.

Some return migrants, typically women, reported coming to the United States, at their children's request, to care for their grandchildren. They too stressed non-interference. Mrs. Jiang, in her sixties, had relocated to Taiwan with her husband five years before our interview but continued to plan trips to the United States around her children's schedules. Offering short-term, intensive care for her grandchildren assuaged her sense of guilt about the geographical distance her relocation had imposed. "Sometimes I do think living in Taiwan is a problem for me because I cannot see my grandchildren as often as I want," she reflected.

> However, whenever my children had urgent needs and asked, I planned a trip to the US in order to take care of my grandchildren for a short period of time. Actually, I have done this several times over the past five years. And I will travel to New York next month. I will stay in my daughter's place in New York and take care of my grandchildren for about a week, because she and her husband are going to San Francisco to attend a wedding and have some vacation. Bringing a one-year-old son and a three-year-old daughter with them is too inconvenient. Similarly, upon hearing that I would be in the States in May, my son immediately emailed and asked me if I can also help take care of their children for several days. My principle is that if my kids let me know they need me beforehand, I will definitely fly back and provide assistance.

Some of the women I interviewed reported that their grandchildren had been sent to stay with them in Taiwan. This practice approximates a common pattern chronicled in the transnational family literature, in which grandparents take care of children left behind when their parents migrate (Dreby 2010; Fonseca 2004; Gilbertson 2009; Øien 2006; Orellana et al. 2001; Smith 2006; Yarris 2017). Among the respondents, eight return migrants (four couples) had grandchildren who had stayed with them in Taiwan. For them, the arrangement had been short term but had helped to compensate for their absence in the United States. Mrs. Tong's daughter had entrusted her with the care of her granddaughters for a couple of weeks so that her daughter could go on a business trip to China. "The biggest regret that I have about relocating to Taiwan is that I have been so far away from my grandchildren," Mrs. Tong reflected.

> I am happy to help look after my grandchildren in Taiwan when my children ask me to do so. It only happened a couple of times, but I really enjoyed it. I had a great time with the grandchildren when my daughter was on a business trip to China. After my daughter came back from China, she checked in with me and asked me, "Did the kids cry and look for Mommy?" I was like, "No, not at all. The kids are very happy with me around." [*Laughs*] Of course, my daughter was disappointed, but she is also glad to know the kids and I had a wonderful time together. My daughter is also very grateful to me.

Managing Intimacy across Borders

Temporalities of migration influence the ways returnees considered intimate relations with their grandchildren. Many of the returnees I met hoped to have meaningful and memorable relationships. They also believed that modern intergenerational intimacy requires effort (Giddens 1992). Lacking opportunities to establish intimate connections through face-to-face interaction, therefore, most returnees developed tactics to participate in their grandchildren's lives and maintain family ties. Some used communication technologies to maintain contact. This strategy was common when grandchildren were preschoolers, but it was also practiced with older grandchildren.

Mrs. Kuan, in her sixties, reported talking with her three grandsons regularly through instant messaging and internet phone calls. Her oldest grandchild was seven, the middle one five, and the youngest only a few months, and she regretted missing the opportunity to watch them grow up. Fortunately, she explained, technology allowed her to "see" her grandsons often and to establish intergenerational relationships across borders. "My husband and I talk to our grandchildren very often," Mrs. Kuan reported.

> In order to talk to them, I started using instant messenger and Skype. I asked my neighbor to set up a video camera for us. You know there is a time difference between Taiwan and Boston. When we are in the evening, they are in the morning. We usually talk after my grandchildren wake up. After talking with them, it's about time for us to go to bed. Actually, my lifestyle is totally messed up by my grandchildren's schedule. Sometimes, my grandchildren do not wake up until ten or eleven a.m. In order to talk with them, we have to wait to go to bed.

KS: What do you usually talk about?

Mrs. Kuan: My grandchildren usually start with hello, *A-ma* [grandmother, in Taiwanese]. . . . Then they tell me what happened recently. Last time when we talked, they brought a children's book in front of the camera, showing me the pictures in the book and explaining the story to me. Sometimes, they sing me a new song they learned and dance. Sometimes, they play piano for us. Sometimes, they tell me what they learned at Sunday school. They also show us new shoes and clothes that they got from their parents.

Technology, however, could not replace in-person contact. Returnees who struggled with their health or had trouble with long-distance flights encouraged their children to bring their grandchildren to visit. Mrs. Chin had trouble walking without a walker and needed regular treatment, so her son and daughters brought her grandchildren to visit once a year. From Mrs. Chin's perspective, visits mattered because they helped her grandchildren remember and love her, even though she was far away.

Returnees who remained healthy and mobile preferred to travel to the United States, where they cherished their family time. Mr. Qi, in his sixties, described flying back and forth between the United States and Taiwan twice a year to see his grandchildren, even though he routinely used Skype to communicate with them. "A grandfather who existed only on the screen" wasn't enough, Mr. Qi explained. "My grandchildren are very close to me. We talked over phone and Skype very often. Sometimes we were worried whether our grandchildren would think Grandpa and Grandma only exist on the screen. My wife and I still think it necessary to visit them in the US, to let them know that we are real people. [*Laughs*] . . . When we see our grandchildren, we bring them to restaurants, to get ice cream and to toy stores. We always have a great time with our grandchildren."

Gifts provided another way to become visible to grandchildren and maintain intergenerational ties. Near the end of my fieldwork in Taiwan, Mr. and Mrs. Kim, both in their seventies and living in Kaohsiung, asked me to bring gifts to their grandchildren in Boston. To assure me that the packages contained nothing illegal or dangerous, Mrs. Kim showed me the clothes, hats, and shoes with popular Japanese cartoon figures, such as Astro Boy, Doraemon, and Pocket Monster. I was more than happy to bring these gifts to their grandchildren, but I asked why they did not instead bring them on their planned visit four weeks later. Mrs. Kim responded, "I don't want to wait that long. These clothes are summer clothes. You know summer in Boston is really short. I want my grandchildren to wear them this summer. And yesterday, my grandchildren just told me, 'We really miss you,

Grandma. When are you coming back?' I want to send these gifts to them and let them know that I miss them and think of them." Mrs. Kim was not alone in using gifts to reaffirm connections with grandchildren. Scholars of transnational families have written about migrant mothers seeking maternal visibility by sending their children expensive gifts (Baldassar et al. 2016; Peng and Wong 2013). Using gifts as reminders, grandparents like Mrs. Kim similarly attempted to overcome physical distance and establish a sense of virtual presence to her grandchildren.

Cultural Mediation from a Distance

Temporalities of migration shaped returnees' thinking about passing ethnic traditions to their grandchildren. Like respondents in the United States, those in Taiwan expressed a desire to become cultural mediators, both because of their attachment to Taiwan and because of their assessment of their grandchildren's future on a global stage. Like their coethnics in the United States, the returnees I encountered hoped to prepare their grandchildren for various opportunities that might appear across time and borders. Recognizing China's rising global prominence, virtually all the returnees I interviewed in Taiwan expected their American-born grandchildren to learn to understand Mandarin Chinese and to read at least some written Chinese (also see Lan 2018). Of course, not all identified as Chinese, and some strongly opposed the notion of Chinese sovereignty over Taiwan. All, however, agreed on the importance of language skills.

Mr. and Mrs. Shen, both in their sixties, were strong supporters of Taiwan's independence movement. As international students in the United States, they had been active in organizations promoting Taiwanese independence and democracy. In 1996, right before Taiwan's first presidential election, China had launched missiles in the nearby sea, and Mr. and Mrs. Shen had begun participating in protests, both in the United States and in Taiwan. At the time of our interview, they encouraged me to sign a petition opposing the Taiwanese government's plan to participate in the Economic Cooperation Framework Agreement (ECFA), a preferential trade pact with China, because they were reluctant to see Taiwan's increasing economic dependence on China's labor and consumer markets. Yet they admitted that learning Mandarin Chinese would be beneficial for their American-born grandchildren.

As strongly self-identified Taiwanese citizens, Mr. and Mrs. Shen wanted their grandchildren to speak Taiwanese/Fujianese, but as grandparents concerned for their grandchildren's future, they thought Mandarin Chinese would be more useful. Their grandchildren "looked" Chinese, they explained, noting their grandchildren's phenotypical features, and would have better chances than people of other racial and ethnic origins to succeed in China. As Mrs. Shen articulated their rationale,

> I thought a lot about the language issue. Taiwanese is my mother tongue, but it is not as widely used as Mandarin. Now except for English, Chinese is the most popular language in the world, right? For the future of my grandchildren, I should encourage my children to teach Chinese to my grandchildren. My children agree with me on the importance of Chinese in the twenty-first century too. We have Oriental faces. It might be easier for us than those white Americans to blend in better in China. My grandchildren might have a lot of opportunities in China after they grow up. It is so much easier for kids to pick up language, you know.

My respondents also sought to instill values, like thrift, which they attributed to their Taiwanese heritage. Mr. Kuan echoed his coethnics in the United States when he emphasized industriousness—or more precisely effort, persistence, and perseverance—to explain having accumulated considerable wealth and achieved a middle-class life in a relatively short period (Lee and Zhou 2015). Mr. Kuan adamantly wanted his grandchildren to appreciate the virtue of industriousness, which he considered central to his immigrant identity and experience. Cultural values like thrift had helped him succeed, and he hoped to pass this virtue to his grandchildren. "The reason why immigrants like us can become successful in the US is our virtue of industriousness," he maintained.

> Unlike Americans, Taiwanese culture very much emphasizes the importance of this virtue. We were always careful about how to use the money we earned. If we earn one dollar, we will save fifty cents. If we earn one million dollars, we will save five hundred thousand dollars. Yet now in the US, and even Taiwan today, people are encouraged to buy things they don't need. If they earn one dollar, they will use a credit card to spend two dollars. That is why a lot of people today have a lot of debts. We really want our grandchildren to learn the importance of being thrifty.

Immigrant narratives like Mr. Kuan's supported most of my respondents' efforts to be cultural mediators for their grandchildren, pointing to the ways their experiences as newcomers at an earlier life stage shaped their identities as grandparents later in life. Return migrants, however, had developed specific strategies for mediating culture from a distance. Some assisted their children in teaching their grandchildren linguistic skills. When I met Mrs. Dai, who had relocated to Taiwan seven years before our interview, she was busy selecting Chinese instruction books and other children's books written in Chinese, and she excitedly showed me the videos and textbooks she had purchased for her grandchildren. With them, Mrs. Dai explained, her children could more easily teach her grandchildren both the Chinese language and Chinese cultural values. "I bought and sent a lot of Chinese instructional materials to my grandchildren from Taiwan in order to create an ideal environment for my grandchildren to learn the language," she elaborated. "I just bought and sent *Benesse* [a popular Mandarin-language cartoon much like *Sesame Street* and *Teletubbies*] to my grandchildren this month. I sent my grandchildren other Chinese storybooks, textbooks, and Chinese-language cartoons, tapes, and videos before. I just try my best to help my daughter raise my grandchildren. Kids learn things really fast. These materials might help my grandchildren learn things unconsciously." Mrs. Dai reported that her children in the United States had affirmed the importance of sustaining her grandchildren's connections to Chinese culture, especially Mandarin Chinese, and her daughter had therefore asked her to find materials that native Taiwanese parents use to educate their children. Mrs. Dai had thus collaborated with her daughter to facilitate cultural connections.

Relocation to Taiwan also constituted a particular structural context, creating opportunities for grandchildren to visit. Young children came with their parents, but older children and teenagers could travel alone. As Robert Smith (2006) argues, many in the second and third generations regularly travel to locales where their parents and grandparents have settled in later life. Some of the respondents in Taiwan reported visits from grandchildren during vacations. These were moments for teaching, during which they communicated with their grandchildren in Mandarin Chinese and sought to reinforce the cultural values and practices that they wanted their grandchildren to learn. Mr. Kim's teenage granddaughter, a junior in high school, was about to visit him several weeks after the interview and, Mr. Kim reported, would stay for about two months, as she had in an earlier summer. Together with his son, he had already registered his granddaughter for summer language classes. By spending time with family and friends, he explained, his granddaughter could improve her language abilities and gain greater cultural familiarity with Taiwan. He added, "My granddaughter will come back alone to Taiwan next month. She will stay with us for the entire summer. My granddaughter is very excited about returning and staying with us this summer. She will take summer courses from the Mandarin Training Center at National Taiwan Normal University. At the same time, she can spend more time accompanying us, knowing her family members here, visiting her homeland, practicing Chinese, and getting to know Taiwan better."

To be sure, predicting the long-term effects of homeland visits is difficult. Much research has found that transnational connections become mostly emotional and symbolic (rather than tangible) among second- or third-generation descendants of immigrants (Kasinitz et al. 2008; Waldinger 2015). Other migration studies have found many younger people ambivalent about homeland trips (Kim 2009; Reynolds 2010). Whereas some members of later generations do feel reconnected to the homelands, others feel deeply alienated and out of place, refusing to call their parents' or grandparents' homeland "home" (Kibria 2002; Kim 2009; Louie 2004). The efforts of return migrants like Mr. Kim, however, are a response to a time-migration configuration with which later generations must grapple, even if they are visiting the "homeland" simply because their grandparents live there.

How Gender Shapes Grandparenting

Gender shapes dynamics within kinship networks (Di Leonardo 1987; Hansen 2005). Among immigrants in the United States, gender differentiates the participation of women and men as they care for their grandchildren. Women, especially mothers, are the primary caregivers for children, both in Taiwanese immigrant families and in Taiwan (Gu 2017). The careers and employment status of their daughters or daughters-in-law thus influence the extent to which grandmothers provide hands-on care. If daughters or daughters-in-law are stay-at-home mothers, grandmothers feel less obligated to care for their grandchildren than they do when daughters or daughters-in-law have paid jobs. From their perspective, their contributions replace a mother's care. Virtually all of my respondents considered grandmothers, rather than grandfathers, in charge of caring for young children.

Gendered Division of Labor in the United States

Arlie Hochschild's (1989) concept of "gender strategy" can explain the operation of gender ideology in these families. In *The Second Shift*, Hochschild (1989) applied the concept to the rationalization of a domestic division of labor. A gender strategy, she elaborates, is "a plan of action through which a person tries to solve problems at hand, given the cultural notions of gender at play" (Hochschild 1989, 15). As Cameron Macdonald (2011) further found, daily tasks involved in the care and protection of small children are typically regarded as mother's work. Many of the respondents rationalized the gendered division of labor they practiced by contending that experience as a mother better prepared them for hands-on care. Men involved in caregiving typically assumed the role of assistant. Notably, my respondents referred to the physical care of infants—especially cooking, feeding, and cleaning—as "women's domains."

Unlike their wives, most of the grandfathers I interviewed offered little detail about their grandchildren's physical care, and none reported cooking for their grandchildren. They were more interested in answering questions about their grandchildren's education. Mr. Hsiu aggressively interrupted and chided me for asking "trivial" and "womanish" questions about the provision of hands-on care and advised me not to write about these minor themes. He wanted to tell me about his strategy for raising his grandchildren as culturally Chinese. For him, some domains, especially cooking and cleaning, were solely the province of women.

This gendered division of labor evolves as grandchildren grow up. Grandmothers might continue to provide childcare assistance, often after school, but care for older children entailed less time and attention. Grandfathers might also assist with older children, perhaps playing with them or driving them to or from class. Both women and men also reported teaching Mandarin Chinese and ethnic values that they deemed central to their grandchildren's identities. Unlike hands-on care, however, cultural education was a shared project for women and men, and I found little evidence of a gendered division of labor in the ways the respondents in the United States described their efforts to provide it.

Gendered Division of Labor among Return Migrants

As return migrants struggled with spatial distance from their grandchildren, they, too, maintained a gendered division of labor. Grandmothers took on most emotional care and made most of the effort to sustain cross-border intergenerational ties. Expressing a sense of guilt more often than grandfathers, return migrant grandmothers also more often traveled back and forth between the United States and Taiwan to provide short-term support. Women, more than men, executed tasks to establish affective ties with their grandchildren. Grandmothers, for instance, typically spoke regularly with their children and children's spouses, and they took responsibility for selecting and sending gifts. Most of the return migrant women I interviewed emphasized their child-rearing experience as a qualification for picking the "right" gifts and communicating more comfortably than their spouses about their grandchildren's needs and desires.

I was surprised when Mrs. Kim chose clothes for her grandchildren with Japanese cartoon figures because even I, growing up in Taiwan, was unaware of this part of popular culture. Mrs. Kim, however, had seen a friend's grandsons wearing the same clothes and had asked her friend where to buy them. Her husband, she told me, paid no attention and was uninvolved in these minor details. "We women talk mostly about family and children when getting together, and our husbands are only interested in discussing politics," she emphasized. She may have overgeneralized, but her account vividly highlights a common perception of family as women's responsibility. Mrs. Kim talked at length, with concrete detail, about the places she went for gifts, the prices she paid, and discussions with neighbors, relatives, and friends about this process. In contrast, Mr. Kim offered little detail and mentioned no conversations about gift giving. Rather, he suggested that I refer these questions to his wife.

The grandfathers I interviewed were thus similar to the fathers described by Annette Lareau (2000, 408), who found that fathers "do not know very much about the details of their children's lives because, relative to mothers, they did not provide very much day-to-day care." Relying on their wives, return migrant men like Mr. Kim could still establish a rapport with their grandchildren halfway around the globe. Indeed, both the men and women whom I interviewed sought to practice grandparenthood in a transnational context. Migrant grandmothers, however, performed most of the related tasks. In this respect, the notion of mothers as primary providers of care became an ideological mechanism that rendered migrant women responsible for doing grandparenthood.

Gendered Conflicts

Whether in the United States or in Taiwan, grandparents engaged in nuanced gender dynamics. Partly because caregiving is deeply gendered and partly because older women (mothers-in-law) in Chinese patriarchy typically supervise younger women (daughters-in-law), conflicts are most common between mothers- and daughters-in-law. Mothers-in-law in Chinese families are often described as guardians of patriarchal order, thereby creating much stress for their daughters-in-law (Gu 2017; Shih and Pyke 2016). Yet many grandmothers I studied also have to negotiate with their daughters and daughters-in-law about involvement in their grandchildren's lives. Given the cultural divisions across borders and between generations, serious conflicts between two generations of in-laws can ensue.

Emphasizing the importance of speaking Mandarin Chinese at home, Mrs. Ma had created fissures in her relationship with her daughter-in-law. Both her son and her daughter-in-law agreed about exposing their children to the language, Mrs. Ma reported, but her daughter-in-law was America born and felt more comfortable speaking English. Mrs. Ma often reminded her daughter-in-law that speaking Mandarin could help her two grandchildren pick up Chinese, but after several exchanges, her daughter-in-law seemed annoyed and yelled at her in front of her husband and children, screaming, "These are my children. I know how to teach them. This is the United States, not Taiwan. You should not teach me what to do." Her daughter-in-law's behavior made her disappointed and upset, Mrs. Ma recounted, and she emphasized that she was always polite. Even though the relationship had been repaired, she had become more cautious about noninterference in her daughter-in-law's child rearing.

Among the return migrants I met, assumptions about the gendered division of labor oriented interaction with their children's families. Returnees typically expected their daughters or daughters-in-law to shoulder primary responsibility for raising their grandchildren and so checked in with their daughters or daughters-in-law, rather than their sons or sons-in-law, as Mrs. Peng maintained:

> We typically talked to my daughter-in-law about how our grandchildren are doing. . . . Mothers definitely take on the biggest responsibilities for children. Fathers are important too. Fathers definitely need to work with mothers to educate their children. . . . However, fathers are the breadwinners and have the responsibility for raising the entire family. Fathers are often busy with their work and spend less time at home. Mothers should and in general do take more responsibilities for the children. After all, mothers are the ones who spend more time with kids. Mothers of course should supervise the development of children. If we had any question about my grandchildren, we would talk to our daughter-in-law about it. And she would fill us in.

Most of the return migrants I interviewed were satisfied with the ways their daughters and daughters-in-law cared for and educated their grandchildren, but a few grandmothers reported conflicts. Some stemmed from the assistance they provided or the unsolicited advice they offered. Mrs. Quian, in her early seventies, reported flying to the United States to help care for her granddaughter when her daughter-in-law was about to give birth. Mrs. Quian believed she had tried her best to help, but her daughter-in-law still found her presence intrusive, and Mrs. Quian described a fierce fight. "Before my first son's daughter was born, I flew to the United States to provide my son and daughter-in-law with some short-term help," she told me.

> I gave all of my attention to my granddaughter. Then my daughter-in-law was unhappy about how I took care of my granddaughter. She was like, "She is my daughter. How come she is always with you?" My daughter-in-law was very Americanized. She was very opposed to my intervention in her and her kids' lives. I remembered that the first month after my daughter-in-law gave birth to our granddaughter, we wanted to give her time to rest. So whenever the baby cried, I ran to see her. I was totally well intentioned. Then one day, she cried and was screaming at us like crazy. She accused me of stealing her daughter away from her. I was really appalled. I did not know what was going on with her.

We have a neighbor next door, Mrs. Lin, who took care of her grandson for her daughter five days a week. And her son and daughter picked
up their kids on the weekend. I never heard Mrs. Lin fight with her
son or daughter-in-law. It is just pretty common [for grandmothers to
handle newborn baby care] in Taiwan.

Mrs. Quian assured me that she held no grudges against her daughter-in-law
and remained close to her grandchildren. She attributed her daughter-in-law's
confrontation to postpartum depression. From then on, however, she had tried
not to give her daughter-in-law advice about child rearing.

Temporalities of migration significantly influenced the respondents' strategies
for participating in the lives of their grandchildren. Their understanding of intergenerational responsibilities shaped the meanings of grandparenthood and
revealed a wide range of practices that these aging migrants use to "be there" with
their children and grandchildren. Central to doing grandparenthood, therefore, is
making sense of the intersection between migration and time. Key for the respondents was their experience as newcomers to the United States, their cultural
ideals of family, their views of modern intimacy, and the survival strategies they
used in a changing global environment.

The respondents' accounts reveal three grandparenting styles: minimal grandparenting, active grandparenting in place, and grandparenting from afar. Minimal grandparents had little to do with rearing their grandchildren, either by choice
or through exclusion. Geographic distance, health conditions, notions of responsibility, and preexisting relationships with their children and children's spouses
explained minimal involvement for some of the respondents. In contrast, more
respondents were actively engaged in grandchild care. The practice of grandparenting depended on proximity, but grandparents in both the United States and
Taiwan grappled with structural constraints as they assessed their past, their
children's present, and their grandchildren's future.

As immigrants of color who had struggled with work and family obligations
at an earlier life stage, immigrants in the United States cared for their grandchildren to relieve their children of responsibilities in a context that was sometimes
hostile. They learned, however, not to interfere in their grandchildren's lives,
adopting what Cherlin and Furstenberg (1986) termed the dominant American
style of grandparenting. In contrast, those who had returned to Taiwan had far
fewer opportunities to interact with their grandchildren and so devised strategies—
money sent to their children, grandmothers flying to provide short-term care,

and grandchildren visiting Taiwan—to compensate for their inability to provide routine, hands-on care.

In both the United States and Taiwan, intimacy with grandchildren was a concern for the respondents. In the United States, however, the immigrants I interviewed expected their grandparenting to differ from their own experiences as children. Highlighting the effort modern intimacy requires, they hoped to establish rapport through hands-on care. Respondents in Taiwan who wanted to help with care fostered alternative strategies, typically through communication technologies, international flights, and gifts sent to maintain connections. Grandparenting from afar, they sought to compensate for spatial distance and create a symbolic presence in their grandchildren's lives.

Respondents further sought to act as cultural mediators, instilling values and practices from their homeland in their grandchildren's everyday lives. Language and thrift were two key features of their accounts. Those who provided hands-on assistance had many opportunities to transmit the Taiwanese or Chinese cultural practices that they deemed important. Those who assisted from afar typically sent books and other culturally significant materials or exposed their grandchildren to Taiwanese culture during visits. Notably, grandparents on both sides of the Pacific promoted the acquisition of Mandarin Chinese, a language they considered most useful in a changing global environment, even if they had spoken a different language in Taiwan.

Gender shaped the dynamics between the respondents and their children's families. Women in the United States typically offered to share responsibilities with their daughters or daughters-in-law, and those in Taiwan offered what assistance they could provide. As a "women's domain," however, caregiving could engender conflicts, usually between mothers-in-law and daughters or daughters-in-law, which deeply affected the women I interviewed. Amid the challenges and structural constraints that these immigrants encountered, therefore, they continued to do grandparenthood in ways that remained highly gendered.

NAVIGATING NETWORKS OF SUPPORT

Social networks are key to the social and psychological well-being of aging populations. Older people's ties to community members can keep them from feeling lonely, give them a sense of purpose and belonging, and offer the concrete support they need (Ajrouch 2005; Zhang and Zhan 2009). As Meika Loe (2011, 27) argues, "the value of social networks translates into safety nets, a sense of belonging, and decreased isolation"; for her research participants (people eighty-five and older), "combinations of socioeconomic status, loose intergenerational networks, family connections, and membership in at least one organization added up to social advantages over time." Just as older people value their connections to immediate and extended family, they also rely heavily on their community members. Therefore, many older people carefully consider, cultivate, and maintain certain social relationships.

This chapter shifts the attention from family to networks of support. Here I analyze the ways temporalities of migration shape older immigrants' management of intimate relations with community members. In both the United States and Taiwan, the experiences of lifelong immigrants shape their strategies to navigate community life across borders. The mutual shaping between time and migratory experience was evident in my respondents' memories about their homeland, the paths they took within US society, and their experiences of a changing Taiwan. More specifically, the ways in which these older immigrants organized social relationships to acquire company, advice, hands-on care, and emotional as well as moral support were deeply affected by their migratory trajectories. While those who *age in place* developed a sophisticated understanding of their standing within ethnic communities, those who decided to spend their retirement life transnationally grappled with their connections to the "homeland."

Despite their distinct struggles, long-term migration left an inerasable mark on these migrants' sense of belonging. Like other older individuals, my respondents articulated a sense of community in which they embedded themselves. Yet they differed from nonmigrant older people in their status as long-term migrants. Nonmigrant elders also need to build communities as their independence diminishes, children move away, and work is no longer the main source of social interaction, but the respondents addressed these changes within a web of connections to communities established in two regions over time. For these migrants, who had spent most of their working years abroad, adaptation to the United States had meant profound self-transformations while Taiwan had undergone dramatic sociocultural changes as well.

In addition, moving into any new community, within the same country or across national borders, requires relearning a place and reestablishing social ties. I found that older immigrants who moved within the United States to be closer to their children or grandchildren had an easier time adapting to life in their new communities than those returning to Taiwan. Compared with their coethnics in the United States, return migrants were more eager to discuss the difficulties that they faced and the efforts they made when trying to integrate themselves into a new community. This finding suggests that cultural familiarity or identification with a society constitutes an important part of migrants' experiences with community life.

The strategies with which respondents managed their networks depended significantly on whether they had returned to Taiwan. Those who had stayed in the United States could draw on knowledge accumulated over years of residence, but those who returned had often found a homeland with which they were unfamiliar. As older immigrants in the United States considered their connections to their homeland communities, those in Taiwan reflected on their ties to their coethnics in the United States. Despite the divergent directions of their transnational ties, both groups of respondents felt a strong sense of hyphenated identity as Taiwanese immigrants or Taiwanese Americans.

Embedded in networks, aging migrant populations often grapple with their social belonging and their sense of community (Hansen 2005; Purkayastha et al. 2012). Drawing on their experiences in the United States, respondents who remained there could *know their place*, for example, by applying trajectories of socioeconomic incorporation (joining the American middle class or becoming an immigrant entrepreneur) and ethnic origin (born in Taiwan or mainland China) to organize social relationships. As long-term immigrants, they also held long-lasting memories about homeland politics and perceived class differences that shaped their construction of support networks. In contrast, those who had returned to Taiwan were trying to *relearn their place* as they reintegrated into their ancestral society and faced a culture now changed by decades of industrialization and modernization. After a long stay in the United States, they perceived that they had become Americanized or Westernized too. Against this backdrop returnees devised strategies—such as recruiting other return migrants, resocializing themselves, and compartmentalizing different life domains—to construct networks of support in Taiwan.

Scholars of migrant transnationalism underscore the possibility that immigrants' social networks extend across borders, further sustaining migrants' sense of belonging to communities in both their home and host societies (Levitt 2001; Reynolds 2006; Smith 2006). My research corroborates these findings. Cross-border relationships, I find, motivated my respondents in both the United States and Taiwan to rethink their status as long-term migrants living overseas. In most cases, living in a transnational community distinguished them from their nonmigrant community members, further reinforcing their identities as Taiwanese Americans or Americanized Taiwanese. This identification not only mirrored older immigrants' sense of community but also influenced the extent to which they could turn their social ties into tangible and emotional support. In comparison with immigrants who stay in the United States, returnees had fewer people they could turn to for help and sometimes felt "out of place" because of their interaction with local people in the homeland.

Constructing Networks of Support: Two Tales from the Field

On a freezing New England winter morning, I sat in a tailor store owned by Mrs. Liao's sister and listened to her vividly describe her adventures since migrating to the United States. Mrs. Liao had moved to the United States in 1972 and ran various small businesses in the Greater Boston, New York, and Los Angeles areas. Migrating, she told me, had been challenging but fulfilling. Excitedly, she related stories about borrowing money from relatives for the move, about her small business that had gone through ups and downs, and about raising five children while working exceedingly long hours. Mrs. Liao was widowed and lived alone; all of her children had moved out after going to college or getting married. Like many migrants I interviewed, she claimed that to survive as an immigrant in a new country required her to stay strong and independent. She stressed that she did not like to burden other people, including her children, relatives, and friends. Rather, as chapter 2 elaborates, she preferred to be self-reliant and planned to stay that way as long as she could.

Yet Mrs. Liao soon revealed more details about the support that she received from her community, despite her wishes to retain self-sufficiency. Since a stroke in 2003, Mrs. Liao had faced limited physically mobility and could not drive or walk without crutches. Yet she lived in a suburban area with limited public transportation, and the Taiwanese church she attended was at least an hour's drive from her home. Given these conditions, I probed, "So how did you come here [her sister's tailor shop] today?" Mrs. Liao replied, "Oh, Lucas [another Taiwanese immigrant from her church] gave me a ride today. I have several nice friends who are willing to help me get around. In the winter, they would also get together in my house, because they know I am not very mobile." Mrs. Liao further emphasized, "These Taiwanese immigrants are long-term friends; we have known each other for decades. We are all like members of one big family. We help each other a lot."

For Mrs. Liao, social networks had played a particularly important role in life-and-death situations, and she described her communities in the United States as "God's blessing." For instance, her husband had passed away on a Sunday morning, when she was in her sixties, after reminding her the night before that commitments at church meant they needed to attend that morning. When trying to awaken him, she had found him unresponsive. Mrs. Liao immediately called several of her friends at church, and they helped her communicate with the police, the hospital, and the funeral home. This support was critical, because most of her children, including her son in a nearby town, were unavailable. Support was also critical on the morning of her stroke, when she fainted in church. Parishioners immediately called an ambulance, she recounted, and once she was in the hospital, they checked in regularly. Mrs. Liao still looked frightened as she recalled those moments, emphasizing, "God really loves me. Without those people, I do not even know what would happen to me then and what kind of situation I would face now."

Mrs. Liao's network of support was not coincidental. Rather, as a long-term immigrant in the United States, she had long-standing ties to a community of Taiwanese immigrants. In addition, because she knew her coethnics well, she consciously selected the community that she wanted to join and carefully considered the organizations in which she wished to participate. For example, Mrs. Liao insisted on going to a Taiwanese-speaking rather than a Mandarin-speaking church. Although many immigrants from Taiwan use Mandarin Chinese, Mrs. Liao was willing only to attend a Taiwanese-speaking church because she did not wish to risk encountering or having conflicts with people who might disagree with her about politics in Taiwan. Mrs. Liao maintained that, as a former small business owner, she understood and respected people who had different political views, but she preferred to spend time with people who were "like-minded."

Mrs. Liao differentiated the church she attended from the other Taiwanese-speaking congregations. She had intentionally joined a Taiwanese-speaking church more than an hour's drive from her home rather than one that was only a twenty-minute drive because she believed the Taiwanese immigrants in the nearby church were "just not my people." To Mrs. Liao, most of the people attending the other Taiwanese-identified church were "elite people," who had come to the United States as international students and then landed professional jobs. As a person who had barely finished high school, Mrs. Liao perceived herself as less educated and less accomplished than her professional middle-class coethnics. More importantly, she often sensed a deep social gap that left her feeling intentionally dismissed. The church she had chosen was easier for her because most attendees were small business owners or people with lower-middle-class jobs. She felt more at ease around these people. They liked her, she thought, and they were also like her.

In contrast, Mr. Hsu had returned to Taiwan and talked of his relationships with community members after he was divorced from his wife. Since his return, Mr. Hsu had reactivated ties to old friends and started to meet new people, and he now spent much time hanging out with classmates, neighbors, and colleagues. When living in the United States, Mr. Hsu related, he had been occupied with professional and personal commitments and separated from friends by geographical distance. Now, resettled in Taiwan and freed from the demands of career and child rearing, he had plenty of time to reconnect with community members and had joined various activities and programs. For example, he had been learning and practicing tai chi in a park nearby and had joined community learning programs for elders. He was making new friends, some his age and some younger.

In Taiwan, Mr. Hsu had constructed a community that for him served both material and symbolic functions, and he was grateful to this community for the many forms of assistance it offered. For instance, his friends had introduced him to a doctor he could trust and continued to see for all of his routine medical care. Mr. Hsu also told of the help he received from his younger friends when he moved into a new apartment and set up a new computer with a wireless internet network. He had also received much emotional and moral support from his friends in Taiwan. Friends were important at his life stage, he maintained, because his children and grandchildren lived in the United States and were busy with their own professional and personal commitments. Therefore, the company of his friends kept him from feeling lonely or becoming socially isolated.

But Mr. Hsu missed his family and friends in the United States tremendously. Relocating, he had searched for a new community in a rapidly changing homeland, and he often struggled with profound differences he perceived between himself and local Taiwanese people, including his relatives and friends. These social and cultural differences seemed significant partly because of cultural changes during his three decades in the United States and partly because of the personal transformation he had experienced there. For Mr. Hsu, not only had his home-land changed, but he had also become a person different from friends who had never lived abroad for a long time. Now he often felt more socially and culturally similar to his coethnics in the United States. This sentiment—"returning home, but home is no longer the same"—captured a complex sense of belonging. Mr. Hsu felt not only that he had to reacculturate himself but also that he needed to construct a new community.

Politics of Belonging in Host and Home Societies

Two stories—Mrs. Liao's and Mr. Hsu's—point to the temporalities of migration that provoke the complex emotions and struggles that many respondents de-scribed. Constructing networks of support was necessary because these networks helped them secure resources they needed and desired. Yet staging networks of support—just like managing any social relationship—is never easy. The effort re-quires cautious thinking, planning, and strategizing. Mrs. Liao, as a long-term im-migrant, had established, maintained, and relied on her coethnics in the United States for decades. In constructing a community, she had adopted an approach I call *knowing their place*. This approach refers to the intimate understanding—the particular, unique knowledge (Zelizer 2005)—that immigrants have about their ethnic communities after spending most of their working years in the United States. Older immigrants like Mrs. Liao know their communities not only because they understand the micropolitics among Taiwanese immigrants but also because they have a clear sense of the networks in which they feel comfortable.

As migration scholars indicate, many newcomers bond with their coethnics in receiving contexts and foster new social networks to acquire various forms of assistance, including money, food, housing, information, and moral support (Bashi 2007; Kibria 1993; Massey et al. 1998; Menjivar 1997; M. Zhou 1992). As research reveals, this circulation of resources allows newcomers not only to sur-vive but also to thrive, even "get ahead" socioeconomically in host societies (Dominguez 2011). This ability to activate ethnic networks also suggests that im-migrants like Mrs. Liao understand their communities. With decades of experi-ence interacting with other newcomers, they have an intimate understanding that informs the ties they choose to forge.

By way of contrast, to manage his social life in Taiwan, Mr. Hsu had adopted an approach I term *relearning their place*. This approach refers to the ways in which return migrants grapple with their sense of belonging to the new community they encounter in the homeland. Temporalities of migration profoundly affect returnees' sense of community both in Taiwan and transnationally. For returnees like Mr. Hsu, moving back to Taiwan meant moving away from the immigrant communities in which they had been embedded for decades. Sensing unexpected but profound differences with local nonmigrant populations, they recognized changes both in themselves and in Taiwan.

As the growing literature on return migration shows (Erdal and Ezzati 2015; Hunter 2011; Tsuda 2014; Zontini 2015), spending an extended period in another society transforms expatriates' worldviews so that returnees feel dissimilar from community members back home (Fitzgerald 2013). For some, this sense of dissimilarity is compounded by what scholars have termed compressed modernity—rapid economic, political, social, and/or cultural changes—in the homeland (Kyung-Sup 2010). For most of the returnees I met, navigating social life in contemporary Taiwan had been an experience of entering a liminal place, where they were forced to rethink who they were and where they belonged. Their reported struggles may not always accurately reflect the social and cultural landscape in Taiwan, but their accounts do point to the negotiation of their perceived American superiority over nonmigrant populations back home.

"Knowing Their Place": Navigating Networks in the United States

The respondents stressed the importance of their ethnic communities from earlier to later life stages, revealing the intertwined relationship between time, migration, and ties to coethnics. Many emphasized ties to other Taiwanese immigrants who had provided them essential support when they had first arrived in the United States. Some reported that they, in turn, had offered help—including money, advice, and accommodation—when they had settled and could assist other newcomers. For many, the company of their coethnics had greatly eased their nostalgia. Early on, the material and symbolic support they acquired had been an essential part of their daily lives, but it was indispensable as they aged. The importance of ethnic communities thus intensified after these immigrants retired from work.

Mr. Guo, in his seventies, described finding most of his connections to the "mainstream" United States through his work as a professor and then as an engineer. His career had offered him many opportunities to make friends with native-born Americans. When he was younger, Mr. Guo had been eager to establish himself professionally by impressing his American colleagues. His work, he emphasized, had deepened his understanding of US society. To understand and communicate with his American colleagues, Mr. Guo had watched CNN, read the *New York Times*, and listened to National Public Radio every day. The news had helped him engage in conversation. Mr. Guo reported having learned much from his colleagues about American perspectives on various issues, including immigration. As he grew close to retirement, however, he had become less ambitious and felt less impelled to monitor events in the United States. He had also lost contact with his former colleagues for a while. Connections to his ethnic community had become more important.

Echoing her husband, Mrs. Guo confirmed the importance of their connections to ethnic communities especially at a later stage of life. Having graduated from the top law school in Taiwan, she had received a master's degree in business administration in the United States. As a mother actively involved in her children's school and as a real estate agent, Mrs. Guo had found ample opportunity to interact with people of various racial, ethnic, and cultural backgrounds. As one of the few Asian faces in her workplace and her children's school, she had worked hard to gain respect from her mostly white American colleagues, her children's teachers, and other parents in the neighborhood.

Yet after her children had left home and after she decided to retire, Mrs. Guo had increasingly lost her connections to what she described as mainstream US society. Now, she told me, she interacted mostly with other Taiwanese immigrants. This postretirement transition would have been inconceivable when she was younger, Mrs. Guo explained, because she used to "have a lot of contempt" for people "stuck in Chinatown," who were never integrated into the mainstream United States. Embracing the idea of a model minority, she differentiated herself from other Chinese immigrants, whom she perceived as an underclass. She thus displayed much pride in socioeconomic success and ethnonational identity as a newcomer from Taiwan. Over time, however, she had come to feel like "one of those people trapped in Chinatown" as she interacted with Taiwanese people most of the time. "When we [she and her husband] just arrived to the US, we saw the lives of Chinese people living in Chinatown." Mrs. Guo elaborated,

> They lived in the US for their entire lives, but they still could only speak their native languages, such Cantonese, Teo Chew dialects, Taishen dialects. We used to mock those people and thought that they were so pathetic. But right now, look at us. My husband and I talked about this: We are becoming the people we used to despise after retiring from work. Our dentist is a Taiwanese immigrant, our family doctor is a Taiwanese immigrant, and all of the social activities we attend are predominantly Taiwanese. Most of the friends we hang out with are Taiwanese. We [she and her husband] sometimes look at each other and wonder what happened and how this happened: Are we becoming those older Chinese people we used to despise?

Mrs. Guo was not alone in placing greater importance on her ethnic communities. Most senior migrants with whom I talked expressed a similar sentiment. To avoid social isolation, they sought to construct networks of interdependence for themselves and their loved ones, and they relied on coethnics to whom they were not biologically related. For most of the immigrants I interviewed, family members to whom they felt close had remained in Taiwan, and although some of the respondents did have close relatives in the United States, they were usually living far away. These migrants had thus turned to their coethnics or "chosen families," who were often people they had known for several decades of living in the United States.

Mrs. Guo talked of long-standing connections, recalling that when she initially arrived, other Taiwanese immigrants had picked her up from the airport, taught her to drive, and helped her find accommodations. Aside from the instrumental support, Mrs. Guo considered her coethnics emotional and symbolic anchors. Whenever she felt homesick, she would gather and chat with other Taiwanese immigrants. They could relate to her struggles and were great sources of comfort. This support dated from her early years in the United States but had become indispensable now that she was older, all but replacing her biological family. Coethnics who shared her immigrant narrative had become her adopted family.

As they grew older, many of the immigrants I met had started to cultivate new social relationships with their coethnics. They reported seeking these connections, whether they were aging in place (i.e., continuing to stay in the same neighborhood) or moving to be physically closer to their children. When Mr. and Mrs. Yang had moved from Los Angeles to Boston for their grandchildren, the first thing they did was to look for Taiwanese immigrant organizations in which they could participate. By joining their high school and college alumni associations in the Boston area, Mr. and Mrs. Yang not only met coethnics of their generation but also got to know younger Taiwanese immigrants.

Mrs. Yang had also newly begun participating in Taiwanese immigrant organizations. To expand her social network, she had become an active member in a church, although she was not Christian and had no intention to be baptized. She even expressed resentment toward some Taiwanese Christians she encountered, describing them as selfish and self-righteous. The church, however, offered an active community, as Mrs. Yang explained. "We regularly went to church after we retired. We live a very simple life. In winter, if we don't go to Taiwanese church, we probably stay at home the entire week. We don't even drive our car. But if we go to church, we have somewhere to go and something to do every week. It is a church, so they have activities every week, and during the weekdays, a lot of retirees also have Bible studies and get-together." Like many immigrants I interviewed, Mrs. Yang used a family analogy, such as brothers and sisters or *jia-*

ren (family members) to describe relationships with coethnics (also see Bashi 2007; Kibria 1993). Now in retirement, she considered many members of her network, especially those older, "like a family."

Mrs. Yang reported ethnic ties with people younger and older. She described relying on those younger and stronger to help her move and to install a new air conditioner. She had also found ways to help others. During my fieldwork, Mrs. Yang often opened her home to international students and younger Taiwanese immigrants, especially on weekends and holidays like Thanksgiving and Christmas. She usually cooked and served traditional Taiwanese food to comfort recent arrivals, who might be experiencing homesickness. Mr. and Mrs. Yang also helped the sick with rides, visits, and shopping. These forms of assistance were not only instrumental but also emotional and social. By offering support, they developed familiarity, intimacy, trust, and a sense of belonging to a Taiwanese immigrant community.

Long-standing Impact of Homeland Politics

The construction of networks always involves processes of inclusion and exclusion. For Taiwanese immigrants, coethnics might serve as extended or adopted family (Espiritu 1996; Kibria 1993), but not everyone could be accepted, at least not easily. For the respondents, ideologies having much to do with memories about homeland politics were central to the construction of community. To be sure, homeland politics always play an essential part in migrant communities (Fitzgerald 2004; Siu 2005). Taiwan's history, however, had generated deep social divisions for the immigrants I met, and their identities often depended on both their ethnic backgrounds and their political views. Intergroup tensions thus suffused their interactions and determined the company they kept.

As chapter 1 elaborates, Taiwan's recent history had shaped an earlier stage of life for many of the respondents. Large-scale migration from mainland China to Taiwan was, after 1949, followed by the Kuomintang government's differing treatment of waishengren (mainland Chinese migrating to Taiwan) and benshengren (native-born Taiwanese). Overlying social identities (Taiwanese, Chinese, or both), therefore, might be support for a political party, either the Kuomintang or the Democratic Progressive Party. For the immigrants I interviewed, as for people in Taiwan, the global rise of China had further complicated identity and politics. Some strongly opposed the possibility of Chinese rule; some questioned the feasibility of Taiwan's independence. Others felt ambivalent about Taiwan's connections to China.

Conflicting views of homeland politics filtered into the everyday lives of the respondents, creating factions in the Taiwanese immigrant community. As

Mrs. Liao astutely observed, Taiwanese immigrant communities were not immune from homeland politics because the diverse range of immigrants reflected Taiwanese society. For her, political and social differences had long influenced social ties. She explained,

> Many of my old friends are from the Taiwanese Association of America. I also joined Taiwanese chambers of commerce and make many friends there. Yet in Boston, there are two different chambers of commerce from Taiwan. One is pro-China and supports the Kuomintang, and the other is pro-Taiwan and supports the Democratic Progressive Party. These things are not just about business. People who only speak Taiwanese and strongly identify themselves as Taiwanese typically go to a Taiwanese church. Other people [from Taiwan who] do not feel strongly about these things might go to a Chinese church. There is nothing we can do. The Taiwanese American community just mirrors what kind of society Taiwan is.

For Taiwanese immigrants, Mrs. Liao makes clear, political affiliation determines membership in commercial, social, and religious organizations.

Among the respondents, divergent memories about homeland politics and different political ideologies exerted a persistent influence on community dynamics, informing their choices for affiliation and friendship. Mr. Wu identified himself as benshengren (native-born Taiwanese) and had long been an advocate for Taiwan's independence. He emphasized having met some "really kind and nice waishengren [people who relocated to Taiwan from mainland China]" in the United States, but most of his friends were benshengren, who shared his political, social, and cultural identities. "In my opinion, birds of a feather flock together," he told me. "Like-minded people are close to each other. This is why we are not particularly close to waishengren, because our political views are different. It is a point of fact. They consider their ancestral land as China, while I think of my ancestral land as Taiwan. We will end up having conflicts. Our friendship lacks depth at the end of the day. That is why I mostly hang out with other Taiwanese who identify with Taiwan."

Mr. Tan, on the other hand, agreed that identity "naturally" fosters community. Many members of his community were, like him, veterans (rong min) from Taiwan, and he cited associations of Taiwanese veterans in Boston, New York, and Washington, DC. Mr. Tan's other social ties, however, depended largely on shared political views. To me, he claimed that "politics is never a problem" and that he "always had a lot of Taiwanese friends" before the "Democratic Progressive Party intentionally manipulated ethnic conflicts to their advantage." In answering my questions about whether he had any close friend who was a supporter of the Democratic Progress Party or who supported Taiwan's independence movement, he paused, hesitated, and finally told me that he could not think of any. While denying the primacy of political affiliation, Mr. Tan acknowledged that most people in his social circle agreed with him or, perhaps, rarely talked about politics. History and politics thus shaped community in the Taiwanese diaspora.

Unlike Mr. Tan, some immigrants explicitly acknowledged efforts to exclude those with differing political views. After our interview, Mr. and Mrs. Guo invited me to a restaurant for lunch. As we considered places to go, I mentioned a Taiwanese restaurant nearby, noting, "I heard that they have great Taiwanese dishes, such as clay oven rolls and fried bread sticks [shao bing you tiao]." But Mrs. Guo immediately rejected my suggestion, saying adamantly, "We will not let Chinese people earn a cent of our money." Though I understood their sentiment, I was surprised because I knew this restaurant was owned by Taiwanese, rather than mainland Chinese, immigrants. Feeling somewhat confused, I answered, "Oh, I think the owner is from Taiwan." But Mr. Guo explained, "Yes, they are from Taiwan, but they are waishengren." For Mr. and Mrs. Guo, not everyone from Taiwan counted as "Taiwanese." Those they considered inauthentic were excluded from their community.

The same logic can be detected in Mr. and Mrs. Guo's friendships. In retirement, they explained, they had become even more selective.[1] "Life is short, and we do not have much time left. Why do we spend time arguing with people we don't like?" they responded to one of my questions. Indeed, during my fieldwork, I learned that they were active members of Taiwanese organizations that opposed the Kuomintang, supported Taiwanese independence, and resisted China's political influence over Taiwan. Mr. and Mrs. Guo sometimes argued with their friends about political issues but, having embedded themselves in a politically homogeneous community, engaged only in narrow disputes about strategy.

Supporters of the Kuomintang and reunification with mainland China had similarly constructed communities that shared their views. When I interviewed Mr. Chao about his social circles, he quickly responded, "I have many different friends. Some of them are from mainland China, but most of them, especially those who I feel close to, were from Taiwan." Mr. Chao identified as Chinese and thought that "Taiwanese were also Chinese." Many of his friends were concerned about Taiwan, he explained, and watched news about Taiwan through satellite TV almost every day. Mr. Chao was deeply worried that the independence movement and corresponding nationalism were exacerbating intergroup relations in Taiwan and negatively affecting economic connections to mainland China. In response to my inquiries, he noted, "Most of my close friends and I share similar political opinions. We occasionally know that someone here belonged to another political camp. Then we avoid talking about politics, but it is rare."

To be sure, not every immigrant I interviewed had strong political views. Some had social networks that extended across the political spectrum and had made friends with coethnics of various backgrounds. Even when uninterested in discussing homeland politics, however, these immigrants were cautious. For example, Chi Dance, a dancing club that I joined and observed, consisted mostly (but not exclusively) of immigrant retirees from Taiwan, mainland China, and Hong Kong. Participants practiced a type of dancing that, they claimed, incorporates components of tai chi and qigong (systems of movement and breathing). According to a director of Chi Dance, himself Taiwanese, core members of the group I observed were from Taiwan, and to avoid disputes, they had unwritten rules forbidding discussion of politics, both in person and online through group email or social media. During my fieldwork, I witnessed a first-time participant asking regular members about the difference between this group and Falun Gong (a self-defined Buddhist organization that challenges the legitimacy of the mainland Chinese government). One of the instructors quickly and nervously responded, "No, no, no, we are *not* Falun Gong. We welcome everyone. We are neutral about politics. And we do not talk about politics here."

The respondents had also joined some groups and institutions for apolitical reasons, such as personal interest or self-care, and they expected to encounter people of diverse social, cultural, and political backgrounds. In such settings, they might suppress their views, often reminding others to be cautious among immigrants from different Chinese societies (e.g., Hong Kong, Taiwan, and mainland China). Mrs. Hua reported avoiding discussions of politics with all but a few close friends, but because she was a fan of choral music and tango, she had joined several social clubs, all consisting primarily of ethnic Chinese. Singing and dancing with others had thus forced Mrs. Hua to engage with coethnics who might have opposing views, so to avoid conflict, she had tried to stay neutral about political issues. Even so, Taiwanese politics mediated her relationships with coethnics in the United States.

Migration Trajectories and Perceived Class Differences

Socioeconomic incorporation into receiving contexts profoundly shaped the respondents' communal lives. During my fieldwork, I found undercurrents of social class divisions within Taiwanese immigrant communities, which the respondents had long perceived. In their accounts, tension was particularly evident between professional middle-class professionals and those who were lower-middle or working class. Professional middle-class immigrants had usually come to the United States as international students, often after graduating from elite universities in Taiwan, and had usually received advanced educations that had led to professional jobs. In contrast, most working-class or lower-middle-class immigrants who had come to the United States for family reunification or had come as labor migrants lacked educational credentials recognized in the United States. They may have worked as hard as their professional middle-class coethnics, but when it came to professional status, they lacked a narrative of immigrant success.

The professional middle-class immigrants I interviewed had often lived on meager incomes when they first arrived, but they had accumulated human, social, and cultural capital over time and tended to maintain close ties to coethnics with similar backgrounds. They also told similar narratives about themselves. Most believed that diligence and competence had propelled them up the socioeconomic ladder, and in many ways, they perceived themselves as the embodiment of the American dream. Their accounts of "making it" in the United States—told with relief, pride, and confidence—were usually stories about arriving with limited resources and overcoming barriers. For them, past struggles were indispensable to explaining their success.

The attitudes that these more elite immigrants exuded, however, made their less privileged coethnics uncomfortable. When in their company, the lower-middle-class and working-class respondents often felt marginalized. Mr. Fong described feeling invisible to the coethnics whom he perceived as elites. Before moving to the United States for his children's education, he had worked as a civil servant in Taiwan. In the United States, however, his educational credentials were unrecognized, and his English-speaking ability, limited, and he had experienced downward mobility. Mr. Fong had taken daytime menial jobs (such as work in a Chinese restaurant) while attending evening programs at a community college, and after graduating, he had worked as a hospital health inspector. The job was less prestigious and lower paying than the occupations of many other Taiwanese immigrants, but Mr. Fong was satisfied with what he had accomplished. He felt, however, that the professors, engineers, accountants, attorneys, and medical doctors in his ethnic community thought little of him.

Mr. Fong expressed frustration with "elite" coethnics who seemed dismissive, quickly lost interest in conversing, or seemed to prefer talking among themselves. They rarely asked his opinions, he noted, and their conservations were typically brief or lacked follow-up questions or clarifications. Mr. Fong had therefore decided to distance himself and had left organizations in which he and his wife had participated. "I can explain our relationship with other elite Taiwanese Americans in this way: Birds of a feather flock together, and people who belong to the same groups gather together too [*Wu yi lei ju, ren yi qun fen*]," he observed.

> Don't you think people from [a Taiwanese organization] are all of a higher-class background? They always look down on people inferior to

them; their eyes are actually on top of their head [*yan jing zhang zai tou ding shang*]! When they are in a good mood, they will say hello to you. When they are in a bad mood, they will just ignore you. You are invisible to them. I will not say all of them are arrogant, but many of them are arrogant. These people were not my friends before, and they are still not people whom I want to interact with now.

Similarly, Mrs. Hua talked of unpleasant experiences with Grace Church (a pseudonym) and described members of this Taiwanese immigrant congregation as an "elite class." Before retiring, Mrs. Hua had worked as an insurance agent, and most of her clients had been Taiwanese and Chinese immigrants. To enhance her visibility and strengthen her niche in the insurance business, she had often made trips to Taiwanese and Chinese organizations. She had been reluctant, however, to attend Grace Church. There she often felt excluded by the elitism its members projected, either intentionally or unintentionally. The church might have expanded her networks, but over many years, she had refused to join its activities.

Mrs. Hua was a divorced single mother who had completed vocational school in Taiwan and received a business diploma in the United States. She had once overheard someone at Grace Church talking loudly about her, in a tone she interpreted as accusatory, saying, "How come this woman showed up again? She is only here for our money." Mrs. Hua had attributed this unpleasant experience to her occupation, which she believed had raised suspicions about her motives. If she had held a professional job that required an advanced degree, she maintained, she would not have been perceived as someone seeking to manipulate social relationships to make a profit. Accordingly, people at Grace Church seemed to her entitled and inclined to "boss people around," acting as if they were superior.

This unpleasant impression had persisted into Mrs. Hua's life in retirement. She was similarly opposed to joining a wide range of activities organized by members of Grace Church, and so she eschewed hiking, singing karaoke, and talks on Taiwanese history and contemporary Taiwan. As she said to me, "People at [Grace Church] are higher class and different from me. We don't belong there and should not go there to annoy them." Invoking the class differences that she considered the cause of ill treatment, Mrs. Hua actively drew the line between herself and these church members, constraining her social networks and organizing her social life accordingly.

Some of the less-educated immigrants I interviewed did maintain friendly connections with more elite coethnics, but they too had learned to suppress their opinions among those they sometimes described as strong-willed. Despite her working-class background, Mrs. Tseng regularly attended Grace Church but observed that many well-educated churchgoers tended to believe they could "out-smart" other people. This attitude, she felt, explained the many unresolved conflicts in Taiwanese immigrant communities. "The Taiwanese American community is relatively small," Mrs. Tseng commented, "but can you imagine how many splits each organization, especially churches, go through? Four or five times since I lived here [in the 1980s]! Each time when people fight, a group of people leave and start their own organization."

Mrs. Tseng reasoned that many Taiwanese immigrants were "too well edu-cated" and thought "their way is the best way." She had therefore become more reserved around her more elite coethnics, even as she sustained connections. "The Taiwanese immigrant community is a family to me," she reflected. "People in the same family listen and talk to each other. But look at our community, and you will soon realize that many highly educated people have trouble understand-ing and communicating with each other well. Many coethnics focus on them-selves. . . . I am a simple-minded person, and I did not receive much education. But I am willing to learn, and I am willing to put myself in other people's shoes. I think many well-educated Taiwanese have a hard time doing it." By way of con-trast, immigrants who arrived to the United States as international students and later joined the American professional middle class rarely expressed explicit con-tempt for less-educated coethnics. Often, however, they praised other Taiwanese immigrants—typically of their generation—who could claim exceptional profes-sional accomplishments but seldom expressed similar admiration for those who were less educated and less "successful" by conventional social definitions.

Apart from explicit class-based biases, the cultural advantages of my more elite respondents might well have excluded others, however unintentionally. During my fieldwork, I regularly attended a Bible study group organized by Taiwanese retirees, who also organized outdoor activities such as hiking and picnicking as well as outings requiring more economic capital. Mr. Chang, a core member in this group, asked me to give a talk on Max Weber's *The Protestant Ethic and the Spirit of Capitalism*. I was surprised by this request and asked Mr. Chang why he was interested in this topic. He replied, "I saw Max Weber's work in my annotated Bible, so I wanted to know more. Since you are a sociologist, you are the perfect person to introduce Weber's work to us." So I gave an hour-long talk, after which participants asked about Weber's evidence, the causal connections in his argu-ment, and the applicability of his work to contemporary China and Taiwan. Ini-tially, I found these questions surprising, but I quickly realized that the participants all had advanced degrees and experience with academic analysis, which might also have created invisible barriers for my less privileged respondents.

Exceptions for Individuals

The quality of relationships could trump political or class differences among my respondents. Mrs. Yang had been an active member in a Taiwanese immigrant organization well known for supporting Taiwan's independence movement. Participation allowed her to make many like-minded friends, including those at the level of leadership, who shared not only her political stance but also her class standing as a well-educated professional. Yet Mrs. Yang reported intentionally distancing herself from segments of this organization because "some people had a big ego and were bossy, and some quickly took credit they didn't deserve when they only offered lip service." Mrs. Yang attributed these unpleasant characteristics to individual personalities. For her, shared interests were helpful but insufficient criteria for inclusion in her network of friends.

Although Mrs. Yang usually avoided coethnics with whom she disagreed politically, she made exceptions for a few high school and college classmates. Acknowledging a few fights with these friends, she had also decided to reconcile because she believed they genuinely cared about her. Mrs. Yang recalled friends on the other side of the political spectrum who had picked her up from the airport and listened to her when she felt lonely. She spoke highly of some successful Taiwanese immigrants who also were "nice and caring," despite their high occupational status and advanced education. In particular, she praised a former client, a CEO in a well-known Taiwanese corporation, and his wife for "not putting on airs." Interpersonal boundaries could thus be fluid and volitional, and microdynamics could transcend class divisions.

Relearning Their Place: Navigating Networks in a Changing Homeland

Like my respondents in the United States, those in Taiwan grappled with their sense of community through myriad dimensions of time and migration. Though relocated to Taiwan, the returnees I interviewed reported an evolving sense of belonging to the United States. Mr. Lee had arrived as an international student and had later established himself professionally. Most of his connections to what he called US society had been established through work, while most of his personal and close friends were Taiwanese immigrants. Mr. Lee's distinction between his white American colleagues and his Chinese and Taiwanese friends had become particularly salient after his retirement, when contact with his former colleagues ceased. "I feel that many of the Chinese immigrants in the United States are often middle class or professionals," he reflected.

They might be very accomplished in their fields but have trouble fitting in with mainstream American communities and cultures. Take myself as an example. I spent twenty-eight years in the US and have many colleagues. But I feel like I lack significant connections to these white colleagues. This is a very sincere reply. I still prefer to make friends with other Chinese. Chinese tend to get together, form a community, have their children attending a Chinese language school, or get together on the weekends. I believe this is a cultural thing. And after I retired, I don't really keep in touch with my colleagues in the workplace.

Having moved away from their long-established ethnic communities in the United States, returnees had to reorganize their social networks in Taiwan. Some of the respondents had maintained contact with friends in Taiwan during their decades in the United States, but even they faced challenges reconnecting with old ethnic communities and meeting new people. They had returned at a later life stage, usually with greater social status, and personal changes had also affected their positions in networks of friends and kin. Returnees thus needed new communities. Some had reconnected with relatives, classmates, and former colleagues. Some had made new friends in local neighborhoods, institutions (e.g., church, temple, volunteer programs, and work organizations), and activities (e.g., hiking, sports, shopping, dancing, and tai chi). No matter the strategy for constructing communities, all had to stage social networks that could provide company and resources.

Mr. Sun had reactivated connections to relatives, neighbors, friends, and colleagues, but he also participated in a local sports center, where he had made new friends with other senior citizens. With all of his children in the United States, Mr. Sun explained, he needed people to turn to at critical moments and considered his friends in Taiwan the people he and his wife could rely on. "I think that people of the same age should get together and take care of each other rather than relying on children," he asserted.

I am playing Ping-Pong every morning in [a community sports center]. We are all retirees, and our age ranges between sixties and seventies. We hang out a lot, and we keep each other company. I think this is great. There is no need to stick to the children; we should set them free. . . . You don't have to worry if I die in my apartment [and] nobody will know it, and my body ends up perishing. If I do not show up for the Ping-Pong game on a particular day, my friends will call me immediately or try to find me in the apartment.

For return migrants, however, noticeable—and sometimes disturbing—differences with local people could confound efforts to establish community.

Not only had they changed over time, but years of modernization had also changed Taiwan. The respondents thus grappled with their sense of social belonging. Like their counterparts in the United States, they cited a political stance and perceived class differences as factors shaping their social circles, and most preferred to spend time with people who shared their views and backgrounds. Encountering political disagreements, they, too, tried to suppress their feelings and remain polite. Compared with immigrants in the United States, however, the returnees I interviewed expressed stronger sentiments about cultural differences separating them from their nonmigrant associates. For returnees, the experience of migration had opened a cultural chasm and thus had become the main obstacle to reestablishing their lives in Taiwan.

Tension about a Changing Homeland

Temporalities of migration mediate the processes through which return migrants positioned themselves in relation to their communities in Taiwan. A small portion of the returnees I interviewed lamented the loss of important cultural values in the process of Taiwan's modernization. These respondents typically distinguished between the Taiwan they had left and the country they now encountered, and they saw themselves embodying precious traditions to endure the hardships and even "make it" overseas. Their narratives about the loss of traditional values became particularly salient when discussing differences with younger generations. After returning, Mr. Xia had joined activities sponsored by a church, community center, and community college and, since the early 2000s, had made many new friends—both young and old—at a local community center. He got along well and, he reported, spent a significant amount of time with his new friends. Furthermore, after a career in the United States, he was often regarded as successful and invited to advise teenagers and young adults.

Mr. Xia did enjoy advising younger people, but he also detected profound differences between their experiences and his. He had grown up in a Taiwan that was socially and economically underdeveloped and, like many people his age, had experienced a childhood without material abundance. His father had earned only a meager income, and his family had often struggled with limited means. These experiences, Mr. Xia believed, had taught him to endure hardship and work hard. By contrast, he felt that younger people who had never faced such hardships took material abundance for granted. In his eyes, they were indolent and sometimes shortsighted. "I feel like our generation came of age when the economy of Taiwan was about to take off," he mused. "People were able to work hard and endure hardship. But the past few years of living in Taiwan made me feel that the younger generation in Taiwan now are completely different from us. They are used to living a comfortable life. They are eager to get things done or get the things they want without putting in enough effort. They are materialistic but not very down-to-earth."

Modernization was thus perceived as a source of moral corruption and had damaged the traditional Taiwanese society that some returnees remembered. Although older generations in Taiwan who never migrated might express similar sentiments, older returnees like Mr. Xia could stake claims about homeland traditions inherited from Taiwan that had prepared them for success in the United States. As Mr. Xia indicated, he had "made it" in the United States because of the many virtues he learned growing up in Taiwan. On the other hand, even though I did not formally interview nonmigrant elderly people in Taiwan, I often heard people express admiration for the respondents who had successfully established a career and family in the United States, a country that many local people perceived as superior to Taiwan.

Tension about Americanized/Westernized Selves

Most of the returnees I met emphasized that the social and cultural barriers they had encountered when establishing new communities stemmed from their degree of sociocultural assimilation into US society. Long-term migration had transformed their worldviews and sense of who they are. Framing themselves as Westernized expatriates, they described norms learned abroad that now distanced them from contemporary Taiwan. Comparing life in the United States and Taiwan, Mrs. Ou Yang described feeling uncomfortable about the ways friends and relatives understood "personal boundaries." Having returned to Taiwan with her husband, she respected other people's personal lives and, she maintained, rarely arrived on a friend's doorstep without giving notice. She also tried to avoid sensitive topics, like finances, with all but a few close friends. She had learned these norms in the United States, but in Taiwan, many of her new friends thought differently about personal boundaries. They might show up at her door or bring uninvited guests, people she did not know, without letting her know in advance. "When we lived in the US, people rarely called after 9:00 p.m.," Mrs. Ou Yang recalled. "We planned our activities in advance, and we were cautious about respecting other people's private life."

Mrs. Ou Yang had been especially shocked to find local people whom she just met tell her detailed personal information, including stories of conflict with their children or their children's spouses. These exchanges, she complained, would have been inconceivable in the United States. In Taiwan, however, "many Taiwanese people had little respect for other people's privacy; once they get to know you, they suddenly become your best friends and do not respect your personal boundaries." Acknowledging the influence of what she considered Western culture,

Mrs. Ou Yang concluded, "Perhaps I am too Americanized, so I am so picky [*tiao san jian si*] about Taiwanese people."

Mrs. Ou Yang also felt frustrated when trying to expand her network in Taiwan. At her church in the United States, she had been responsible for student fellowships and charitable activities, and she wanted to manage similar activities in Taiwan. She soon realized, however, that her lack of personal connections to religious organizations made this role difficult. She had contacted a number of congregations about the possibility of establishing new fellowships and fundraising for disadvantaged youth, but in Taiwan, she lacked *guanxi* [personal networks of influence]. After more than two decades in the United States, she felt like a migrant all over again. She lamented, "Churches in Taiwan have their own systems. Denominations like the Taiwanese Presbyterian Church have their own programs to take care of young people. Denominationally independent congregations in Taiwan, such as the Glorious Church, have their own philosophies and people to run fellowships for children and youth. For them, I am just an older woman from the US. . . . So it's hard for me to blend in. After all, I am new to them, and I don't have much guanxi to them." Perhaps the relative importance of social networks in Taiwan or the extent to which altruistic systems, like volunteering or donating, are formalized better explains the obstacles Mrs. Ou Yang had encountered. Yet like many returnees I interviewed, she attributed her difficulties to cultural differences that relocation had made salient.

Some of the returnees I interviewed described feeling so Americanized that they sometimes felt like outsiders in their homeland. Their experiences had certainly been influenced by the number and the length of return visits, but almost all—including those who regularly visited Taiwan when living in the United States—reported that adaptation to Taiwan had taken some time. This sense of outsider status was particularly strong when interacting with community members who had no experience in Western societies. Mrs. Shen clearly articulated the cultural influence of US society, citing privacy and personal life as areas with contrasting interpersonal norms. These perceived cultural differences had hampered her communication with friends in Taiwan. "We sometimes get together with our old classmates," Mrs. Shen reported. "But if they never lived abroad before, we felt a gap between us. I feel that people living in the US for a long time share similar values, and we are interested in different conversational topics. Very often, we have issues with certain topics, but local Taiwanese are fine. Like . . . we don't like talking about money, and we respect other people's privacy. But Taiwanese people are comfortable asking about your financial situation or your investment plans."

The ways in which return migrants talked about the differences between the United States and Taiwan were not neutral, and returnees often blamed their co-ethnics in Taiwan for not being Westernized enough. Comparing countries, they contended that their families and friends should incorporate Western sensibilities. In their view, material life in Taiwan might now approximate or even exceed life in the United States, but socially and culturally, Taiwan remained "backward." Mrs. Ou Yang criticized her community members for their superficial understanding of Western democracy and told me that she had been politically resocialized as an international student in the United States. Taiwan was still under martial law before she left Taiwan, Mrs. Ou Yang, explained, and the Kuomintang dominated the political landscape. Only in the United States had she seen the way politicians in a "truly democratic" society expressed, exchanged, and debated ideas.

Mrs. Ou Yang spoke highly of the mass media, citing National Public Radio and the *Washington Post*, which she felt provided in-depth and balanced analysis of political and social issues. In Taiwan, however, she had found these features of democracy still unavailable. Friends who lacked her political socialization usually based their opinions on the information gleaned from local politicians and news media, and these sources, she argued, often asserted claims without providing evidence. For Mrs. Ou Yang, the "democratization" of Taiwan had provided only the right to vote. Missing was a more comprehensive understanding of the meaning and operation of democracy.

Mrs. Ou Yang further cited limited English fluency among her local friends, which precluded them from accessing international news media or attending to developments outside Taiwan. She exemplified this observation with her friends' English pronunciation: "Do you expect them [her friends in Taiwan] to watch *Meet the Press* [a weekly US news/interview program]? They don't even pronounce Godiva [a chocolate brand] correctly. It is 'God-ai-va,' not 'God-ee-va'!" Mrs. Ou Yang found most members of her Taiwanese community incapable of conversation about events outside Taiwan. She illustrated this point with the US election of 2012, when Barack Obama was running for reelection as president, lamenting, "My friends could not even have a decent conversation about the US presidential election, and they have no idea about the implications of this election for Taiwan and for the world."

Of course, Mrs. Ou Yang's friends in Taiwan had no reason to master English or to have a sophisticated understanding of US politics. Bilingual skills and the ability to navigate two social worlds are also forms of privilege. Yet what Mrs. Ou Yang perceived as a schism with her coethnics in Taiwan *felt* real. Here, the respondents' definitions of modernization in Taiwan was volitional and could reference anything they disapproved of (e.g., lack of English proficiency, media literacy, or democracy). Indeed, these judgments were often used as boundary markers to differentiate "us" from "them" (see Lamont 2000). For the respondents, the infrastructures in Taiwan (e.g., public transportation or medical systems) might have been modernized, but the cultural orientations of Taiwanese people had yet to catch up with the country's material development. The symbolic boundaries that Mrs. Ou Yang articulated—and the underlying rules governing these boundaries—thus informed her views of local populations and shaped her perceptions of contemporary Taiwan. Grappling with the differences they experienced, returnees were also proudly asserting their superiority over the perceived less cosmopolitan people they now encountered.

This critique of insufficient Westernization was particularly explicit in the accounts of respondents who had returned to "improve" their homeland. Mr. Shih was a physician who had worked in Taiwan after retiring in the United States. Initially, he had been eager to point out many problems in Taiwan's medical system. Doctors in Taiwan consulted with too many patients, he believed, and gave each insufficient attention. He had tried to introduce protocols learned in the United States to his office in Taiwan but felt like an outsider trying to stake insider claims. While his professional status was prestigious, therefore, it also created social barriers. Mr. Shih reported becoming quieter in meetings, to avoid appearing arrogant or contemptuous, and he remained frustrated with his "insufficiently Westernized" colleagues. As he elaborated,

> Initially, I made lot of suggestions and proposed lots of changes. But when I talked too much, some of my colleagues started to think that I am an American, so I was very arrogant and despised them. . . . I feel like a lot of times, my colleagues in Taiwan don't understand what I am saying and do not appreciate my advice. Increasingly, I feel like it's difficult to reform Taiwanese hospitals entirely based on my experiences in the US, and it is impossible for me as an individual to change the entire medical and cultural system in Taiwan.

Notably, Mr. Shih's discontent with his professional community was mixed with pride in his own career accomplishments. He believed in his own judgment and faulted his colleagues for ignoring his advice. Asserting the benefit of his experience for Taiwan, however, he had also forfeited an insider claim to his homeland.

Adaptation to a Changing Homeland

To address their sense of foreignness in an evolving homeland, most respondents stressed the quality of their relationships with individual friends and family members. Even if they could not change local people or local ways, they could still find people they liked. Some return migrants thus selectively reconnected with relatives and old friends and, through these networks, had expanded their social circles. They emphasized selectivity in establishing relationships and focused on characteristics they appreciated in the people they knew while downplaying aspects they disliked. In assessing their networks, therefore, they sought to compartmentalize conflicting feelings and perspectives and to dissociate themselves from elements of Taiwanese life.

Here, aging and life course are central to understanding the ways the returnees I interviewed maintained a boundary between what they could change and what they could not. Mrs. Shih emphasized spending time with friends she genuinely liked and noted that, as an older person with limited remaining years, she was reluctant to waste time "dealing with" people she disliked. By the same logic, Mrs. Shih commented, her limited time left in this world was reason to ignore difficulties with relationships and focus on positive features of her network connections. "Sometimes situations in Taiwan make me emotional," she reflected.

> But you know, for people at my age, we do not have much time, and we do not expect much. I know there are problems everywhere, and there are politics and issues everywhere. I live in the present, I live day to day. If I was younger, I would probably worry more and try to think about my life differently. But now, I no longer fight for my family. . . . I already fought my fight. At this point, even if there are things I don't like, I no longer care. . . . I can focus on the people and the things I like and overlook others I don't.

About half of the respondents had formed communities partly through networking with other migrants who had moved back. Returnees, they explained, shared a perspective on the evolution of Taiwan and had also known similar struggles abroad. Many experiences offered commonalities: managing linguistic barriers, raising children in a foreign society, adapting expectations for their children, and living with racial discrimination in white communities. Some return migrants knew others who had relocated from the United States to Taiwan, and some had found other returnees through referrals in the United States. Mrs. Shen, for example, had organized a social life for herself and her husband around return migrants from the United States, Canada, and Australia. She appreciated her local friends in Taiwan but felt that they had difficulty understanding important aspects of her life. She reflected, "I think my friends in Taiwan and my friends in the US are different. My friends in Taiwan are childhood friends or classmates, while my friends in the US are the people I met as an adult. My friends in Taiwan know who I was prior to my departure for the US, but my friends in the US know who I have become after spending so many years in the US."

Still, some return migrants told me that time—from several months to several years—had helped them overcome discomfort. In general, the longer they stayed in Taiwan, the better they felt interacting there. For Ms. Ho, interacting in Taiwan had initially made her feel "American." Significant differences, she noted, were the ways she and her friends thought about personal boundaries and relationships with adult children. Yet over time, she had come to accept her community members. "Just as when we initially moved to the US, we had to adjust ourselves to many new things and new people," Ms. Ho asserted. "Now, we are moving back, and we need to adapt again." Migrating to the United States had taught her the importance of adaptability. Returning to Taiwan, she had to relearn to be Taiwanese in her society of origin.

Membership across Borders

What I term temporalities of migration shape respondents' reactions to cross-border ties they sustain from afar. As scholars of transnational migration have demonstrated, immigrants can maintain communities in both sending and receiving societies (Levitt and Schiller 2004; Schiller and Caglar 2010). Indeed, many of the immigrants I interviewed in the United States talked of precious memories with friends, colleagues, classmates, and relatives. For some, communication technologies (e.g., email, Skype, and Facebook) had made communication easier and cheaper, with an intimacy unavailable when they initially arrived (Baldassar et al. 2016; Foner 1997). Retiring from work had also provided more time for communication and travel.

Cross-Border Ties from the United States

One-third of respondents in the United States had traveled back to Taiwan at least once a year, and about three-fifths mentioned regular exchanges with communities there. Networks provided emotional and social support, and a few migrants, like Mr. Wen, even claimed that geographical distance had drawn friends and family closer. "I don't know how to describe this connection," Mr. Wen said.

> There is a saying that "absence makes heart grow fonder [*xiao bie sheng xin hun.*]" Perhaps that's not the right way to put it, but the sentiment is very similar. When we live there [in Taiwan], we do not have time to get together often. But now, whenever we go back, we will have a lot of meetings and gatherings. . . . Your friends become more appreciative of you, perhaps because seeing each other is getting difficult. Friends in Taiwan are old friends. We rarely come to each other for practical needs. We just get together and talk about trivial things or recall what happened in the past. It is very bittersweet since so many decades have passed by.

Perhaps surprisingly, for the respondents, cross-border interaction intensified their identities as immigrants. Trips to Taiwan, planned as temporary breaks from life in the United States, also heightened awareness of their status as expatriates. Mr. Guo described being treated like a "guest" in Taiwan. There, he was free from major obligations and had only to enjoy himself during stays that he and others knew would be brief. For example, his siblings had no expectation that he would care for elders back home, and friends, too, asked little in the way of practical support. For Mr. Guo, therefore, interaction with his homeland community highlighted his loss of membership there.

Respondents usually attributed their sense of separation to US cultural influence. Mr. Luo told me of his deep concern with Taiwan's politics. In the United States, he read online news, watched Taiwanese programs on satellite TV, and kept in touch electronically with friends and family. After retiring, he and his wife had traveled to Taiwan once or twice every year. She always returned to vote in presidential elections, and as a top engineer in his field, he was often invited to consult in Taiwan. Nonetheless, Mr. Luo felt a disjuncture when interacting with colleagues, relatives, and old friends there. He had been "Americanized," he told me, influenced by a US culture of "directness" and "toughness." After three decades of living, studying, and working in the United States, his interactional style had become "straightforward," and in Taiwan, his approach to professional issues was sometimes deemed "confrontational." "I always told my colleagues and friends here [in Taiwan], 'Don't take my comments personally,'" he jokingly commented. "They [community members in Taiwan] know I am a good person, and I am trying to help. But I am from the US. I am not Americanized. I *am* American."

Mrs. Luo also reported a similar sense of disjuncture. She joked that her friends in Taiwan were surprised to find that, as a baseball fan, she had not supported Chien-Ming Wang, a leading Yankees pitcher recruited from Taiwan. "I was torn," she recounted, "but I just could not cheer for Chien-Ming Wang. The Red Sox is my team! The Yankees are the enemy! I want to see Chien-Ming Wang score, but I want the Yankees to lose, especially when they were competing with the Red Sox!" For Mrs. Luo, Taiwanese identity was no longer the priority. A long-term resident in Boston, she had developed another sense of belonging, one surprising to her community in Taiwan.

Living abroad for many years could also challenge the legitimacy of membership back home. Deeply concerned about politics in Taiwan, Mrs. Guo reported sometimes debating with friends there. One remark, she told me, could leave her speechless. "If you love Taiwan so much, why do you live abroad?" she was sometimes asked. Pushed to reflect on her sense of belonging, she had reconsidered her right to claim an interest in Taiwanese politics and society. In the eyes of her community, Mrs. Guo realized, she had left long ago and now only returned and departed at will. "I used to debate with my relatives in Taiwan," she elaborated.

> And they can basically shut me up with one sentence: "You are very eloquent. Then why don't you move back and fight for your homeland? It is better for you to do something here rather than judge from the outside." Another relative of mine said to me, "OK. Tell me where you will be when mainland China launches missiles against Taiwan. Taiwan or the US? Will you continue to stay here? Or will you move back to the US eventually?" I feel like my relatives really hit my Achilles' heel. What my relatives said to me is true. We are not in Taiwan. We should respect Taiwanese people's choice.

Cross-Border Ties from Taiwan

The return migrants I interviewed actively sustained relationships with their coethnics in the United States. Most returnees valued connections forged while living abroad and readily traveled and used communication technologies to maintain cross-border ties. Maintaining their networks affirmed a sense of ongoing membership in their Taiwanese-American communities, and many reported greater commonality with coethnics in the United States than with those in Taiwan, who rarely understood the experience of navigating two social and cultural worlds. Returnees also recalled the money, information, or emotional support they had received abroad and saw cross-border ties as a form of reciprocity.

Mrs. Lee, in her sixties, had left Taiwan after graduating from college and had experienced many life transitions in the United States (e.g., getting married, acquiring her PhD, starting to work, purchasing her first house). These experiences, Mrs. Lee believed, had been central to her personal development but were better comprehended by Taiwanese immigrants who had either shared them or, in some cases, provided concrete or symbolic assistance. She vividly recalled those who had taught her to drive and cook, helped her shop for her first car and house, or comforted her when she encountered racism and sexism. For Mrs. Lee, these people were irreplaceable lifelong friends, as she reflected: "When we were in the US, we regularly met with other Taiwanese immigrants. Perhaps because we were all migrants outside the homeland, we understood each other's homesickness and went through a lot of similar struggles, experiences, and food. In Taiwan, I feel that people lacked similar experiences or motivations to form a tight community."

Navigating across cultures also promoted common experiences among the respondents. For example, many struggled to adjust expectations for their children and their children's spouses. These struggles offered an easily relatable subject for discussion across borders because, as Mrs. Shen indicated, friends in Taiwan rarely understood the struggles of a mother and mother-in-law with children growing up in the United States. Echoing his wife, Mr. Shen noted that friends in Taiwan typically lacked "double vision," the ability to see beyond Taiwan and understand different social worlds (Collins 1986; Du Bois 1903). He especially enjoyed getting together with friends visiting from the United States, with whom he could discuss their experiences as newcomers, their encounters with overt and subtle racism, and their struggles raising children. "If you never lived in the US, you could not really understand what it is like living there," he asserted, "just as if you never experienced the winter in the Midwest, it is hard to explain to you how to manage your life in an ice box."

Many returnees also proudly identified as both Taiwanese and American, able to navigate two different worlds. Located in Taiwan, they were still emotionally and symbolically attached to the United States. Maintaining connections thus confirmed an immigrant narrative (M. Waters 1999, 144). Taiwanese immigrant friends were "their own people," with whom they carved out in-group and out-group distinctions. Having survived—and usually then thrived—overseas, they believed themselves culturally different, even superior to those who had remained in Taiwan. Mr. Qi asserted this difference:

> I, of course, keep in touch with my [Taiwanese immigrant] friends in the US. Whenever I get together with them, we talk for hours and do not feel tired. We were very cosmopolitan [*si hai wei jia*]. We moved as international students to pursue opportunities. We have been flexible and are used to adapting to all kinds of different situations. I think this is a feature that you can find in a lot of early Taiwanese immigrants like us. The mentality [*xin tai*] and temperament [*qi zhi*] of people who always lived in Taiwan and never step out of their comfort zone of course differ drastically from ours.

A small portion of respondents in Taiwan had experienced a weakened connection to their Taiwanese friends in the United States. Several told me that life routines—working, socializing, caring for themselves or for their loved ones, receiving medical treatment—had left them little time to maintain cross-border relationships. A couple of returnees, however, felt ashamed of their situations in Taiwan. Mr. Leung—whom we met in the introduction—had worked in the United States as a waiter in various Chinese restaurants. Single and childless, he had tried to find a wife through a match-making agency and had met a mainland Chinese woman. They had become engaged, he recounted, but she then stole a significant portion of his savings and eloped with someone else. Mr. Leung then lost more of his savings while gambling away his troubles. Around the same time, the Chinese restaurant where he worked went out of business after a shooting.

Mr. Leung's friends in the United States had persuaded him to move back to Taiwan. There he could manage with a lower cost of living and public benefits for which he qualified. Through the referral of an acquaintance, he now worked in Taiwan as a janitor and had accumulated enough resources to rent an apartment and sustain himself in Taipei. He was highly reluctant, however, to maintain contact with friends in the United States. He no longer had "the face to talk with my friends" and was unwilling to let them see where he lived and worked. Mr. Leung wanted to avoid the contempt his US friends might now have for him. Describing his ordeal as "like a nightmare," he had opted to sever ties to his former community, to help him move on.

This chapter has examined the strategies through which older migrants in the United States and Taiwan relate to their communities in both home and host societies. Varying time-migration configurations, I argue, led these migrants to manage their networks and grapple with complex social dynamics. The interplay between time and migratory experience profoundly affected the networks they maintained and the relationships they sought to establish. Two approaches— knowing their place and relearning their place—distinguish immigrants in the United States from those who had returned to Taiwan. As these migrants moved into a later phase of life, they increasingly felt a sense of disconnection from what they perceived as mainstream US society. In this context, their relationships with other Taiwanese and Taiwanese immigrants became more important.

As long-term members of their ethnic communities, older immigrants knew their communities. They had an intimate understanding of their coethnics and could assess the micropolitics of their social networks. Homeland politics and perceived class differences constituted two significant dimensions through which these older immigrants carved in-group and out-group distinctions and decided whom they wished to befriend. In some cases, intimacy could trump political and class divisions so that individuals forged friendships, but respondents tended to frame these relationships as exceptions. Even those without strong political views or class consciousness were aware of these undercurrents and described cautiously managing their behavior when navigating their social lives. No matter what their strategies are, interpersonal dynamics at the communal level point to insider status in their ethnic networks.

Many years of living in the United States had made return migrants feel like "new arrivals" in their homeland, and they often described themselves as migrants once again. Inevitably, returnees met new people and made new friends, but

Taiwan's profound modernization, together with returnees' acculturalization into US society, generated consciousness of cultural differences. Many returnees experienced emotional difficulties and felt out of place after moving back to Taiwan. Return migrants thus had to relearn their place by developing strategies to manage a web of social relations. While some tried to adjust conflicted feelings about their network connections, others coped with their emotions by choosing whom they wished to befriend (e.g., other returnees or old friends). Reacculturating into contemporary Taiwanese society, they sought to improve their connections to friends and relatives. Their different strategies point to returnees' outsider status and highlight the processes through which they constructed social networks.

In line with the literature on migrant transnationalism (Levitt and Jaworsky 2007), these migrants lived in cross-border communities and maintained cross-border ties. Managing these transborder relationships then pushed them to reconsider community membership. For most, cross-border connections confirmed a sense of membership in the Taiwanese diaspora while challenging the legitimacy of their social citizenship in Taiwan. Returnees' local interactions revealed them as "Americanized," orienting them toward their coethnics in the United States. Long-term migration had thus changed their self-perception and cultural disposition. Transnational communities, in turn, transformed their sense of membership in a social field, and cross-border networks strengthened their identities in both sending and receiving societies.

This changing sense of social belonging has profound implications for the emotional and social support that older returnees could acquire from their communities in Taiwan. As research has shown (Loe 2011), social networks can help migrants better cope with concrete and psychological issues by offering various forms of support and resources. For these returnees, the most trustworthy network connections were typically other Taiwanese immigrants in the United States whom they had befriended for decades rather than the local people in contemporary Taiwan. This distinction explained returnees' accounts of having fewer friends to whom they could turn for advice, information, and comfort than they had when living in the United States. Conversely, my respondents living in the United States described having a more stable sense of community.

ARTICULATING LOGICS OF SOCIAL RIGHTS

The nation-state provides valuable resources that could protect aging migrant populations (Blakemore 1999; Estes et al. 2006; Gardner 2002; Gilbertson 2009; Lamb 2009). Existing scholarship, however, offers a limited understanding of the ways senior migrants make sense of governmental support. This oversight is particularly evident with long-term migrants who relocated to their host societies during younger adulthood. As a result, we have only rudimentary ideas about the interplay between time and migratory experience. Such factors as length of stay, employment and migration history, and changes in a migrant's homeland might influence relations with the nation-state. Older migrants' changing sense of social belonging might also influence their perspectives on tax-funded social programs.

In the United States, views of public benefits for immigrants focus largely on recent arrivals and tend to be polarized.[1] Older immigrants are framed either as undeserving and greedy or as vulnerable and victimized (Gardner 2002; Purkayastha et al. 2012). Existing literature has demonstrated stakeholders' constructions of the degree of deservingness of migrant groups in the United States (Brown 2011; Deeb-Sossa and Mendez 2008; Horton 2004; Marrow 2012). Some scholars have been particularly attentive to the framing of older immigrants in media and public debates. For instance, in the debate surrounding the 1996 welfare reform, policy makers often represented aging immigrants as "non-contributing members of U.S. society" and a burden on taxpayers (Fujiwara 2005; Yoo 2001). In the same debate, however, activists and health service providers sought to show that older newcomers deserved a federal safety net by representing their economic and social needs to the mass media and to policy makers (Wong 1999; Yoo 2008).

This body of literature reveals stark differences in the articulation of social membership for migrant populations. As institutional actors employ contrasting frames to promote policy outcomes, however, the voices of older immigrants, especially long-term migrants, are missing. Yet the processes through which aging migrants grapple with their social membership are related to questions of state support. As reflexive social actors, older immigrants think about their rights, duties, and privileges in their adopted society. As Irene Bloemraad (2018, 5) maintains, "the concept of citizenship makes appeals to, or demands on, further normative ideals and values, both vis-à-vis the state and with respect to other citizens."

Despite a long-established concern about the role of the state in the lives of elderly immigrants (Estes et al. 2006; Purkayastha 2012), few researchers address the rise of state support in some of these migrants' home societies. Taiwan, notably, has established its own public benefits programs, with National Health Insurance providing medical services to citizens since 1995 and passage of the Senior Citizen Pension Law in 2002 (Lin 1997; J. Wang 2004). With recognized dual citizenship, even Taiwanese migrants who have become US citizens can use their homeland's public health care system. More affordable medical resources are thus a rationale for overseas Taiwanese to return, either temporarily or permanently (S.-C. Liu 2014).

In this chapter, I examine the logics of social rights through which older immigrants justify their use of public benefits, both nationally and transnationally. The ways in which aging migrant populations define, deliberate, and stake claims about their social rights can explain much about their perceptions and self-presentations as deserving or undeserving citizens. As time and space positioned my respondents in a transnational social field, their accounts reveal discursive patterns of emphasis. In the United States, many emphasized rights earned through years of hard work. In Taiwan, returnees debated their rights and sought to justify claims to deserving public benefits.

This chapter makes two analytically distinct but empirically related arguments. First, perceived socioeconomic incorporation into the United States influences older migrants' sense of responsibility, entitlement, and belonging. Asserting their entitlement to state aid, the immigrants I interviewed presented themselves as full US citizens who had nonetheless been obliged to earn their legitimacy as a basis for public benefits. This logic of social rights, however, involved the disparagement of "undeserving others," whose entitlements are presumably unearned. When justifying their access to tax-supported programs in the United States, therefore, my respondents constructed moral and cultural boundaries to distinguish themselves from other migrants. Most, if not all, of these claims are based on stereotypes or emotional appeals rather than empirical evidence. As Purkayastha and her colleagues (2012, 124) argue, the allocation of public benefits is one of the best examples of "us versus them" boundaries because these issues often provoke strong political feelings in the broader public. Viewed in this way, my respondents' comments about other migrant groups mirror their desire to prove their belonging and moral worth as Americans.

Changing structural features—such as new public benefits in Taiwan—offered these older migrants possibilities and resources, both to pursue an ideal later life and to rethink social membership in their homeland. Wherever they lived, my respondents claimed to have earned social rights in the United States. They differed, however, in the logic they applied to entitlements in Taiwan. These varying logics of rights delineated the construction of social membership across a transnational field. The same logics also pointed to structural positions and identity politics that allow these older migrants to represent themselves as respectable citizens rather than calculating actors seeking only to access public services.[2]

Public Benefits in a Transnational Social Field

The US government differentiates entitlements from means-tested welfare programs. Supplemental Security Income (SSI) provides cash benefits to recipients—such as low-income elderly, disabled, and blind citizens, together with qualified resident aliens—and also enhances access to the Food Stamp and Medicaid programs (Elder and Powers 2006). Medicaid, another means-tested program, offers medical services to low-income citizens and legal residents, including eligible senior citizens. The elderly in the United States who qualify can apply for such entitlement programs as Medicare and Social Security. Medicare provides health insurance for US citizens and legal residents age sixty-five and over, as well as some individuals with disabilities or permanent kidney failure (Field, Lawrence, and Zwanziger 2000).[3] Social Security offers retirement benefits to senior citizens who have worked for more than ten years in the United States and paid taxes into the system (Fenge and Pestieau 2005).

As research has shown, the American public is generally less supportive of means-tested welfare than entitlement programs, "largely because beneficiaries of means-tested programs are viewed as not earning their right to benefits" (Silverstein et al. 2000, 271). Animosity toward means-tested beneficiaries was evident, for example, in debates surrounding the 1996 welfare reform, in which the aged were sometimes singled out as public charges. Indeed, since the 1980s, all benefits for the elderly have come under attack. As Merril Silverstein and his colleagues (2000, 272) note, "framed as a debate about 'generational equity,' claims were made that the U.S. allocated too large a proportion of its public resources to the elderly at the expense of the young." Stigma is greater, however, for seniors receiving means-tested benefits. As several scholars point out (Hudson 2012; Yoo 2001), the perception that older people might gain something for free contrasts with entitlement programs, such as Medicare and Social Security, which have elements of self-financing.

Older immigrants who access welfare benefits encounter more public skepticism than native-born elderly in the United States. Older immigrants also differ from other stigmatized groups accused of "milking the system" in that the legitimacy of their social membership is often questioned (Purkayastha et al. 2012, 127). As Kenneth Neubeck (2006, 103) notes, in addition to assuming that senior newcomers to the United States seek welfare dependency rather than self-sufficiency, some political elites further contend more broadly "that public expenditures on benefits and services to support immigrants outweighed their contributions to the U.S. economy." These critics also frame older immigrants (especially Chinese immigrants) as social outsiders who have contributed little or nothing to the US economy but have become public charges in their later lives (Yoo 2001, 2008). Against this backdrop, aging immigrants often encounter suspicion about their social rights and access to public benefits.

Across the Pacific, Taiwan has followed in the footsteps of many Western countries and established its own government-run entitlement programs and welfare system to provide a safety net for its citizens (Lin 1997). In particular, the National Health Insurance established in 1995 has attracted attention among Taiwanese emigrants. Other forms of state support—such as monthly pensions provided by central, municipal, and county governments—are also available for senior citizens in Taiwan. Yet for most of my respondents, the pension for senior citizens provided by the Taiwanese government (which typically ranges from $150 to $200 per month) was not enough incentive to prompt relocation. Rather, deteriorating health and the expense of health care in the United States had led them to consider whether public benefits in Taiwan might help them in a later phase of life.

The distinctive designs of health care systems in the United States and Taiwan structure different resources on which aging expatriates can draw to protect themselves and their families. Since 1965, Medicare in the United States has provided health insurance for most Americans age sixty-five and over; it has since been extended to some people with disabilities (Pearman and Starr 1988). Medicare is a multitiered system that contains four parts: hospital insurance (part A), which covers "inpatient hospital stays (at least overnight), including semiprivate room, food, and tests" (Stephens 2013, 306); medical insurance (part B), which pays for outpatient services and products not covered by part A (Field et al. 2000); a privately run option (part C), known as Medicare Advantage, which combines parts A and B (Kronenfeld 2011); and prescription drug coverage (part D), established in 2006 with various plans covering drugs that insurers "wish to cover, at what tier they wish to cover" (Stephens 2013, 307).

Medicare is financed by payroll taxes. Enrollment is voluntary (Aaron, Lambrew, and Healy 2008). Part A is free to eligible beneficiaries; parts B and D require monthly premiums, as do many part C plans. Failure to pay will result in the interruption of coverage. From the outset, services provided by Medicare have focused on the "coverage for hospital, physician, and certain other services that are 'reasonable and necessary for the diagnosis or treatment of illness or injury'" (Field et al. 2000, 1). By this logic, Medicare does not cover most preventive or dental care. Those who want comprehensive coverage must purchase supplemental insurance.

In Taiwan, National Health Insurance is a single-payer universal insurance system under the jurisdiction of the Department of Health (J. Wang 2004). The program provides extensive services for Taiwanese citizens and permanent residents and has a high level of patient satisfaction (Cheng 2009). It pays for "outpatient service, inpatient service, emergency care, dental treatment, eye care, maternity delivery, rehabilitation service, preventive medical service, Chinese medicine and prescription drugs" (Chen et al. 2008, 502). The system is financed by premiums collected from employees and employers and by other government revenues. Policy makers can impose copayments and adjust premiums to avoid financial deficits (Chen et al. 2008), but severe resistance by politicians and the public prevented any increases before 2002. Since 2001, the sustainability of the system has been a concern "because of foreseeable financial deficits of the program in the near future that have neither [been] generally agreed upon nor politically feasible solutions" (Deng and Wu 2010, 897).

Many policy makers, scholars, and laypeople in Taiwan blame older return migrants—including those who return to visit and those who return to settle—for exploiting public health insurance. Indeed, public opinion research regarding National Health Insurance has found widespread discontent with migrants who settle abroad but fly back to access the benefits of public insurance (I-C. Liu 2010). Some media have been explicitly hostile. Editorials of major Taiwanese newspapers— such as *Apple Daily, United News, United Evening News,* and *Liberty Times*—have criticized overseas Taiwanese for manipulating public health insurance by paying minimal fees and shifting their medical cost to other local taxpayers (see Sun 2014b, 541–542).

The skyrocketing expenditures for the system have also led many local people to blame returnees for taking advantage of public benefits without contributing to their financing. Overseas Taiwanese do not pay taxes—which cover a significant portion of expenditures for National Health Insurance—but can access the same benefits earned by local taxpayers (Kan and Lin 2009).[4] Moreover, some returnees—especially those with high-paying jobs outside Taiwan—pay little in monthly premiums, which are calculated according to income and require employers to pay a portion. While not age specific, these attacks have become a source of social stigma for older return migrants (I-C. Liu 2010).

Earning Social Rights in the United States: From Aliens to Deserving Citizens

The intersection between temporalities and migration shaped the respondents' construction of their social membership and the legitimacy of their rights to public benefits. Having lived and worked in the United States for decades, most of the immigrants I met considered their membership in US society an achievement. To them, long-term residence, even as naturalized citizens, could not automatically confer legitimacy. Rather, membership came through working hard and shouldering responsibilities. They had won social rights, they asserted, not only by meeting formal criteria but also by deserving public benefits. Predominantly middle-class, most of my respondents focused on earned entitlements for which they qualified rather than means-tested welfare support. With this logic, they framed themselves as deserving newcomers.

The divide between entitlements and means-tested programs profoundly shaped their thinking. Few considered themselves deserving of welfare support for low-income seniors. To be certain, they often used the term "welfare" to describe all public benefits. For many, welfare stood in opposition to private support, typically from their families. They were clearly aware, however, of distinctions among benefits programs. Some older immigrants, I was told, had accessed means-tested support by transferring assets to their children. This practice, perhaps legal under certain circumstances (Krooks 2012), was against the law, and the respondents considered it a violation of a moral boundary of respectable citizenship that rendered the recipient undeserving.[5] Most notably, my respondents were sensitive to accusations that foreign migrants had become a financial burden to the United States, and they derided attempts to "steal extra welfare." Several further worried that abusing the welfare system threatened the sustainability of US entitlement programs on which they now depended.

Mr. Tsai, at age sixty-seven, had been naturalized in the 1970s and reported always striving to fulfill his civic obligations by following the law and paying taxes. His efforts, he believed, granted him the right to receive public support. The Social Security checks he received each month were delayed payments, saved from his salary, and Medicare was the social care that he had earned through taxation. As a middle-class citizen, however, he had no claim to welfare support, such as SSI for low-income seniors. Any such claim would violate his notion of decency and render him an undesirable alien. "Legally, I am also an American citizen," he explained.

> I realize my civil responsibilities and obligations to the US. I always think that since I decided to be a citizen in this country, I should act like a decent American citizen. I pay taxes. I follow the law. I clean up the fallen leaves in the yard before my neighbors complain. I already get my Social Security money every month. The US government is doing a great thing, and I earned it myself. . . . Since the US government is already so considerate of senior citizens, we should not take advantage of the US welfare system. That is not right. That is not moral. How can we try to steal money that did not belong to us? How can we abuse the welfare resources in a society that is willing to receive newcomers like us?

Most return migrants expressed a similar appreciation. The United States had provided opportunities to migrate and "succeed" and now offered entitlement programs for seniors. Against this backdrop, they viewed attempts to qualify for means-tested welfare as a mark of disloyalty to their adopted country, as Mr. Shih, a respondent in his seventies, asserted.

> We really appreciate the US taking care of us in our later life. I have lived in the US for more than thirty years. The US gave newcomers like us opportunities when we were younger. Now we are old, and the US government supports us. . . . My wife and I get Social Security checks every month. We got about four thousand dollars in total. We also have our own house, savings, and other assets. And we are both healthy at this point. So materially, our life is pretty carefree. . . . I don't really expect the US government to do more for us. How could we gain so many benefits and manipulate the system at the same time?

Beyond the ethics of claiming additional benefits, exploiting the welfare system might have complex legal and social ramifications. For example, migrants I interviewed in both the United States and Taiwan considered transferring assets to their children, a risky strategy for claiming means-tested benefits. Support for low-income seniors, they noted, was barely sufficient, and as chapter 2 explains, most of these immigrants were reluctant to exchange their self-sufficiency for family care. Many, however, also feared losing control of their assets. Having money at hand meant avoiding dependence on their children, who might demand a say in financial planning. Some even worried about whether their children would abandon them.

Mr. Hsiu, in his seventies, told me horror stories he had heard from friends and read in ethnic newspapers about children who had mistreated their aging parents after receiving their inheritance. Any welfare check he might receive, he explained, would be less than his income from savings, and any transfer of assets would likely disrupt family relationships. "We have income and savings," Mr. Hsiu reflected.

> It's impossible for us to have access to welfare support for the low-income seniors. . . . First of all, I am not going to use up all of my money in order to receive government funding. This is a big gamble, and the money provided by the US government is not sufficient either. Second, I am not going to transfer all of my money to my children in order to qualify for some welfare support. I don't like depending on my children. And this is a huge risk. Have you read the newspapers? How do you know that your children will not abandon you after they get all of your assets? What am I going to do if my children spend the money in ways I disagree with? I am not that stupid!

Mr. Lam, a returnee in his sixties, was most concerned that his children could gain control over his money. He had no confidence that they would care for their parents or respect their financial wishes. Observing social changes in Taiwan, he believed elderly parents could no longer rely on their children and, during our interview, several times cited a news report about elder abuse of parents by their children. "Have you read the newspapers in Taiwan?" Mrs. Lam asked. "There are lots of children abusing, abandoning, or even killing their parents. I am not saying that I don't trust my kids. I actually have a very good relationship with my children and their spouses. But if I keep money in my account, I have absolute control over how the money should be spent. The times have changed. Old people like us had better learn to be self-reliant. You never know how our children will treat us after they get our money."

Two of my respondents, both middle-class, admitted that they received welfare for low-income seniors. They also expressed guilt and emphasized desperate circumstances. Mrs. Ma, in her sixties, had placed her husband—who had passed away at the time of interview—in assisted living after a stroke, and the facility had cost about eight thousand dollars per month. To make her husband eligible for government assistance, she had divorced him. The alternative was to use all of her savings, sell her house, and become a "burden" to her children. Mrs. Gao had faced a similar dilemma. Her husband suffered from Alzheimer's disease, and to receive support for assisted living, she had transferred most of her assets to her children.

For Mrs. Gao, the assets that she and her husband had saved embodied her dreams of establishing a new home in the United States, and she wanted to avoid spending most of her money on her husband's care. Yet she was reluctant to violate her notion of good citizenship by "cheating" the US government. To relieve her sense of guilt for securing government support for her husband, she had decided not to apply for SSI for herself. Mrs. Gao thus still framed herself as a respectable citizen and her act of gaining additional support as excusable. "I know I should not do this to the US government," she exclaimed.

> I don't want to bring down the US government. It's like a family. If a family is running out of money, everyone in the household needs to save rather than waste money, right? . . . Some people told me that I should apply for SSI, but I don't want to get any other welfare money from the US government. They already take care of my husband. . . . I do get Social Security money, but I do not get any SSI. I am legally qualified for it, but I don't want to apply for it. I feel like the US government is running out of money. I am not one of those people who are rich but still try to suck blood out of the US government. This is not how I perceive myself in American society.

By contrast, none of the return migrants I interviewed reported qualifying for public support by transferring assets to their children. With a cost of living significantly lower in Taiwan, they could access affordable old-age facilities. Several self-employed business owners, however, admitted that they had underreported their income while working in the United States and so received meager Social Security benefits. Asserting that self-sufficiency was their responsibility, they expressed little interest in applying for additional assistance. As Mr. Xia maintained, "I decided to keep my money in my pocket, and then I had no right to ask or expect the US government to provide additional support for me." Tax evasion, Mr. Xia knew, marked a moral line for receiving public benefits, a distinction between entitlements and means-tested programs.

Stratified Migrants: Identifying Undeserving Others

The sociologist Hana Brown (2013) differentiates two frames that have been evoked to construct the moral worth of immigrants in debates about welfare reform: the "racial frame" and "legality frame." The racial frame directly challenges the deservingness of immigrants (mostly Latino/as), further scapegoating them for the suffering of white Americans (Brown 2013, 291). By contrast, the legality frame underscores "moral boundaries based on legal status, lauding the contributions of *legal* immigrants while chastising their illegal counterparts" (Brown 2013, 291). Building on her insights, my research points to a third frame, *rights of long-term citizens*, with which my respondents represent themselves as more deserving of public benefits than many other immigrants.

Constructing themselves as worthy newcomers in their host society, most of the migrants I interviewed reacted strongly when asked about those whom they perceived as undeserving. Here, the intersection of their status as long-term immigrants and other stratifying forces—such as class, race/ethnicity, and life course—is key to understanding the migrants whom my respondents considered troublemakers or free riders. Slightly more than half of my respondents identified three groups of immigrants who, they believed, exploited the welfare system: poor seniors, unauthorized immigrants, and recently arrived seniors. Like many other anti-immigrant politicians and activists, they contrasted their differences with those they deemed undeserving. Drawing comparisons allowed them to claim moral and social superiority over other immigrants, further pointing to the ways temporalities of migration had affected their self-perceptions. Although their depictions of these other immigrants are mostly unsubstantiated claims, the ways my respondents tried to prove their value as long-term US citizens reflects deeply ingrained biases against newcomers across racial, ethnic, and national lines (Brown 2013).

Many respondents were eager to differentiate themselves from poor elderly migrants. Largely professional or middle-class, these respondents emphasized their financial and social independence and stressed their superiority over poor older immigrants whose claims could exacerbate US finances. Although many respondents' comments pointed to the threshold criteria for (and inadequacies of) public benefits programs in the United States, they typically focused on defining themselves as more deserving than those who relied on government funding. This sense of moral superiority was infused with dissatisfaction that those they perceived as less deserving might receive more governmental support than they did. Mr. Lai, in his eighties, was proud not to depend on welfare checks but pointed to old-age homes, to which he considered relocating, as an example of unfair treatment for middle-class immigrants like him. "This is how the US government treats immigrants," he complained.

> If elderly immigrants have little money or assets, then the US government will take care of them. But unfortunately, we are not poor! We have to take care of ourselves. Nursing homes are a case in point. If only we had little money in our account, we could move to a government-funded nursing home. Yet we are middle-class and cannot have access to those welfare resources. We would have to pay at least seven or eight thousand dollars per month to live in a decent nursing home. . . . I don't really remember exactly how much money it would be, but it's a lot. Because we

are middle-class and because we are decent people who abide by the law, we are actually being punished in a lot of ways. How is this fair?

The return migrants I interviewed also sought to distinguish themselves from economically disadvantaged migrants in the United States. Many returnees claimed that, compared with low-income immigrants, they received little attention and assistance from the US government. Mrs. Ho considered herself a responsible citizen who had fulfilled her legal and social duties and had become self-sufficient, and she decried that immigrants in economically precarious situations might receive generous support. Middle-class migrants, she asserted, were treated unfairly. "I think middle-class immigrants like us are really outside of the radar of the US government," she lamented. "We worked diligently. We obeyed the law. We paid taxes. We paid Social Security for the checks we received every month. However, poor senior immigrants can get free money and free services from the US government. They can get SSI. They can live in government-funded nursing homes. But how about us? The US government should think about what kind of assistance middle-class immigrants like us need. I think this is really important. We are not poor, but we should not be ignored either."

Working-class respondents also noted that they were not poor enough to qualify for welfare available to low-income seniors. Like their middle-class counterparts, they complained of a lack of attention from the US government, but they also emphasized that, by remaining self-sufficient, they caused no problems for the United States. As Mrs. Fong maintained, she and her husband had worked hard and tried to save money but faced a dilemma: unlike older immigrants who were "really poor," they could not access SSI or government funding for an old-age home. Yet Mrs. Fong was happy not to be a "troublemaker" who strained public funding. "The US is the family we chose," she reflected. "I am not going to bring down my own family. I will sustain myself as much as I can." Although Mrs. Fong's comments point to threshold criteria for public benefits and could apply more broadly, she underscored her moral and social superiority by comparing herself with immigrants who relied on governmental support. This rhetoric constitutes what Natasha Warikoo and Irene Bloemraad (2018) call defensive incorporation, a strategy that immigrants use to portray themselves as contributing members rather than a burden to American society. This strategy, however, allowed my respondents to construct their respectability at the expense of immigrants who were in extremely economically precarious situations.

Many of the immigrants I interviewed further distinguished themselves from undocumented (or unauthorized) migrants who, they presumed, abused public services. To be clear, most means-tested welfare in the United States is contingent on citizenship and unavailable to newcomers who have not become naturalized.

In addition, undocumented immigrants pay taxes and so contribute to a system from which they cannot draw benefits (Gonzales 2016; Marrow and Joseph 2015). This anti-immigrant labeling, however, is common in the United States and clearly reflected in the accounts of many respondents. Research on public opinion has shown many Americans attributing welfare expenditures, as well as crime, to an influx of undocumented immigrants (Sanchez and Sanchez-Youngman 2013). An economic recession and financial crisis in the United States exacerbated this critique. As Kitty Calavita (1996) contends, targeting immigrants and other minority groups as the cause of fiscal drain during times of drastic social change is a symptom of "balanced-budget conservatism." Anti-immigrant sentiment, especially stereotypes against Hispanic newcomers, is typically mobilized through a heightened focus on legal status (Marrow and Joseph 2015).

My respondents illustrated this observation. Underscoring their own hard work, they believed unauthorized immigrants contributed little to US society. Influenced by politically conservative views on US immigration, many cited news reports to argue that an influx of illegal immigrants was depleting the US welfare system. Many of my respondents emphasized that, unlike unauthorized immigrants who, they believed, exploited US welfare, they had earned access to entitlement programs, as sixty-five-year-old Mr. Zhang contended:

> The US believes in meritocracy. They received immigrants from all over the world. They gave immigrants opportunities to be trained and to be successful. A lot of top scientists, scholars, medical professionals, et cetera are excited to come to the US and end up staying here. That is also why we came to and stayed in the US. And immigrants like us definitely reciprocate for the US with our talents and abilities. Immigrants like us and early immigrants from Europe contributed to American society in so many significant ways. However, illegal immigrants are another story. These illegal immigrants come to the US for work and abuse the welfare system. They go to the hospital without paying the bills. They give birth to children to get welfare checks. But they don't have to pay taxes.

Comparing himself with European immigrants to the United States at the turn of twentieth century, Mr. Zhang implied a distinction between "good" and "bad" immigrants, decrying those who lacked documentation.

Not every respondent was hostile to undocumented immigrants; indeed, some were sympathetic. But even they claimed that, unlike unauthorized immigrants, they had worked hard in exchange for access to government programs for senior citizens and were therefore more deserving of support. An influx of unauthorized migrants, they claimed, would have a negative impact on the assistance they deserved. As seventy-year-old Mr. Jiang adamantly maintained, undocumented immigrants had no right to US welfare because they had assumed no civic responsibilities. Rather, he worried, entitlement to programs like Medicare might be undermined by unauthorized immigrants. "Illegal immigrants shouldn't have any access to welfare," he asserted.

> They don't have any right under the Constitution except basic human rights. . . . I know a lot of illegal immigrants are in a vulnerable position and suffer from double jeopardy: because they are illegal immigrants, their employers can exploit them, and they are outside the Social Security system. Just like I told you, I am sure that a lot of immigrants suffer a lot. And they take over lots of jobs that no Americans want to do. I don't think that there is any easy solution or a quick fix to the problems surrounding illegal senior immigrants. However, I think there needs to be a fair system. After all, immigrants like us paid taxes for our benefits in later life. They [illegal immigrants] did not pay, and they, of course, shouldn't get the benefits. It is unfair for taxpayers like us to support them. We earned our right to access government programs for senior citizens, and they didn't. The US government should not support illegal immigrants at the expense of our well-being.

In Taiwan, return migrants similarly cited unauthorized immigrants as a cause of trouble for the US welfare state, and some returnees feared that expenditure on unauthorized immigrants would impinge on US entitlement programs for senior citizens. Most returnees told me that, given the income disparities between the United States and Taiwan, the Social Security they received from having worked in the United States covered most of their living expenses. Asserting that an influx of illegal immigrants would exacerbate a financial crisis, Mr. Yeh, in his seventies, thought the government should prioritize the needs of legal over unauthorized immigrants. "The American government is in trouble now," he stated.

> Legal immigrants like us waited in line in order to become naturalized citizens. We work hard. We abide by the law. We contributed our working years to the American society. . . . The Social Security checks we received from the US government are the money we saved throughout our lives. However, since the 1990s, a lot of illegal immigrants secretly travel across the borders. They caused a lot of problems for the US government. Because the US is a humanistic country, it still provides a lot of assistance for these illegal immigrants and their children. This actually encouraged more illegal immigrants to come to the US in order to access the welfare resources. It's such a vicious circle. And it's not fair for immigrants who follow the rules like us.

The interplay of my respondents' notions of gender and race further complicated the ways in which some described undocumented immigrants. A few targeted unauthorized migrant women, especially those of Latina descent. Mr. Fang,
in his sixties, believed Latinas avoided paid work and gave birth to children in
the United States so they could receive welfare benefits. Without evidence, he assumed that many Latina immigrants in the United States were both undocumented and welfare recipients. Encountering women who appeared to fit his
stereotype, Mr. Fang constructed a moral hierarchy of migrant groups. "Many
Hispanic illegal immigrant women came to the US in order to take advantage of
the US welfare system," he insisted.

> They know that the US government very much cares about supporting
> their American-born children. They tried to give birth to lots of kids in
> the US in order to get free money from the US government. If you walk
> in Brooklyn in the afternoon, you can see many Hispanic women fool-
> ing around with their children on the street. Yesterday afternoon, I saw
> a pregnant Hispanic woman bring two other little kids with her on the
> subway.
>
> KS: How do you know she is an undocumented immigrant?
>
> Mr. Fang: It's simple logic. How can a normal person of her age work
> and walk around on the street at the same time? They just try to abuse
> the US welfare system. . . . We are not like these illegal Hispanic immi-
> grants. We came here when we were young. We worked very hard
> throughout our life. We earned our right to resources such as Social
> Security and Medicare. You have to document this in your research
> and let Americans know that we are decent immigrants!

My respondents also cited the time that they had spent in the United States as
a rationale to distance themselves from immigrants who had arrived later in life.
To be fair, older people who are not US citizens have difficulty accessing public
benefits. Whether aging immigrants who are recent arrivals can receive welfare
benefits in the United States depends on both their citizenship status and their
economic situation. In fact, lack of access to public benefits—especially medical
care—constitutes the primary reason that older parents decide to stay in their
homeland rather than reunite with their children in North America (Sun 2017;
Y. Zhou 2012). Blaming older newcomers for accessing public benefits is also
problematic because this claim not only underestimates the difficulty of relocating to a new society later in life but also overlooks the contributions of aging
immigrants to unpaid caregiving in their own communities (Dossa and Coe
2017). Nonetheless, the accusation that the US government is too generous to

recently arrived seniors illuminates the ways my respondents conceptualized their legitimate, long-term membership in US society.

Mr. Yang, an immigrant in his sixties, objected to unconditional support for aging immigrant newcomers, asserting that those who had arrived later in life had not contributed in their prime and thus deserved a lesser degree of welfare. The failure of US policy to make this distinction, he argued, created financial problems for taxpayers. "The influx of elderly immigrants causes a lot of problems in the US society," Mr. Yang argued.

> These recent senior immigrants have a huge impact on the budget of the US government.... But to be quite frank, I think the States receives too many recently arrived old immigrants. You know, the US has a great welfare system for senior citizens. And the US is a powerful country. It always takes on the moral role of world police that tries to solve everyone's problems. The US is a really great society with a superior sense of justice and human rights. However, we have to understand that supporting senior immigrants who did not work in the US when they were younger is really unfair for us and other taxpayers. We paid taxes, and those recently arrived old people did not. The burden of raising them falls on people who are currently paying taxes. It is not really fair.

Notably, my respondents often targeted recently arrived older newcomers from mainland China, claiming that they exploited the US welfare system. Just as immigrants of Latino descent are often racialized as illegal, aging Chinese immigrants who come to reunite with their children are often stereotyped as free riders in the United States (Fujiwara 2005). Political tension between Taiwan and mainland China might have influenced some of my respondents' accounts, but those born in China and highly supportive of China-Taiwan reunification expressed similar resentment toward recently arrived Chinese. These immigrants, they argued, took advantage of US welfare.

Mrs. Tan, at eighty-one, was a so-called mainlander, or waishengren, in Taiwan, someone who had moved from China to Taiwan after 1949. She strongly identified as Chinese yet fiercely criticized the increasing number of older immigrants from mainland China for raising US welfare costs. Mrs. Tan believed that many elderly immigrants had migrated strategically to gain illicit access to welfare benefits. To her, recent arrivals who might "enjoy" welfare checks were morally unacceptable, and to be "fair" and "just," US policy should differentiate newcomers from earlier immigrants like her. "A lot of elderly Chinese immigrants from mainland China have moved to the US in their later lives," Mrs. Tan said.

These elderly Chinese immigrants really abuse the US welfare system. They live in government-funded old-age homes. And because they don't have assets in the US, they are qualified for government funding like SSI. So lots of old people from mainland China really like coming to the US. Like European countries, the US has a really solid welfare system for old people. Yet it's very difficult to migrate to the European countries. In contrast, the US has a relatively lax immigration policy, which opens the door for many calculating elderly Chinese immigrants. I find it very unfair. Why do I and my children pay taxes for these elderly mainlanders who never fulfilled any obligation to the US?

Many returnees similarly blamed later-life immigrants from mainland China for abuse of the US welfare system. Rather than poor, my respondents told me, recently arrived Chinese immigrants had left their assets in China so that they could access welfare resources in the United States. Quite a few returnees expressed contempt for Chinese immigrants in the United States, who had, presumably, contributed less to US society than they had. Mrs. Yeh, a seventy-year-old returnee, contended that an inflow of older Chinese immigrants had significantly changed the ethnic enclave where she shopped. These immigrants behaved and talked differently and were not earning the right to Social Security and Medicare, as Mrs. Yeh lamented:

When we just arrived in the US, most *huaren* [overseas Chinese] were from Hong Kong and Taiwan. Very few Mandarin-speaking people were from China back then. But over the past ten years, a lot of older immigrants from mainland China have moved to the US through their children's sponsorship. Now when you walk in Chinatown or Flushing, you can hear lots of Chinese seniors from China act rude, talk loud, and speak Mandarin at such a high pitch. A lot of them are very rich in China, and their children have high-end jobs and lots of money. However, they still applied for welfare for low-income senior citizens. I think those people are pretty shameless. They have not done anything to American society but gain welfare support for free.

Several of my respondents expressed similar resentment toward recent Taiwanese immigrants who had accessed or tried to access welfare. Some new Taiwanese arrivals, they maintained, were wealthy but still sought assistance for low-income seniors. Most respondents, however, expressed less contempt for Taiwanese immigrants than for those from mainland China. They argued, correctly, that in the early twenty-first century, the United States had been receiving more immigrants from mainland China than from Taiwan (Gu 2017; Lan 2018). They also noted Taiwan's entitlement programs for seniors, available to dual citizens (J. Wang 2004). Many contended that now, with entitlement programs in Taiwan, older Taiwanese lacked incentives to relocate to the United States to receive the governmental support. Mrs. Tong, a returnee in her seventies, commented,

> Taiwanese immigrants are different from Chinese immigrants from mainland China. Today, few elderly Taiwanese people like to migrate to the US in their later lives partly because of the economic development of Taiwan and partly because of the development of the welfare system in Taiwan, such as the National Health Plan. I don't think that old people want to move to the US today. Migration is never an easy thing, especially for old people. The Taiwanese government also provides good support for graying populations. Most elderly people in Taiwan are reluctant to move to the US even if their children move to the States. . . . As far as I know, the social security system in China is not as good as that in Taiwan. So many elderly Chinese with children in the US try very hard to move to the US. They would rather stay in the US rather than mainland China. The governmental support for the senior citizens in the US is so much better than that in mainland China.

Respondents' hostility toward other migrants vividly reveals their quest for respectability as deserving newcomers, morally charged with civic duties in their adopted country. Rarely, however, did they compare their sense of deservingness with native-born Americans. Notably, even though public discourses often stigmatize black Americans (especially black women) as undeserving welfare recipients (Collins 2000), few of my respondents criticized African Americans as outsiders who lacked legitimate social membership. Instead, their notions of perpetual foreigners were Asian and Latino/a immigrants (Kim 2008; Tuan 1998). Many of the immigrants I interviewed did express common stereotypes that associated black Americans with poverty, criminality, violence, and indolence, but they rarely framed African Americans as foreigners or newcomers who stole wealth from the US government without earning their social rights.[6]

Positioning themselves as deserving, therefore, many of my respondents consistently compared themselves with older newcomers and those who, from their perspective, had not performed well enough to deserve government support. They differed, however, in the strength of their condemnation for "undeserving foreigners." Those in the United States typically expressed fiercer disapproval of groups they perceived as illegitimately using US welfare, and their depictions were more emotionally intense—in tone, volume, and facial expression—than their counterparts in Taiwan. Most notably, my respondents in the United States spent much more interview time blaming newcomers whom they deemed unworthy.

The availability of entitlement programs in Taiwan may partly explain return-ees' lesser intensity. Many were more secure in later life because they had state support from both home and host societies. The returnees I interviewed believed they could rely on the social insurance system in Taiwan—especially public health care—even though one day the US government might be in crisis. As Mrs. Sun, a seventy-two-year-old returnee, maintained, the relative security of public ben-efits in Taiwan made Taiwanese immigrants less motivated than those from main-land China or Latin America to "milk the system." "Health is something people of our age usually worry about," she reflected.

> Fortunately, Taiwan has great public insurance system. We are all cov-ered by National Health Insurance and have access to various medical services. It took me about five minutes to go to [Hospital A] by car within five minutes. I can walk about fifteen minutes to [Hospital B]. Because of the National Health Insurance in Taiwan, the service is almost free. And it is convenient to consult with a doctor or receive any diagnosis or treatment in Taiwan. . . . It's such a relief for people of our age. . . . Even without the help from the US government, I will still be doing fine today. If anything happened to me, I still have Taiwan's National Health Insurance to count on.

Challenging Rights to Public Benefits in Taiwan

Long-term migration, along with the evolution of their homeland over time, influ-ences the processes through which my respondents articulated their sense of social rights transnationally. The immigrants I interviewed in the United States did criti-cally rethink deservingness in their homeland. Among respondents in the United States, ten reported using public health care (e.g., dental surgery or medical exami-nation and treatment) in Taiwan. Traveling back once or twice per year, they could combine vacations in Taiwan with "medical tourism." Conflating their legal and social rights, six respondents claimed that Taiwanese citizenship made accessing public health care in Taiwan both legal and acceptable. Other immigrants framed these practices as exceptions or emphasized that they might use medical services in Taiwan only in specific situations. For example, Mr. Lai had used public health care when he was a visiting scholar in Taiwan. Mrs. Tsai had decided to fly back to Tai-wan for chemotherapy because her siblings could help take care of her there. With her children far away and involved with their own careers and families, accessing the health care in Taiwan made family members' lives easier.[7]

Many of my respondents in the United States, however, had little interest in Taiwanese health care. Many believed that depending on medical services in Taiwan had become unrealistic after 2006, when the government limited access to migrants staying at least four months per year. The threshold for benefits then rose to six months in 2010 (S.-C. Liu 2014). Returning only for short-term visits, therefore, most immigrants living in the United States were ineligible for medical care in Taiwan. Rather, they worried about medical emergencies halfway around the globe. Some also reported greater confidence in medical services in the United States, lauding the quality of the US medical system even as they complained of its unaffordability. Some questioned whether medical professionals in Taiwan could truly attend to all patients' needs.

Mr. Zhang, an immigrant in his sixties, described perceived differences between medical systems in the United States and Taiwan. When visiting family members in Taiwan, he had seen doctors several times and was generally satisfied, but he felt that he would have been better treated in the States. As a consumer, Mr. Zhang believed people got what they paid for, and he disparaged Taiwan's system of public insurance, which he thought made doctors prioritize efficiency over patient care. Taiwan's cheaper medical services, he maintained, could compromise his well-being. "Doctors in Taiwan take care of too many patients," he asserted.

> They are also very impatient. If a patient asks too many questions, he or she becomes impatient. Doctors in Taiwan don't care about what we think or want. They just focus on their own diagnosis, because they need to manage a lot of patients within a couple of hours. Given the system of National Health Insurance, doctors in Taiwan are forced to see a lot of patients per day. In the US, doctors give patients plenty of time and consider symptoms carefully. This is why the medical expense in the US is so high. If you want to talk, American doctors will definitely spend time with you. They want to know your specific needs before they come to any conclusion.

Many more immigrants in the United States raised questions about their right to benefits in Taiwan. Several asserted that, having left years earlier, they had no claim on public health care there. Mrs. Liu, in her late sixties, emphasized her contributions to US society and anticipated using Medicare in the United States. "I am a decent person. I have a clear conscience," she maintained.

> I know some people move back to Taiwan after they retire from work. Then they can use the National Health Plan as well as perhaps other forms of governmental support in Taiwan. I have great contempt for those people. This is how I feel: We have stayed in the US for about

twenty, thirty, or forty years. We earned money in the US. We paid taxes in the US. We contributed to the US. It makes sense that we use resources in the US. But it's wrong to ask the Taiwanese government to support us in our later life.

While echoing Mrs. Liu's reasoning, many of my respondents further sought not to burden the Taiwanese government. Mrs. Guo, an immigrant in her sixties, used a family analogy, in which Taiwan was a parent and its citizens children who should consider their parents' needs, as she elaborated: "I feel like we earned money and fulfilled our responsibilities and obligations here. We should use the US government's money. We should not use the Taiwanese government's money. . . . More important, I still feel like being part of Taiwan. I still feel that I am a Taiwanese inside my head. In comparison with Taiwan, the US is much wealthier. The US is an international superpower after all. . . . I often compare Taiwan with our parents. As children, we always try to save rather than waste our parents' money, right?"

Quite a few respondents in the United States criticized their coethnics who had returned to use public health insurance in Taiwan. Some expressed resentment, arguing that Taiwan's system belonged to the citizens who had contributed to it. For Mr. Guo, immigrants using public benefits in Taiwan, whether visiting or settling there, were transgressing moral boundaries. The sustainability of National Health Insurance, he believed, depended on Taiwanese taxpayers, and those who had paid taxes in the United States had no right to public health care in Taiwan. Any migrant who accessed these benefits was thus despicable to him. "How can we dedicate the prime of our lives to the US and utilize Taiwan's resources in our twilight years?" he argued. "I know some people paid a fee for National Health Insurance, but they only paid a couple of hundred Taiwanese dollars per month now. They did not pay taxes before. They did not serve Taiwanese people. How is this behavior moral? You are a sociologist; you tell me!"

Justifying Use of Public Benefits in Taiwan

For most returnees, National Health Insurance was an important incentive for relocation or extended return visit. Indeed, deteriorating health and the rising cost of health care in the United States had led a great many of my respondents to reconsider the potential benefits of public health insurance in Taiwan. Many praised the medical services they had received in Taiwan and emphasized the lower cost. Mrs. Qi, a return migrant in her seventies, had needed regular physical therapy after falling down the stairs and breaking her leg "Medical services in Taiwan are very affordable," she reported. "I fell and broke my leg here once. I was very satisfied with the physical therapy I received after surgery. In the US, even if I was covered by Medicare, I still had a forty-dollar copay each time I saw my therapist. In Taiwan, I paid, like, one hundred twenty Taiwanese dollars [about four US dollars]. And my therapists here are very responsible. They perform electric muscle stimulation first, then massage my legs a little bit. In the US, I paid a lot more. . . . That is why I very much appreciate living in Taiwan."

Return migrants' finances shaped their response to health insurance in Taiwan. Those who struggled with money were typically forthcoming about their concerns over the cost of health care in the United States. Even with Medicare, these financially disadvantaged returnees worried about deductibles and copays. Mrs. Sun, a seventy-two-year-old returnee, reported paying thousands of dollars when her husband was hospitalized after a car accident, even though he was covered by Medicare. In Taiwan, she said, she would have paid two-thirds less. Other return migrants noted that, unlike Taiwan's National Health Insurance, Medicare did not cover vision or dental care, hearing aids, routine doctor visits, and Chinese medicine. Therefore, a root canal in the States might cost more than a thousand dollars but was almost free in Taiwan.

The absence of a language barrier with Taiwanese medical professionals made health care in Taiwan even more appealing. A few of the returnees I interviewed, especially those with working-class backgrounds, reported discomfort when interacting with US health care professionals. Return migrants with limited vocabulary or English fluency had often been frustrated in their attempts to communicate with doctors in the United States and reported problems understanding diagnoses and treatments. Mrs. Chin, a return migrant in her seventies, jokingly expressed her frustration with medical professionals in the United States. "Right now," she explained, "at least I might know what doctors would do to my body. I had no idea what my doctor in the US was talking about if my children were not around!"

In Taiwan, some return migrants could communicate without "bothering" their children every time they sought medical services. They also had a wider range of options for health care. Like other Taiwanese, many had developed the habit of "shopping" for doctors. Many also countered the view, common in the United States, that public care is inefficient and stressed that they had received medical attention more quickly in Taiwan, an observation supported by research showing improved hospital efficiency with National Health Insurance (Chen et al. 2008). In Taiwan, Ms. Ho had experienced shorter waiting periods for appointments. "I think the National Health Insurance in Taiwan is really fantastic," she asserted.

> It's very cheap. And the medical professionals in Taiwan provide excellent services too. In the US, you have to make an appointment, and sometimes you have to wait for months. Even if you have a toothache and cannot sleep at all, you still have to wait for a long time to see a doctor . . . unless you are in an emergency situation. I remember once waiting for about two weeks to get the annual check on my teeth done. In Taiwan, if I had a toothache, I walked in, and my dentist took care of my problem right away.

For return migrants, the cost and accessibility of Taiwan's National Health Insurance created a secure environment for aging.

The stigma attached to return migrants who "manipulate" the benefits of public health care constitutes a "status paradox of migration"—that is, a "transnational dynamic of losing social status and gaining it at the same time" (Nieswand 2011, 3). Existing literature argues that loss of social status in receiving communities drives many economically disadvantaged labor migrants to strive for social and economic success that can restore their respectability in sending communities (Kronenfeld 2011; Thai 2014). But the return migrants I met struggled with a different dilemma. Having spent most of their working lives in the United States, they lost status in Taiwan when they were perceived as opportunists taking advantage of public benefits. Against this backdrop, many of the return migrants I interviewed sought to justify their right to National Health Insurance.

Many therefore sought to highlight their reciprocity from afar, stressing their loyalty and contributions to Taiwanese society, even from the other side of the globe. Political engagement was one form of reciprocity. Some respondents claimed they had expressed ongoing concern for their homeland or had donated money to parties and politicians. Some reported protesting US policies toward Taiwan or engaging in US politics on Taiwan's behalf. To support Taiwan, Mrs. Wu, a sixty-eight-year-old returnee, had become heavily involved in US politics, together with her husband. "We are always trying to help Taiwan even if we don't live in Taiwan," she reported.

> For example, in Massachusetts, we raised lots of money for Senator Edward Kennedy. I remember we raised about fifty thousand dollars at one dinner party. It's just one night. Massachusetts is a blue state. No matter what happened, Kennedy would be elected. We knew what we did might have little impact on how he voted. But we still wanted to try our best to make politicians be friendly to Taiwan. When China did things to hurt Taiwan, we at least had some congressmen to speak for us. My husband and I even went to DC to lobby several times. Back then, we were actually very busy with children and work. What we did in the past might be of

little use, but we never abandoned Taiwan. We still tried very hard to do something for our homeland. We are definitely not free riders who only want to take advantage of the National Health Insurance.

Facilitating the flow of people, goods, and information between the United States and Taiwan was another form of reciprocity. Helping newly arrived Taiwanese immigrants could thus represent attachment to their homeland. Mr. Chao, a sixty-six-year-old return migrant, had felt deeply offended by accusations that returnees like him were using public health care in Taiwan without having performed their civic duties. Contending that he could be a loyal and reliable citizen without residing in Taiwan, Mr. Chao cited having helped newcomers from Taiwan, among them international students, visiting scholars, migrants, and tourists. As a good citizen who had helped other overseas Taiwanese, Mr. Chao believed he had proved himself loyal, as he elaborated:

> When I was in the US, I still very much cared about Taiwan. I watched *World Journal* [one of the major Chinese newspapers in North America] to understand what happened in Taiwan. . . . I also opened my house to host many immigrants and international students from Taiwan. I taught them how to drive. And I helped them find apartments. My house is like a hotel. Many people stayed in my house in the US. Some people even joked that I was the underground mayor of [our city]. And I never charged them a cent. I did this because I love Taiwan and because I try to help my coethnics. I was always a citizen of Taiwan. And I always did things for Taiwan. I was just millions of miles away.

A few returnees cited the expertise they had brought back to Taiwan as a contribution to their homeland. In particular, migrants with professional-class backgrounds rationalized their entitlement to public resources as compensation for knowledge, ideas, practices, technology, and information transferred from the United States to Taiwan. These constituted what the sociologist Peggy Levitt (2001, 11) calls "social remittances . . . the ideas, behaviors, and social capital that flow from receiving to sending communities." For recognized experts in their fields, these social remittances demonstrated that they had neither abandoned Taiwan nor returned merely to use its more affordable public health care.

Mr. Lu, age seventy-two, a psychiatrist who had moved back to accept an offer from a Taiwanese hospital, reported his ongoing concern with the professionalization of psychiatry in Taiwan. When in the United States, he explained, he had always tried to keep his colleagues in Taiwan updated with developments in US psychiatry, and he refused to see himself as a strategic migrant, returning to take advantage of social insurance. Rather, he emphasized his attachment to Taiwan as motivation for contributing expertise to Taiwanese society. "It is very unfair to say that we did not contribute to Taiwan when we were younger and moved back to use the public health care here," Mr. Lu contended.

> When I was in the US, I was still very much involved in the professional development of psychiatry in Taiwan. I was still in contact with my colleagues in Taiwan. If I went to a conference and knew any new information, I would definitely bring the most updated information back to Taiwan. Back then, we still did not have the internet. I told my colleagues in Taiwan what was going on in [the] US Psychiatry Society. . . . I am still doing the same thing after relocating to Taiwan. If I learn anything from my colleagues in the US, I will still keep my colleagues in Taiwan updated. My heart is always with Taiwan no matter where I live. And I contributed to Taiwanese society no matter where I lived.

To be sure, not every return migrant with whom I talked could offer examples of reciprocity from afar. A few were instead seeking to compensate for their access to National Health Insurance and so highlighted their plans to contribute to Taiwan. Here, too, returnees' strategies constituted a moral narrative that affirmed their contributions to Taiwan and claimed their entitlement to governmental support. Mrs. Lam, age sixty-three, acknowledged that National Health Insurance had been a reason she and her husband had returned but stressed that they also tried to reciprocate and, in effect, earn their right to governmental support. With their privileged class background, Mrs. Lam believed they could contribute knowledge, wealth, talents, and skills to Taiwan and were positioned to serve vulnerable populations. "We never want to be a free rider in the national health care system in Taiwan," she related.

> We are indeed covered by National Health Insurance in Taiwan. But we are also trying to reciprocate for Taiwanese society in our later life. We contributed most of our working years to the US. We thought we might be able to do something for Taiwanese society. In the US, we could probably only do things like donating money or to a food bank. Yet in Taiwan, we could teach English and math in orphanages and elementary schools, helping those kids in need. Because we gave the prime of our lives to American society, we wanted to do something for Taiwan in our later life, too. It's not all about taking advantage of Taiwanese government. This is not true.

Deflection is yet another strategy with which returnees articulated their entitlement to public services. Deflecting concerns about free riding, some of my respondents highlighted other returnees' contributions, thereby suggesting that

elderly returnees are in general respectable citizens. Return migrants who struggled with health issues often had trouble establishing their sense of entitlement to
government programs and so focused on others, whom they thought had contributed significantly. Mrs. Chin earnestly reminded me that many return migrants
had done great things for Taiwan, either from the United States or after moving
back, and she mentioned several returnees who had, in the United States, helped to
establish civic, commercial, religious, and nonprofit organizations to help overseas
Taiwanese. She spoke of elite returnees, including the dean of a major hospital in
rural Taiwan, who had given up high-salary positions to serve local people. For her,
these examples served to counter criticisms of returnees using public health care.

Other respondents defended their entitlement by differentiating themselves
from nonmigrant Taiwanese, sometimes claiming social and cultural superiority
in their use of public resources. Several stressed that they used public health care
responsibly, without abusing its services. Having lived in the United States, they
understood that health care could be expensive and claimed that they approached
medical professionals only when necessary, unlike local people who often took
the public insurance system for granted and used it unnecessarily. Emphasizing
their appreciation for Taiwan's social insurance, they implied that they were responsible citizens who deserved Taiwan's public health care. As Mrs. Yeh stated,

> We see doctors in Taiwan, but we never abuse the National Health In-
> surance. Many Taiwanese people have the mentality that since the gov-
> ernment pays the bill and since they have paid the monthly fee, they
> should use medical services as much as they can. Yet they never think
> about how the budget of Taiwanese government comes from taxpayers'
> money. This is why the US government hesitates to have public health
> insurance. . . . We are different. We never abuse public health care in Tai-
> wan. We lived in the US and know how expensive medical services in
> America are. So I always go to see a doctor only when we really need
> help. There is no point of wasting valuable health care resources.

Temporal aspects of migration affect the ways the older Taiwanese migrants I interviewed articulated their responsibilities and entitlements in relation to government support. Having contributed most of their working years to the United
States, my respondents staked claims to public benefits. To them, hard work,
together with legal and civic duties in the United States, had secured their social
membership and rendered them more deserving than other migrant groups. Their
articulation of entitlement to state support was intimately tied to their perceived
incorporation into the United States, which had in turn shaped their choices. Dif-

ferent migration experiences, I argue, promote distinct connections to host societies and affect the ways migrants imagine and construct their later lives across national borders.

The respondents' justifications for receiving public benefits in the United States highlight the boundary-making processes through which long-term migrants seek to distinguish themselves from immigrants they deem less deserving. Believing that they had "earned" access to governmental support, many contended that other immigrants—principally working-class, unauthorized, and recently arrived Chinese—effortlessly received generous welfare without assuming civic responsibilities. Claiming moral superiority over other newcomers, they attempted to justify their social rights to programs for senior citizens. Their sense of rights, responsibilities, and entitlement to resources thus created tension with other migrants, whom some considered undeserving of state aid. Their views thus echo the anti-immigrant sentiments expressed by conservative critics of the US welfare system and mirror larger controversies over immigration.

The establishment of public health care in Taiwan had altered the logic of social rights for these migrants. As Taiwanese citizens, they could gain access to public benefits after a few months of residency. In the United States, most of my respondents were reluctant to claim a resource to which they had contributed little during the prime of their lives. Many further expressed greater trust in US medical professionals. Returnees, however, defended their access to government support, constructing their entitlement by highlighting their long-term loyalty and differentiating themselves from those who, they believed, failed to appreciate public benefits or used them irresponsibly. Yet by moving back, these return migrants had transferred financial and social responsibility for health care from the United States to Taiwan. The seeking of health care transnationally thus contributes to the global restructuring of governmental support for older populations. This phenomenon also raises questions about state responsibility to its foreign-born and native-born citizens.

Representing their entitlements, migrants in both the United States and Taiwan might as well have obscured important elements of their social worlds. As they compared their connections to both societies, for example, they highlighted their social and financial contributions but avoided the contradictions of transnational access to resources. Presenting themselves as morally upright and deserving, they may well have (re)constructed biographies that promoted their sense of entitlement. A cross-border assessment of differences in the identities and practices of migrants requires further comparative research. Nonetheless, the narratives these migrants mobilized to justify their social rights reveal their efforts to establish their membership and their desire to be viewed as respectable citizens in both sending and receiving societies.

CONCLUSION

Rethinking Time, Migration, and Aging

This book has examined the interaction of time and migration in the experiences of older Taiwanese migrants living in both the United States and Taiwan. All had been long-term residents in the United States, having migrated to pursue an education or a career or to maximize their children's life chances. In their transitions to later life, the decisions they faced had prompted a remaking of relations at the familial, communal, and state levels. Echoing other scholars (Dossa and Coe 2017; Gardner 2002; Karl and Torres 2015; Lamb 2009; Näre and Walsh 2016; Purkayastha et al. 2012), this book demonstrates that older migrants are neither guided exclusively by homeland traditions nor rendered vulnerable only to the challenges of human aging. Notable here, however, are temporalities of migration that structure specific opportunities and restrictions to which aging migrants reflexively respond.

More broadly, this book points to the impact of time/temporalities on the identities of immigrants. Existing scholarship has established that relocating to a new society complicates the subjectivities of newcomers, giving them and their children new options for identity in familial, communal, and social settings (Jiménez 2017; Levitt 2001; Roth 2012; Smith 2014; Vallejo 2012; M. Waters 1999). Because of their varying degrees of sociocultural assimilation, immigrants and their children develop not only new identities but also disagreements over related practices (Chung 2016; Espiritu 2003; Foner 2009). Such identity shifts, as I emphasize throughout this book, can be found not only across generations but also over time. Long-term stays in the United States, coupled with temporal variation of transnational contexts, can profoundly transforms immigrants' perspectives across worlds.

Time and Immigrant Incorporation

The notion of temporalities of migration underscores the ways time—including length of relocation, life path, and life transitions—profoundly affects immigrants' incorporation into receiving contexts (Ho 2019; King et al. 2017; Levitt and Rajaram 2013). Long-term migration, along with changing transnational contexts, transforms the ways older migrants address life transitions in such domains as families, communities, and nation-states. Over time and across borders, older migrants reconsider their needs, desires, and roles in relation to a complex constellation of opportunities and constraints. Living in the United States for several decades, the migrants I met had accomplished important life milestones (e.g., raising children, establishing careers, and becoming grandparents). Experiencing these life transitions across borders had required them to develop new cultural repertoires and ways of knowing. Over time, migration had also pushed them to reflect on what they perceived as American modes of aging and to grapple with their membership in a familial, communal, and national setting. These findings caution us to notice the heterogeneity within aging foreign-born populations (e.g., long-term migrants or recent arrivals). They also point to the possibility that immigrants can develop new identities, worldviews, and lifestyles as they mature in the receiving contexts.

The hyperselectivity of immigrants I studied further complicates scholarly understanding of immigrant incorporation and adaptation across life phases. Hyperselectivity—the fact that many Asian immigrants are better educated than both nonmigrant populations in their home societies *and* native-born populations in their host societies—is key to understanding the rapid social mobility that Asian and Asian American families have experienced in the United States (Lee and Zhou 2015, 6–7). Accompanying this socioeconomic mobility are inevitable interactions with US institutions (e.g., school and work) and families with "assimilated" children and grandchildren. The impact of long-term relocation on immigrant newcomers is thus not only accumulated across the life span but also path dependent. At a later life stage, migrants' adaptations to what they perceive as US society are not a choice but a consequence of the decision made when they were younger.

My respondents' perceptions of US culture, however, are partial and even misleading. For example, belief in US individualism, evident in their portrayal of the nuclear family as the prevalent cultural norm, fails to capture the complexity of US family life, as many scholars have documented (Bengtson 2001; Hansen 2005; Klinenberg 2012). Like many native-born Americans (Gross 2005), however, my respondents viewed individualism and the nuclear household as guidelines, which in turn shaped their interactions with their loved ones. Their long-term exposure to the dominant cultural ideal in a host society thus constituted their social worlds, further orienting their efforts to assimilate themselves culturally.

Time in a Transnational Social Field

Myriad temporalities also construct transnational life for immigrants, especially older migrants. For many, career and work, together with raising children, were the primary reasons for relocating to the United States. Yet as children grow up and leave home and they draw closer to retirement age, older immigrants begin to plan their remaining years and rethink their priorities, and against this backdrop, many of the respondents revived ties to their homeland. Some reconnected with their families and friends in Taiwan. Some traveled to Taiwan more frequently. And some decided that their "missions" in the United States had been accomplished and so moved back to the homeland.

Temporality also operated in the development of a transnational social field in which these immigrants could reside. As Peggy Levitt and Nina Glick Schiller (2004) argue, immigrants can incorporate activities, routines, and institutions in their home societies into their lives in host countries. Immigrants can also affect the development of their homeland by sending money, information, ideas, expertise, goods, and people (Fitzgerald 2013; Levitt 2001; Zhou and Tseng 2001). Extending these insights, this book examines a homeland that had experienced significant transformation over time and had spurred migrants to renew their ties to their country of origin. As dual nationals, the respondents could access resources in Taiwan and so considered public benefits, modern old-age facilities, and the demand for international talent as they planned their retirement life.

As the accounts of the respondents make clear, living a transnational life is about more than maximizing individual or family welfare. Rather, later-life decisions can provoke thorny questions regarding personal and national identity, the need for elder care, the support migrants felt they deserve, and their relations with children, grandchildren, and extended family. The questions they must consider in later life had led these older migrants to grapple with their self-respect, with the attitudes of their communities, and with their social and cultural citizenship. Future studies of aging and transnational migration should pay close attention to the temporal dimensions through which older migrants envision, plan, and organize their daily lives and later-life trajectories beyond national borders.

Constructing an Economy of Belonging

The ways in which immigrants articulate their sense of social belonging can vary across life stages. These older migrants enacted an economy of belonging, through which they delineated rationales and strategies to evaluate their well-being and the well-being of their family members. Much as the historical relationship between the United States and Taiwan had informed an earlier decision to migrate, the contingencies of time and place now shaped their decision making. Confronting changing roles, needs, and priorities, together with various constellations of resources, my respondents had come to different decisions about residence and relocation at a later stage of life. Weighing their options, they both constructed and contested an economy of belonging that spanned ethnic cultures and national borders.

Their aspiration to "become American," often well before emigration, was deeply embedded in the historical relationship between the United States and Taiwan. Before they set foot in the United States, many of these immigrants had imagined belonging to US society. The United States' support for Taiwan from the 1950s to the 1970s had encouraged contact, and they knew about the United States through the transnational circulation of people, goods, and ideas. Global mass media and connections with earlier Taiwanese immigrants had led to perceptions of US superiority. Moving to the United States had then marked an important life transition, but only after relocating did they come to understand that the American dream, like any other dream, requires adjusting to realities.

During their working and child-rearing years, these older migrants had placed a premium on class mobility, both for themselves and for their children. Given racial discrimination, xenophobia, and the cultural stereotyping of Han Chinese—which dominated their narratives of life in the United States—they sought to prove themselves worthy by moving up the socioeconomic ladder. Upward social mobility enabled many to resist what they perceived as an unfriendly or even hostile society, and their success then sparked a desire to reproduce class privilege across generations. Having endured hardship, they had reached a class location that would serve their children and grandchildren.

Entering later life, however, prompted these older migrants to rethink their evolving connections to Taiwan. As they retired from work, they reflected on their needs, desires, and priorities. Most had established careers, families, and communities in the United States, together with a strong sense of belonging to the United States. The United States was the new home they had adopted. Taiwan was an ancestral home that they missed and visited, but its socioeconomic development stood in sharp contrast to the homeland that many remembered. Home, in this sense, could be found only in memories now decades old, and for some, it was no longer a physical place to which they wished to return and settle.

By contrast, changes in the homeland profoundly affected the ways many older migrants articulated their notions of social rights and social membership. To secure the right to a stable and desirable life, some migrants moved back to Taiwan. For these aging returnees, relocation was often a way to maximize psychological, physical, and social well-being. Whereas some scholars have found older returnees moving back to pursue lifestyles that are socially and culturally familiar (Gilbertson 2009), I find more complexity among immigrants trying to remake home in their ancestral societies. The respondents did seek traditional components of Chinese-Taiwanese culture, but most had returned because of changes in Taiwan. There they found a newly urban society and accessible public benefits. Some hoped to further still greater change. As migration scholars need to recognize, changing features in a transnational field can profoundly influence migrants' choices and sense of home.

Negotiating Family Intimacy

Acquiring, securing, and exchanging various forms of support required these migrants to renegotiate relationships with family, community, and nation-state. Learning social and cultural norms in the United States had engendered temporal reflexivity. Long-term migration had promoted multiple and sometimes conflicting frames of reference across time and space. Whether remaining in the United States or returning to Taiwan, these migrants had remade family intimacies and reflected on homeland traditions. Rather than remaining "tradition-bound," as many researchers suggest (Hareven 1994; Kamo and Zhou 1994), they had actively drawn on cultural repertoires—perspectives and practices selectively used to foster strategies of action (Swidler 2001)—to give new meanings to their roles as parents, spouses, and grandparents, both nationally and transnationally.

Their decisions to emigrate during adulthood had set a foundation for reconsidering relationships in later life. Having moved away from family members, many of these migrants had been unable to care for their own parents and grandparents in traditional Chinese ways. Family dislocation had thus reduced the constraints imposed by extended families and created the space to concentrate on their own nuclear households. Staying in the United States for most of their working years had, in turn, transformed their belief systems, while socioeconomic incorporation into US society influenced cultural assessments of family. Over time, therefore, geographical and social distance had led these migrants to readjust their expectations of their own children and their children's spouses.

Most grappled with the meaning of Americanization. For some older migrants, claiming to be Americanized helped to maintain desirable relationships with children, children's spouses, and grandchildren. As parents with American children or as Americanized parents, these immigrants emphasized independence and self-sufficiency over intergenerational dependence. As husbands and wives, they adapted to US norms of family, which challenged Chinese gender conventions and promoted an ethos of mutuality, egalitarianism, and emotional expressivity. As immigrant grandparents in the United States, they learned to respect the boundaries of their children's families and avoid undue intervention in their grandchildren's lives. For them, a new cultural understanding of family, together with a later phase of life, mediated the negotiation of roles and needs in the course of human aging.

Their homeland provided points of reference for reflecting on family, but cultural differences between the United States and Taiwan had heightened awareness of norms for family responsibility and hands-on care. For some, the changes in Taiwan that drove the decision to return also determined strategies for sustaining family intimacies, especially with children and grandchildren. Notably, the commercialization of elder care in Taiwan not only challenged ethnic traditions of intergenerational obligation but also offered a solution to a potential "care crisis" for some migrants and their spouses. Turning to old-age facilities, either in the United States or in Taiwan, thus reflected a practical attitude toward issues that come with aging and deteriorating health.

Applying ethnic traditions across an evolving transnational field, many of these migrants had sought to be cultural mediators in the lives of their grandchildren. In both the United States and Taiwan, they selectively facilitated awareness of Taiwanese values and promoted ethnic practices in their grandchildren's everyday lives. They promoted values like industriousness and skills like fluency in Chinese, which they hoped would prepare their grandchildren to be cosmopolitan citizens, able to succeed inside and outside the United States. Their strategies for transferring ethnic traditions might depend on geographic location, but most based their efforts not only on ideology but also on an assessment of requirements for surviving or "making it" in a globally connected world.

Navigating Communities and Citizenship

Long-term migration further affected the exchange of material, emotional, and moral support between these migrants and members of their extended communities. As scholars have long chronicled, newcomers translate ethnic ties into critical resources for everyday survival, creating "fictive kin" by forming networks with trustworthy coethnics (Dominguez 2011; Kibria 1993; Roy and Burton 2007). The accounts of these migrants complicate this analysis. Whether remaining in the United States or relocating to Taiwan, they had navigated complex politics of belonging when constructing larger networks of support. Coethnics in the United States and in Taiwan might be viewed as extended family, but the intimacies that these older immigrants had established, sustained, or severed were also highly selective and conditioned by ethnonational origins, affiliation with homeland politics, and socioeconomic position in US society. For them, long-term residence in the United States, coupled with the transformation of Taiwan, meant some degree of disconnection in both North America and Asia.

State support constituted a larger structural context for the needs of these older migrants. Key for many was the availability of public benefits in the United States or Taiwan. Having spent most of their working years in the United States, most felt entitled to state-sponsored programs and therefore compared themselves favorably to those they considered "undeserving" or "underdeserving." By comparison, their absence from Taiwan rendered rights to social benefits problematic so that they risked critique and stigma in their homeland. These conflicting experiences across borders point to linkages between citizenship and its corresponding rights and responsibilities. For these migrants, becoming American had shifted their perspectives on entitlement to social care. Here, temporalities of migration are manifest in the working histories of long-term migrants and in the social structures that embed them in different societies.

Social Policy, Elder Support, and Transnational Social Protection

The concept of temporalities of migration highlights the institutional support that older migrants need as they reconsider family and belonging across cultures. Whereas many studies highlight the importance of ethnic traditions in elder support (Hareven 1994; Kamo and Zhou 1994), this study emphasizes the contribution of time to the experience of migration. Other than homeland traditions, the ways in which these older Taiwanese migrants conceptualized successful aging are intimately tied to the interaction of time with structural and cultural factors. Long-term residence in the United States had led them to appreciate independence and self-sufficiency, and they had become reluctant to rely on their children. Even among these immigrants, whose culture of origin emphasizes intergenerational care, families required sufficient support. Understanding migrants' diverse needs and wants could help policy makers in the United States reconsider support for older immigrants, who may have arrived at different points in their lives.

A changing Taiwan, especially the growth of public benefits programs and affordable old-age facilities, also offers insights for US policy. The more affordable retirement life available to returnees facilitates the transfer of financial and social responsibility for older migrants from the United States to Taiwan. This phenomenon raises questions about government responsibility for foreign-born citizens who have committed most of their working years to a host society. Older return-ees may have improved their lives by moving back, in part, because of lower costs for housing and health care in Taiwan. Their decisions have contributed, how-ever, to the global restructuring of government responsibilities for older migrants.

Beyond this case, policy makers should consider the ways aging individuals negotiate resources available across a transnational field. Some migrants relocate to pursue new lifestyles and affordable care facilities after retiring from work (Gustafson 2001; Newendorp 2020). Some move back to construct a stronger safety net for themselves and their loved ones (Coe 2017a). Parents left behind and parents migrating to reunite with their children abroad are both anxious about securing the support they need (Lamb 2009; Sun 2012). And millions of domestic workers and health care workers leave their homelands to care for ag-ing populations in other countries (Coe 2019; Hondagneu-Sotelo 2007; Lan 2006; Parreñas 2001; Paul 2017). These different cases document the varying constellations of resources at individual, familial, and (super)national levels and demonstrate their effects on aging individuals and their family members. Aging thus becomes a global issue, and related resources must be reconsidered in a cross-border environment (Levitt et al. 2017).

Future Research on Migration and Time

The intersection of time with structural and cultural factors shaping the immi-grant experience is an area for future research. Comparing recent arrivals with long-term residents, for example, might reveal factors affecting migrants at differ-ent points in their lives. Comparing different sending contexts might similarly identify social and structural differences that construct individual choices and promote migratory patterns. Futures studies should also examine the diversity and dynamics among aging migrant populations. Attention to time-migration configurations—including changing conditions in homelands, immigration his-tories, distinct life paths, and modes of socioeconomic and cultural incorporation—could help capture key factors that affect the psychological, physical, and social well-being of aging migrant individuals.

For older migrants, health and finances are key concerns. Most of the respon-dents in this study were in reasonably good health and able to take care of them-selves and their spouses, even though some were struggling with illness. Many had arrived in economically precarious situations but had become middle-class over time. Nonetheless, they could expect a rapidly rising need for care (Ornstein et al. 2017). Migrants across the spectra of age and socioeconomic status are thus differently equipped to manage biological aging and life transitions. Attention to socioeconomic circumstances, as well as their intersection with time/temporalities, is thus critical to understanding migrants' choices.

Future studies should also consider the time constraints that nation-states impose on aging migrant populations. For example, Alistair Hunter (2018) observes that dependence on noncontributory public benefits in France caused many older African migrants—who initially arrived as laborers in the service sector—to reject the possibility of moving back. Noncontributory welfare resources in France not only fall outside the confines of transferability legislation but also require recipients to maintain "regular and effective" residence their new locales (Hunter 2018, 64). As a result, older working-class immigrants in Hunter's research had difficulty returning to settle in their homelands. The extent to which aging immigrants can live a transnational life is thus deeply influenced by the definition of citizenship and its corresponding rights, obligations, and entitlements in a national setting.

Another important issue is death in a transnational social field. Migrants, especially long-term residents in their respective receiving countries, must grapple with death care—services for transportation and cremation or burial of the dead—together with their family members (Felix 2011). As with caring for the living, death care involves navigating transnational resources. While some migrants decide to be buried or cremated in their receiving countries, others want their remains repatriated to their home societies. Such decisions may well depend on migrants' familial and social networks, their cultural schemas, and their constellation of resources. Future research should consider these questions.

This book has taken a subject-oriented approach to analyzing the influence of time on the ways in which older migrants manage intimacies at familial, communal, and (trans)national levels (Lee and Zhou 2015). I chose this focus because the voices of older migrants have not been heard and carefully analyzed. Expanding this analytical lens to include accounts of the children and grandchildren of older migrants might extend the story with new insights into complex intergenerational dynamics. How, for example, do subsequent generations understand the cultural ideal of the American family? How do younger people view their parents' and grandparents' notions of traditional values? Cross-generational data might also identify additional factors that affect migrants' families and communities. Migration, as this research shows, is an ongoing process, not only across borders but also over time.

Appendix A

REFLECTIONS ON METHODOLOGY AND RESEARCH DESIGN

Entering Taiwanese immigrant communities in the United States was not part of my plan when I arrived in the United States from Taiwan as an international student. The Department of Sociology at Brandeis University had offered me a full scholarship to study abroad, enabling me to realize my dream of a PhD in sociology. Yet the move marked a major life transition for me. I had never left Taiwan and was ambivalent about navigating life in a foreign society. To alleviate my anxiety and encourage me to pursue my dream, a friend introduced me to Mr. and Mrs. Bien (pseudonyms), who were Taiwanese immigrants working in the Boston area and happened to be in Taipei. After we met and had dinner, I felt much more secure about the prospect of my new life in the United States. Mr. and Mrs. Bien seemed like solid people to whom I could turn for help. Back then, I did not expect to be incorporated into their family and community. I also did not foresee that the decision to connect with Mr. and Mrs. Bien would open the gate to enter—and later study—Taiwanese American communities.

Entering the Field

Only after I arrived in the United States did I learn that Mr. and Mrs. Bien were well-known and well-networked people. They were leaders of several Taiwanese immigrant organizations and were committed to incorporating younger people into the Taiwanese American community. I soon came to know many of their friends, and after a year, I started to shoulder some responsibilities for a Taiwanese immigrant organization. As I proceeded with my graduate studies, therefore,

I often communicated with immigrant families. We organized various activities—dinner parties, meetings, study groups—which usually took place in private homes. Gradually, I came to know many Taiwanese immigrants. I listened to their stories about living, working, and raising children in the United States, and I participated in numerous conversations about their connections to the United States and Taiwan.

Back then, I had no plans to investigate communities of older Taiwanese migrants. A significant number of the Taiwanese immigrants I met were age sixty or older, but I rarely thought about their ages. Indeed, I was never exactly sure how old they were. Yet as a younger person engaged with an older generation, I had, in effect, entered the field long before I took on the role of researcher. I knew many older immigrants and had heard about their families' lives well before I officially started collecting data for this book. This long-term connection to the community gave me much intimate knowledge of older migrants' daily lives, providing information I could later use to triangulate with interview and ethnographic data.

From Mr. and Mrs. Bien's interpersonal networks I met many Taiwanese immigrants who were Christian, but only about one-third of the respondents I interviewed identified themselves as Christian. Less than 5 percent of Taiwan's population is Christian, but many Taiwanese immigrants have converted to Christianity in the United States. As the sociologist Carolyn Chen (2008, 2) estimates, "Christians are approximately 20–25 percent of the Taiwanese population in the United States." Church, therefore, featured prominently in the accounts of many respondents. Compared to their non-Christian coethnics, the Christian respondents enjoyed talking about their faith and organized their life around "adopted" families at church, which might also play key roles in secular Taiwanese immigrant organizations.

Many immigrants further recalled receiving critical support—food, accommodation, money, information, and emotional care—from Taiwanese immigrant churches on their arrival to the United States. Even when they did not believe in Christianity, many still talked about their relationship with immigrant churches and their friends there. After they retired, many older non-Christians (with no plans to be baptized) attended Taiwanese- or Mandarin-speaking congregations because church offered activities and stable social networks. Many nonreligious activities (e.g., talks and holiday gatherings) took place at churches because they provided ample space. In this sense, an immigrant church could be a social—rather than spiritual—space.

Positionality in the Field

Throughout my fieldwork (especially in the Boston area), I was what Patricia Hill Collins (2000) calls an "outsider within," living simultaneously in two social worlds. One was the academic world where most of my professors, colleagues, and friends were socially liberal. The other was the world of older Taiwanese immigrants, who were more often conservative regarding gender, race/ethnicity, class, sexuality, and immigration. During my fieldwork, I sometimes heard comments with which I disagreed. For example, in one Bible study gathering, participants talked about organizing a "special prayer meeting" for the Boston area. Virtually all participants in the group were long-term area residents, and they were worried about the implications of legal gay marriage, especially in Massachusetts, the first state in the United States to legalize same-sex marriage.

One of my respondents commented that accepting homosexuality, especially legal gay marriage, fundamentally countered biblical teaching and would have a long-standing negative influence on US society. Another participant added that the public schools in Boston had started to teach their children that "a family might not be composed of one father and one mother but could consist of two mothers or two fathers. Is this the society that we want?" At these comments, other participants sighed and shook their heads. These sentiments contrasted sharply with my academic world, where diversity, including sexual orientation, was often celebrated. As a sociologist heavily influenced by the sociology of sex and gender, I disagreed with these older migrants. Yet I avoided controversy and instead reflected critically on the assumptions underlying their accounts.

I assumed the same critical position as some of my respondents who intervened in my personal life. For example, Mrs. Gao called me almost every Saturday morning for about five months to "chat." During our hour-long conversations, she lectured me about selecting a "good" woman to marry and living an ideal family life. She admonished me to get married as soon as I could because "you need someone to take good care of you." Indeed, because I was single, some respondents were eager to play the role of matchmaker. Some of the dinner parties to which I was invited turned out to be blind dates arranged by the host and hostess. Two of the older migrants I encountered (but did not interview) strongly encouraged me to go out with their daughter. Moreover, it seemed that my marital status was widely circulated throughout transnational Taiwanese migrant networks. As I conducted research in Taiwan, Singapore, and Hong Kong, someone would always want to fix me up.

These experiences taught me to keep considerable social distance from many of my respondents. I learned to reject many requests and invitations gently and to keep my personal and professional lives distinct. Leaving Boston after completing my PhD program helped me manage boundaries with my respondents, and I ended up losing contact with some of them.

My time in the field, however, did sensitize me to their assumptions about age, work, family, and life stage. As a younger coethnic, I appreciated their good intentions, but as a scholar, I remained an "outsider within," keenly aware of my position and the interpersonal boundaries I needed to maintain.

Recruiting Respondents in the United States

Studying older migrants from Taiwan required me to recruit respondents who could help me capture the complexity within Taiwanese immigrant communities. Growing up in Taiwan in a waishengren (mainland Chinese) household, I had learned that older members of my family harbored political views fundamentally different from those of many friends, classmates, and professors, who were largely benshengren (native-born) Taiwanese. Some had family members who had been arrested and executed by the Kuomintang, the political party that withdrew from mainland China and assumed control of Taiwan in 1949. Many of my family members strongly identified as Chinese and were adamant advocates for the Kuomintang, but some of my friends identified as Taiwanese and supported the Democratic Progressive Party. Others were ambivalent or indifferent.

Interacting with Taiwanese immigrants across generations both confirmed and complicated my earlier observations. In many ways, divisions in Taiwanese immigrant communities in the United States resembled divisions in Taiwan over homeland politics and social issues. In the United States, older migrants of different political stances joined different homeland organizations (e.g., churches and *tongxianghui*, or townsmen associations) and formed distinctive communities. I thus tried to recruit respondents from organizations across the Taiwanese political spectrum. I also sought immigrants who had arrived in the United States on different types of visas—for example, as international students, labor migrants, or family members with sponsors—and those who had forged varying life paths.

Initially, I planned to conduct interviews only in Greater Boston, but I decided to extend my fieldwork to New York City for three reasons. First, I had become a member of the Taiwanese American community in Boston, and I was concerned that respondents there might censor themselves with me for fear of exposure to their coethnics. Notably, even though I assured them of confidentiality, quite a few asked me if I would share information with Mr. and Mrs. Bien, with whom I had become close. This concern became particularly pertinent when Mr. and Mrs. Bien left an immigrant organization over major disagreements. I still managed to interview people who had clashed with them, including those who had pushed them out of the organization, but I worried that my ties to the community might affect the data I collected.

Second, the Taiwanese immigrant community in Boston is relatively small, and my respondents and their children tended to know each other. I struggled, therefore, to protect their confidentiality, especially when community members expressed interest in reading my work. Recruiting additional respondents from New

York allowed me to diversify my sample and maintain "plausible deniability"—that is, "the ability to plausibly deny any claim that a particular respondent in my research corresponds to a specific individual in real life" (Marrow 2011, 278). Writing up my findings, I also sometimes changed identifying information to avoid revealing the identity of any respondent.

Third, extending my fieldwork to New York, especially Flushing, Queens, allowed me to include a historically Taiwanese immigrant enclave and to speak with immigrants representing a greater diversity of backgrounds. For example, when conducting fieldwork in Boston, I had trouble identifying migrants who worked or had worked in small businesses in ethnic enclaves. Some whom I did find refused the interview. Yet in New York, where I had no direct connections to the community, I was able to interview several small business owners from Flushing's ethnic enclave. Ultimately, seventeen of my fifty-eight respondents in the United States came from the Greater New York region.

I used two methods to locate respondents in the United States: personal connections and organizations, both Taiwanese and Chinese. Among these were Chinese and Taiwanese churches and the Center of Taipei Economic and Cultural Office. I recruited further through modified snowball sampling, asking respondents to introduce me to their colleagues, friends, or family members. To avoid too insular or homogeneous a data set, however, I interviewed no more than two people from the same referral source. Forty-eight respondents came from middle-class backgrounds and suburban communities; the rest were, in general, working class. I tried to find more economically disadvantaged respondents, but like other researchers (C. Chen 2008; Gu 2006), I had difficulty finding disadvantaged Taiwanese immigrants in metropolitan US cities. The working-class immigrants I did interview provide a comparison for theoretical explanations across the class spectrum (Becker 1998).

All of the immigrants I interviewed in the United States were foreign born and had been granted US citizenship after the age of eighteen. By conducting interviews only with US citizens, I made sure that my respondents had not come to the United States only temporarily but had, indeed, made a commitment to relocating. The length of time they had resided in the United States ranged from twenty-eight to forty-five years. If a respondent was married, I sought also to interview that respondent's spouse. Speaking to both partners, all in heterosexual marriages, allowed me to explore the possibility that older immigrant women and men might respond to my questions differently.

Recruiting Respondents in Taiwan

In Taiwan, I located many returnees through the referrals of my respondents in the States. Many were thus siblings, other relatives, or close friends of people I had met in the United States. I also used my personal connections—friends, family members, and former classmates—to locate return migrants in Taiwan. To diversify the sample, I employed snowball sampling and contacted such organizations as churches, temples, community colleges, and old-age homes to solicit additional respondents. Recruiting returnees was much harder than recruiting immigrants in the United States, not least because, in Taiwan, return migrants did not have their own organizations, institutions, and communities and so were harder to find.

I did meet some return migrants who refused to participate. Several expressed concern about responses from the United States, wondering, for example, whether they might be viewed as "traitors," disloyal to the United States. Several worried that their decision to return would make the US government less willing to receive Taiwanese immigrants. Some working-class returnees insisted that their experiences were not worth documenting and instead suggested that I speak with more affluent, successful, or knowledgeable returnees. For instance, I found Mr. Ko through his sister and knew he had lived in the United States for more than twenty years, but the first time I called him, he denied that he was a return migrant. I asked his sister to remind him of my research and contacted him a second time, but even then, he firmly rejected the interview, insisting that he "was not a good example for this study" and had "nothing interesting to offer." Instead, he suggested that I talk to "other, successful or knowledgeable people who moved back to Taiwan," because "working-class people like me have nothing to contribute to your research."

Similarly, some return migrants I interviewed seemed concerned with being perceived as "losers" who had been unable to survive in the United States. Seeking to show that they had not moved back to Taiwan because they had failed in the United States, they emphasized their "accomplishments" as well as their children's. I therefore heard about the schools they or their children had attended, the cars they had driven, the careers they had pursued, the houses they had owned, the organizations they had established, and the services they had provided for overseas Taiwanese communities. These respondents stressed that they had chosen to return, despite their successes in the United States.

All of the returnees I interviewed were long-term migrants who had settled in the United States for three to five decades and had moved back to Taiwan in the 2000s. All but one were naturalized US citizens who had spent most of their working years in the United States and returned in later life. A lack of statistical information on return migrants in Taiwan makes assessing the overall class distribution of returnees difficult. Among my respondents, however, forty-seven of the fifty-seven returnees were middle class or professionals, and ten had working-class backgrounds. Here, too, I sought to interview spouses of respondents who were married, to explore the ways gender might shape their perspectives and experiences.

Conducting Interviews

I carefully considered the potential influence of gender, ethnicity, and Taiwanese politics on the dynamics of my interviews. I worried, for example, that spouses would censor themselves in front of each other, so when interviewing spouses, I asked to speak to them independently. Some, however, insisted on being interviewed together and, contrary to my expectations, seemed not to silence themselves or suppress their responses. Rather, they often complemented, corrected, or even debated each other in front of me. I typically interviewed respondents in their own homes, even though some preferred coffee shops or restaurants. Speaking in private space, I could better address sensitive issues and assure confidentiality.

I was particularly careful about introducing myself before the interview, when I would intentionally reveal or obscure some of my family background to establish some commonality and initial trust. With respondents who were waishengren, I spoke of my grandparents and my father, who were also mainlanders, but when encountering respondents born in Taiwan, I avoided mentioning my paternal grandparents' ethnicity and instead mentioned my mother, who is native-born Taiwanese of Ha-ka origin. Because my Chinese name is difficult to pronounce in Taiwanese/Fujianese—and also marks me as a descendant of mainlanders—I used my English name "Ken Sun" rather than my Chinese name "Chih-Yan Sun." I believe my strategy encouraged my respondents to be more forthcoming, especially when they had strong views of an ethnic group in Taiwan.

Before each interview, I asked about the language—Mandarin, Taiwanese/Fujianese, or English—in which the respondent felt most comfortable. My Taiwanese is not as fluent as my Mandarin, and I sometimes stuttered as the interview proceeded, but almost all of my respondents appreciated my efforts to communicate in their native language. After finishing each interview, I wrote in-depth field notes right away. There I documented the source of the referral and described the interview setting, the dynamics I experienced with the respondent, the narratives that impressed me during the interview, and any theoretical hunches I had considered during the interview. These notes proved to be extremely useful in constructing my analysis and served as a good record of the development of certain lines of inquiry. I also used these field notes to revise my protocol of interview questions.

Collecting Ethnographic Observation

I complemented my interview data with ethnographic observation in both the United States and Taiwan. Interviewing in respondents' homes provided me with opportunities to conduct what Loretta Baldassar, Cora Baldock, and Raelene Wilding (2007, 18–19) call "ethnographic interview, . . . where it is possible to conduct some, albeit limited, naturalistic participant observation."

Observing the intimate spaces of my US respondents, I had the chance to observe their neighborhoods, the food in their homes, the books and newspapers on their tables and shelves, their pictures of family members, and the TV programs they were watching. I also regularly went to events and activities in which respondents participated.

By contrast, in Taiwan, I lacked similar opportunities to join activities involving return migrants, at least in part because no formal organizations or immigrant centers are focused on returnees. Instead, I met each respondent principally for the interview, without a chance to become better acquainted. I did, however, have opportunities to observe some of their personal and professional lives. For example, I met returnees who were employed in their workplaces (usually their offices) and arrived early to observe their work environments. I also chatted informally with their assistants, colleagues, or students. These observations enabled me to better understand their work and assess the veracity of their accounts.

I also interviewed about one-third of the returnees in their apartments. Meeting them at home gave me the opportunity to observe their intimate lives. For example, I took detailed notes about the pictures, books, magazines, trophies, slogans, and national as well as religious symbols (e.g., national flags and crosses) that my respondents displayed at home. During or after the interviews, many respondents showed me news stories (from newspapers, professional newsletters, magazines, governmental reports, and biographies) about their accomplishments before moving back to Taiwan. These materials helped me to triangulate my respondents' accounts, affirming what they described during the interview.

Analyzing Data

I analyzed the data I collected using a grounded theory approach, which involved "(1) an initial phase involving naming each word, line or segment of data followed by (2) a focused, selective phase that uses the most significant or frequent initial codes to sort, synthesize, integrate, and organize large amounts of data" (Charmaz 2006, 46). In the initial phase, or open coding, I labeled and organized data into themes. Later, I applied focused coding, using the most salient initial codes to sift through data and "determine the adequacy of those codes" (Charmaz 2006, 57). I triangulated these codes with the accounts of various respondents to check their credibility, and I linked codes to develop categories and subcategories.

To test their validity, I then compared my data with these categories and subcategories, applying a process of comparison that qualitative researchers continue until "no new properties or dimensions are emerging from continued coding and comparison" (Holton 2007, 265). After categories were developed, and their characteristics and dimensions (roughly) defined, I applied "axial coding" to "link categories with subcategories, and ask how they are related" (Charmaz 2006, 61).

I sought to understand the larger structural and cultural forces that had shaped and mediated the experiences of my respondents. I thus coded the data comparatively, looking for similarities and differences, among respondents in the United States and those in Taiwan and between these two groups. This approach allowed me to compare divergent accounts and commonalities among older Taiwanese immigrants across a transnational field.

Appendix B

BACKGROUNDS OF RESPONDENTS

Immigrants in the United States

NAME	AGE	PLACE OF BIRTH	TIME OF ARRIVAL IN THE UNITED STATES	ROUTE TO ARRIVAL IN THE UNITED STATES	NUMBER OF CHILDREN	NUMBER OF GRAND-CHILDREN	EDUCATIONAL LEVEL
Mr. Tseng	70	Taiwan	Late 1960s	Family sponsor	3	3	College
Mrs. Tseng	63	Taiwan	Late 1960s	Family sponsor	3	3	Vocational school
Mr. Tsai	67	Taiwan	Late 1960s	International student	2	1	Graduate degree
Mrs. Tsai	64	Taiwan	Early 1970s	Spouse	2	1	College
Mr. Zhang	65	Taiwan	Mid-1980s	Family sponsor	2	0	College
Mrs. Zhang	63	Taiwan	Mid-1980s	Family sponsor	2	0	Vocational school
Mrs. Ro	60	Taiwan	Early 1980s	International student	3	3	Graduate degree
Mr. Hsiu	71	Taiwan	Early 1970s	Economic migrant	3	2	Graduate degree
Mrs. Hsiu	69	Taiwan	Early 1970s	Economic migrant	3	2	College
Mr. Chang	76	Taiwan	Mid-1960s	International student	2	3	Graduate degree
Mrs. Chang	67	Taiwan	Early 1970s	International student	2	3	Graduate degree

(continued)

NAME	AGE	PLACE OF BIRTH	TIME OF ARRIVAL IN THE UNITED STATES	ROUTE TO ARRIVAL IN THE UNITED STATES	NUMBER OF CHILDREN	NUMBER OF GRAND-CHILDREN	EDUCATIONAL LEVEL
Mr. Fang	66	Taiwan	Late 1970s	Family sponsor	2	2	College
Mrs. Fang	61	Taiwan	Late 1970s	Family sponsor	2	2	College
Mr. Tan	83	Mainland China	Mid-1960s	Family sponsor	2	4	College
Mrs. Tan	81	Mainland China	Mid-1960s	Family sponsor	2	4	Vocational school
Mr. Lai	87	Taiwan	Early 1970s	Economic migrant	3	2	Graduate degree
Mrs. Lai	88	Taiwan	Early 1970s	Spouse	3	2	College
Mr. Huang	65	Taiwan	Early 1970s	International student	2	2	Graduate degree
Mrs. Huang	65	Taiwan	Early 1980s	International student	2	2	Graduate degree
Mr. Weng	69	Taiwan	Early 1970s	International student	2	2	Graduate degree
Mrs. Weng	67	Taiwan	Early 1970s	International student	2	2	Graduate degree
Mr. Wu	72	Taiwan	Mid-1970s	International student	1	2	Graduate degree
Mrs. Wu	68	Mainland China	Mid-1970s	Spouse	1	2	College
Mr. Yang	65	Taiwan	Late 1960s	International student	2	2	Graduate degree
Mrs. Yang	65	Taiwan	Late 1960s	Spouse	2	2	College
Mr. Chen	74	Taiwan	Mid-1960s	International student	3	2	Graduate degree
Mrs. Chen	65	Taiwan	Mid-1960s	Spouse	3	2	College
Mr. Chou	72	Taiwan	Mid-1960s	International student	2	2	Graduate degree
Mrs. Chou	70	Taiwan	Mid-1960s	International student	2	2	Graduate degree
Mr. Guo	71	Taiwan	Early 1970s	International student	2	1	Graduate degree
Mrs. Guo	63	Taiwan	Late 1970s	Spouse/ International student	2	1	College
Mr. Liu	74	Mainland China	Late 1970s	International student	2	3	Graduate degree
Mrs. Liu	69	Mainland China	Mid-1960s	International student	2	3	Graduate degree
Mrs. Zuo	76	Taiwan	Mid-1960s	Family sponsor	4	7	High school
Mrs. Ma	65	Taiwan	Early 1980s	Family sponsor	3	4	High school

NAME	AGE	PLACE OF BIRTH	TIME OF ARRIVAL IN THE UNITED STATES	ROUTE TO ARRIVAL IN THE UNITED STATES	NUMBER OF CHILDREN	NUMBER OF GRAND-CHILDREN	EDUCATIONAL LEVEL
Mr. Long	65	Taiwan	Early 1980s	Economic migrant	3	0	College
Mr. Hsieh	67	Taiwan	Late 1970s	International student	2	0	Graduate degree
Mrs. Hsieh	62	Taiwan	Late 1970s	International student	2	0	Graduate degree
Mr. Chao	73	Mainland China	Mid-1960s	International student	2	3	Graduate degree
Mrs. Chao	70	Mainland China	Mid-1960s	Spouse	2	3	Vocational school
Mr. Luo	66	Taiwan	Early 1970s	Family sponsor	3	0	College
Mrs. Luo	64	Taiwan	Early 1970s	Family sponsor	3	0	High school
Mrs. Ho	66	Taiwan	Mid-1970s	Family sponsor	1	0	High school
Mr. Fong	68	Taiwan	Mid-1970s	Family sponsor	2	0	Vocational school
Mrs. Fong	66	Taiwan	Mid-1970s	Family sponsor	2	0	Vocational school
Mr. Lin	72	Taiwan	Mid-1960s	Labor migrant	1	2	Vocational school
Mrs. Lin	70	Taiwan	Mid-1960s	Spouse	1	2	Vocational school
Mrs. Gao	73	Mainland China	Early 1960s	International student	3	5	Vocational school
Mr. Chiang	66	Taiwan	Late 1970s	International student	2	0	Graduate degree
Mrs. Chiang	65	Taiwan	Late 1970s	Spouse	2	0	College
Mr. Liang	66	Taiwan	Mid-1970s	International student	2	3	Graduate degree
Mrs. Liang	64	Taiwan	Mid-1970s	International student	2	3	College
Mr. Gu	70	Mainland China	Late 1960s	International student	2	2	College
Mrs. Gu	68	Mainland China	Late 1960s	Spouse	2	2	High school
Mr. Huo	69	Taiwan	Late 1970s	Family sponsor	2	2	College
Mrs. Hua	67	Taiwan	Late 1970s	Family sponsor	2	2	Vocational school
Mrs. Liao	74	Taiwan	Early 1970s	Family sponsor	4	5	Elementary school
Mr. Ruan	71	Mainland China	Late 1960s	Student migrant	2	2	Graduate degree

Return Migrants in Taiwan

	AGE	PLACE OF BIRTH	TIME OF ARRIVAL IN THE UNITED STATES	ROUTE TO ARRIVAL IN THE UNITED STATES	NUMBER OF CHILDREN	NUMBER OF GRAND-CHILDREN	EDUCATIONAL LEVEL
Mr. Sun	76	Mainland China	Mid-1960s	International student	1	1	Graduate degree
Mrs. Sun	72	Mainland China	Mid-1960s	International student	1	1	Graduate degree
Mr. Deng	80	Taiwan	Early 1960s	Economic migrant	2	2	College
Mrs. Deng	76	Taiwan	Early 1960s	Economic migrant	2	2	College
Mr. Xia	76	Mainland China	Early 1980s	Family sponsor	2	3	Graduate degree
Mrs. Xia	74	Hong Kong	Early 1980s	Family sponsor	2	3	College
Mr. Jiang	70	Taiwan	Late 1960s	Economic migrant	2	3	College
Mrs. Jiang	68	Taiwan	Late 1960s	Spouse	2	3	Vocational school
Mr. Ou Yang	73	Mainland China	Mid-1960s	International student	3	4	Graduate degree
Mrs. Ou Yang	65	Taiwan	Late 1960s	International student	3	4	College
Mrs. Chin	74	Taiwan	Early 1970s	Spouse	2	3	High school
Mr. Qi	66	Taiwan	Early 1970s	International student	2	2	Graduate degree
Mrs. Qi	73	Taiwan	Mid-1970s	International student	2	2	Graduate degree
Mr. Kim	77	Taiwan	Early 1960s	Family sponsor	2	3	College
Mrs. Kim	71	Mainland China	Early 1960s	Family sponsor	2	3	College
Mr. Shih	76	Taiwan	Mid-1960s	International student	2	2	Graduate degree
Mrs. Shih	69	Taiwan	Mid-1960s	Spouse	2	2	College
Mr. Kuan	66	Taiwan	Late 1970s	International student	2	2	Graduate degree
Mrs. Kuan	66	Taiwan	Late 1970s	International student	2	2	Graduate degree
Mr. Dai	75	Taiwan	Early 1970s	Family sponsor	3	2	College
Mrs. Dai	72	Taiwan	Early 1970s	Family sponsor	3	2	College
Mr. Chuan	74	Taiwan	Early 1970s	International student	2	3	Graduate degree
Mrs. Chuan	74	Taiwan	Mid-1970s	International student	2	3	Graduate degree

	AGE	PLACE OF BIRTH	TIME OF ARRIVAL IN THE UNITED STATES	ROUTE TO ARRIVAL IN THE UNITED STATES	NUMBER OF CHILDREN	NUMBER OF GRAND-CHILDREN	EDUCATIONAL LEVEL
Mr. Peng	77	Taiwan	Late 1960s	Family sponsor	2	3	Vocational school
Mrs. Peng	76	Taiwan	Late 1960s	Family sponsor	2	3	Vocational school
Mr. Quian	78	Taiwan	Late 1960s	Family sponsor	3	2	College
Mrs. Quian	72	Taiwan	Late 1960s	Family sponsor	3	2	College
Mr. Yen	75	Mainland China	Early 1970s	Family sponsor	2	3	College
Mrs. Yen	73	Mainland China	Early 1970s	Family sponsor	2	3	High school
Mr. Wei	71	Taiwan	Mid-1970s	International student	2	2	Graduate degree
Mrs. Wei	70	Taiwan	Mid-1970s	International student	2	2	Graduate degree
Mr. Lee	65	Taiwan	Mid-1970s	International student	3	2	Graduate degree
Mrs. Lee	65	Taiwan	Mid-1970s	International student	3	2	Graduate degree
Mr. Lam	65	Mainland China	Late 1970s	Family sponsor	2	1	College
Mrs. Lam	63	Mainland China	Late 1970s	Family sponsor	2	1	College
Mr. Hsu	66	Mainland China	Mid-1970s	International student	2	0	Graduate degree
Mrs. Mei	63	Taiwan	Mid-1970s	Spouse	2	0	College
Mr. Chao	66	Taiwan	Late 1970s	Family sponsor	3	0	College
Mrs. Chao	65	Taiwan	Early 1980s	Family sponsor	3	0	Vocational school
Mr. Hung	74	Taiwan	Mid-1960s	International student	3	3	Graduate degree
Mrs. Hung	64	Taiwan	Early 1970s	International student	3	3	Graduate degree
Ms. Ho	75	Taiwan	Mid-1960s	Family sponsor	0	0	High school
Mr. Wang	66	Taiwan	Late 1960s	International student	2	0	Graduate degree
Mr. Ning	70	Taiwan	Late 1970s	International student	1	0	Graduate degree
Mrs. Gui	68	Taiwan	Mid-1970s	Family sponsor	2	0	Vocational school
Mr. Tam	75	Mainland China	Early 1960s	International student	2	1	Graduate degree

(continued)

	AGE	PLACE OF BIRTH	TIME OF ARRIVAL IN THE UNITED STATES	ROUTE TO ARRIVAL IN THE UNITED STATES	NUMBER OF CHILDREN	NUMBER OF GRAND-CHILDREN	EDUCATIONAL LEVEL
Mr. Shen	66	Taiwan	Early 1970s	International student	2	2	Graduate degree
Mrs. Shen	67	Taiwan	Early 1970s	Spouse	2	2	College
Mr. Lu	72	Taiwan	Mid-1960s	International student	3	2	Graduate degree
Mr. Yeh	70	Taiwan	Late 1960s	International student	3	3	College
Mrs. Yeh	69	Taiwan	Early 1970s	Spouse	3	3	College
Mrs. Tong	70	Mainland China	Early 1970s	Family sponsor	2	2	College
Mr. Bai	66	Mainland China	Late 1970s	International student	2	2	Graduate degree
Mrs. Bai	64	Taiwan	Late 1970s	Spouse	2	2	High school
Mr. Leung	71	Mainland China	Late 1970s	Undocu-mented immigrant	0	0	Middle school
Mr. Du	65	Taiwan	Late 1970s	Family sponsor	2	2	High school
Mrs. Du	62	Taiwan	Late 1970s	Family sponsor	2	2	High school

Notes

PREFACE

1. Civil War in China constitutes an important backdrop to understanding the Chinese diaspora. After the Kuomintang (KMT) lost to the Communist Party in 1949, many people evacuated with the military from mainland China and relocated to Taiwan with the KMT government. These evacuees and their children are so-called *waishengren* (mainland Chinese). By contrast, those who settled in Taiwan prior to 1949 are typically called *benshengren* (native-born Taiwanese). As I discuss in chapter 2, both waishengren and benshengren relocated to the United States, but they did so for very different reasons. Following other scholars (C. Chen 2008; H.-S. Chen 1992; Tseng 1995), this book calls both groups Taiwanese immigrants or immigrants from Taiwan, partly because they are all legally citizens of Taiwan and partly because Taiwan is central to understanding their experiences in the United States and transnationally. For example, both waishengren and benshengren, some of whom have become US citizens, can gain access to public health care in Taiwan.

2. This intergroup conflict escalated and intensified after the KMT government enforced martial law; imprisoned (and executed) many local elites, activists, and political dissidents; and suppressed local Taiwanese culture (e.g., forbidding the use of Taiwanese/Fujianese at school and on TV). Listening to my respondents often reminded me of talking with my grandparents. Many of my respondents told me the reasons they resented Taiwan or had left the mainland, as my grandparents had done. As a researcher, I learned their life stories from multiple perspectives.

INTRODUCTION

1. Marta Bivand Erdal and R. Ezzati (2015, 1210), for example, found that many older migrants in Norway have a hard time relocating to their sending societies because "having spent their entire or most of their lives in Norway, 'returning' to a life that they [migrants] are no longer, or never have been, accustomed to, is difficult to imagine."

2. It is important to differentiate the relationship between intimacy and sexuality. As Jamieson (2011, 1) explains, "closeness may also be physical, bodily intimacy, although an intimate relationship need not be sexual and both bodily and sexual contact can occur without intimacy."

3. Failure to distinguish geographical locations among Chinese migrant populations also runs the risk of obscuring the impact of unique social backgrounds, political and economic systems, collective memories, and colonial histories on overseas Chinese from such diverse areas, such as Taiwan, Hong Kong, Singapore, Malaysia, and different regions of mainland China. As a result, the different levels and dimensions through which migrants' experiences can be examined—(trans)local, (trans)regional, and/or (trans)national—might be conflated rather than disaggregated. As Ien Ang (2001) argues, determining what *is* Chinese and what *is not* is critical to understanding the formation and rejection of the so-called Chinese diaspora. Migrants who are of Chinese ancestry but from different corners of the globe often develop their perspectives and stances on the term "Chinese."

1. EMIGRATING, STAYING, AND RETURNING

1. Several sociologists have pointed out that the globalization of US mass media culture has become vital in spreading and reproducing US racial ideologies—such as white supremacy, stigma attached to blackness, and the use of pan-ethnic labels—in many immigrants' sending communities (Kim 2008; Roth 2012). Before migrating to the United States, some Taiwanese immigrants I interviewed not only developed the notion of US superiority but also—because of their exposure to predominately white US pop culture—implicitly conflated the United States with whiteness. Many stated that they had spontaneously linked the idea (and ideal) of the United States with whiteness, because most movie and TV stars, models, and pop culture icons representing the United States in Taiwan were white. Most notably, some of the respondents vividly used television or movie stars of Caucasian descent to specify their premigratory understanding of US society.

3. REMAKING CONJUGALITY

1. Taiwan was Japan's overseas colony between 1895 and 1945, after China lost the First Sino-Japanese War to Japan during the Qing dynasty and ceded Taiwan in the Treaty of Shimonoseki. After the defeat and surrender of Japan in 1945, Taiwan was placed under the control of the Kuomintang government.

5. NAVIGATING NETWORKS OF SUPPORT

1. This political division can even supersede religious and ethnic identities. For example, some of the immigrant churches I visited were extremely supportive of Taiwanese independence and opposed the idea that Taiwan is part of mainland China. Some embraced pan-ethnic labels, such as *Hua-ren* (ethnic, or Han, Chinese). Still some insisted on not talking or commenting about politics.

6. ARTICULATING LOGICS OF SOCIAL RIGHTS

1. For example, Norman Matloff (1996)—the key advocate urging the government to terminate public benefits for immigrants during Clinton-era welfare reform—testified on February 6, 1996, to the US Senate Judiciary Committee's Subcommittee on Immigration that many elderly Chinese immigrants relocate to the United States to take advantage of US welfare benefits rather than to reunite with their family members. In contrast, many immigrant activists construct aging migrants as victims of anti-immigrant social policy who suffer negative consequences of the 1996 welfare reform (Fujiwara 2005). This framing often highlights the indispensability of welfare benefits and entitlement programs for the social and psychological well-being of foreign-born seniors. Stressing their vulnerability, however, largely sidetracks their agency, reflexivity, and complex experiences. As a result, we have limited knowledge of the ways aging migrants—especially long-term US residents—position themselves with respect to public benefits.

2. Of course, not all older people need medical care, and many people need care at other stages of life (e.g., pregnancy and childbirth). Yet as Greta Gilbertson (2009, 136) argues, a focus on senior migrants is important because "the elderly are more likely than those in other age groups to depend on the state and its institutions for services and sustenance." While National Health Insurance in Taiwan is not solely designed to satisfy the needs of senior citizens, it has great implications for aging migrants because many confront health-related issues in later life.

3. Noncitizens are eligible for Medicare if they meet certain criteria (Olson 2010).

4. In contrast, the US government taxes its citizens working abroad, but US citizens who are taxed abroad can avoid paying taxes twice on the money they earn. If their income is taxed abroad, the United States does not tax the income again.

5. As chapter 1 explains, many immigrants romanticize their connections to the United States, describing themselves as the embodiment of the American dream and depicting the United States as an open society where all have equal opportunities to succeed if they work hard enough. Thus, they might not openly admit in an interview to having gained illicit access to welfare benefits. Their articulation of rights, however, reveals their thinking about obligations to the United States.

6. For instance, at a dinner party during my fieldwork—in which most attendants were older immigrants from Taiwan—several people spoke of a news report that delivery staff in a Chinese restaurant had been robbed and shot to death by a black suspect. I immediately asked, "So the police already caught the suspect?" One of the attendees answered, "No, the police did not catch the suspect yet." I then asked, "How do we know the suspect is a black person?" After an awkward silence during which people looked at each other, another attendee replied, "Oh, we just think that the suspect is very likely to be a black person." In Taiwan, I heard many similar stereotypes describing African Americans as lazy and lacking intelligence. Some returnees even argued that African Americans today had "benefited" from their ancestors' slavery history and were thus "privileged" over white Americans and immigrants with similar or better credentials.

7. Immigrants who gained access to the National Health Insurance in Taiwan might have used difficult situations as excuses to justify their behavior. Their rationales, however, help to explain the larger structural contexts in which Taiwanese immigrants might return to receive public health care in their homeland.

Bibliography

Aaron, Henry J., Jeanne M. Lambrew, and Patrick F. Healy. 2008. *Reforming Medicare: Options, Tradeoffs, and Opportunities*. Washington, DC: Brookings Institution Press.

Ajrouch, Kristine J. 2005. "Arab-American Immigrant Elders Views about Social Support." *Ageing and Society* 25 (5): 655–673.

Alba, Richard. 2005. "Bright vs. Blurred Boundaries: Second-Generation Assimilation and Exclusion in France, Germany, and the United States." *Ethnic and Racial Studies* 28 (1): 20–49.

Alba, Richard D., and Victor Nee. 2003. *Remaking the American Mainstream: Assimilation and Contemporary Immigration*. Cambridge, MA: Harvard University Press.

Ang, Ien. 2001. *On Not Speaking Chinese: Living between Asia and the West*. London: Routledge.

Angel, Jacqueline L., and Ronald J. Angel. 2006. "Minority Group Status and Healthful Aging: Social Structure Still Matters." *American Journal of Public Health* 96 (7): 1152–1159.

Appadurai, Arjun. 1990. "Disjuncture and Difference in the Global Cultural Economy." In *Global Culture: Nationalism Globalization and Modernity*, edited by Mike Featherstone, 295–310. London: Sage.

Arber, Sara, and Virpi Timonen, eds. 2012. *Contemporary Grandparenting: Changing Family Relationships in Global Contexts*. Bristol, UK: Policy Press.

Baldassar, Loretta. 2016. "De-demonizing Distance in Mobile Family Lives: Co-presence, Care Circulation and Polymedia as Vibrant Matter." *Global Networks* 16 (2): 145–163.

Baldassar, Loretta, Cora Vellekoop Baldock, and Raelene Wilding. 2007. *Families Caring across Borders: Migration, Ageing and Transnational Caregiving*. New York: Palgrave Macmillan.

Baldassar, Loretta, Mihaela Nedelcu, Laura Merla, and Raelene Wilding. 2016. "ICT-Based Co-presence in Transnational Families and Communities: Challenging the Premise of Face-to-Face Proximity in Sustaining Relationships." *Global Networks* 16 (2): 133–144.

Barbalet, Jack. 2014. "Greater Self, Lesser Self: Dimensions of Self-Interest in Chinese Filial Piety." *Journal for the Theory of Social Behaviour* 44 (2): 186–205.

Basch, Linda, Nina Glick Schiller, and Cristina Szanton Blanc. 1994. *Nations Unbound: Transnational Projects, Postcolonial Predicaments, and Deterritorialized Nation-States*. Langhorne, PA: Gordon and Breach.

Bashi, Vilna Francine. 2007. *Survival of the Knitted: Immigrant Social Networks in a Stratified World*. Stanford, CA: Stanford University Press.

Becker, Howard S. 1998. *Tricks of the Trade: How to Think about Your Research While You're Doing It*. Chicago: University of Chicago Press.

Bengtson, Vern L. 2001. "Beyond the Nuclear Family: The Increasing Importance of Multigenerational Bonds; The Burgess Award Lecture." *Journal of Marriage and Family* 63 (1): 1–16.

Bengtson, Vern, Roseann Giarrusso, J. Beth Mabry, and Merril Silverstein. 2002. "Solidarity, Conflict, and Ambivalence: Complementary or Competing Perspectives on Intergenerational Relationships." *Journal of Marriage and Family* 64 (3): 568–576.

Blakemore, Ken. 1999. "International Migration in Later Life: Social Care and Policy Implications." *Ageing and Society* 19 (6): 761–774.

Blieszner, Rosemary, and Raeann R. Hamon. 1992. "Filial Responsibility: Attitudes, Obligations, and Roles." In *Gender, Families, and Elder Care*, edited by J. W. Dwyer and R. T. Coward, 105–119. Thousand Oaks, CA: Sage.

Bloemraad, Irene. 2006. *Becoming a Citizen: Incorporating Immigrants and Refugees in the United States and Canada.* Berkeley: University of California Press.

Bloemraad, Irene. 2018. "Theorising the Power of Citizenship as Claims-Making." *Journal of Ethnic and Migration Studies* 44 (1): 4–26.

Bolzman, Claudio, Rosita Fibbi, and Marie Vial. 2006. "What to Do after Retirement? Elderly Migrants and the Question of Return." *Journal of Ethnic and Migration Studies* 32 (8): 1359–1375.

Boris, Eileen, and Rhacel Salazar Parreñas, eds. 2010. *Intimate Labors: Cultures, Technologies, and the Politics of Care.* Stanford, CA: Stanford University Press.

Brijnath, Bianca. 2009. "Familial Bonds and Boarding Passes: Understanding Caregiving in a Transnational Context." *Identities: Global Studies in Culture and Power* 16 (1): 83–101.

Brown, Hana E. 2011. "Refugees, Rights, and Race: How Legal Status Shapes Liberian Immigrants' Relationship with the State." *Social Problems* 58 (1): 144–163.

Brown, Hana E. 2013. "Race, Legality and the Social Policy Consequences of Anti-Immigration Mobilization." *American Sociological Review* 78 (2): 290–314.

Brownell, Patricia, and Robin Creswick Fenley. 2009. "Older Adult Immigrants in the United States: Issues and Services." In *Social Work with Immigrants and Refugees: Legal Issues, Clinical Skills and Advocacy*, edited by F. Chang-Muy and E. P. Congress, 277–307. New York: Springer.

Calavita, Kitty. 1996. "The New Politics of Immigration: 'Balanced-Budget Conservatism' and the Symbolism of Proposition 187." *Social Problems* 43 (3): 284–305.

Carstensen, Laura L., D. M. Isaacowitz, and S. T. Charles. 1999. "Taking Time Seriously: A Theory of Socioemotional Selectivity." *American Psychologist* 54 (3): 165–181.

Charmaz, Kathy. 2006. *Constructing Grounded Theory: A Practical Guide through Qualitative Analysis.* Thousand Oaks, CA: Sage.

Chee, Maria W. L. 2005. *Taiwanese American Transnational Families: Women and Kin Work.* New York: Routledge.

Chen, Carolyn. 2006. "From Filial Piety to Religious Piety: Evangelical Christianity Reconstructing Taiwanese Immigrant Families in the United States." *International Migration Review* 40 (3): 573–602.

Chen, Carolyn. 2008. *Getting Saved in America: Taiwanese Immigration and Religious Experience.* Princeton, NJ: Princeton University Press.

Chen, Feinian, Guangya Liu, and Christine A. Mair. 2011. "Intergenerational Ties in Context: Grandparents Caring for Grandchildren in China." *Social Forces* 90 (2): 571–594.

Chen, Hsiang-Shui. 1992. *Chinatown No More: Taiwan Immigrants in Contemporary New York.* Ithaca, NY: Cornell University Press.

Chen, Wen-Yi, Jwo-Leun Lee, Yia-Wun Liang, Chin-Tun Hung, and Yu-Hui Lin. 2008. "Valuing Healthcare under Taiwan's National Health Insurance." *Expert Reviews Pharmacoeconomics Outcomes Research* 8 (5): 501–508.

Cheng, Tsung-Mei. 2009. "Lessons from Taiwan's Universal National Health Insurance: A Conversation with Taiwan's Health Minister Ching-Chuan Yeh." *Health Affairs* 28 (4): 1035–1044.

Cherlin, Andrew J., and Frank F. Furstenberg Jr. 1986. *The New American Grandparent: A Place in the Family, a Life Apart.* New York: Basic Books.

Choi, Sunha H. 2012. "Testing Healthy Immigrant Effects: Among Late Life Immigrants in the United States; Using Multiple Indicators." *Journal of Aging and Health* 24 (3): 475–506.

Choi, Susanne Y. P., and Yinni Peng. 2016. *Masculine Compromise: Migration, Family, and Gender in China.* Oakland: University of California Press.

Chong, Kelly H. 2006. "Negotiating Patriarchy: South Korean Evangelical Women and the Politics of Gender." *Gender and Society* 20 (6): 697–724.

Chung, Angie Y. 2016. *Saving Face: The Emotional Costs of the Asian Immigrant Family Myth.* New Brunswick, NJ: Rutgers University Press.

Coe, Cati. 2011. "What Is Love? The Materiality of Care in Ghanaian Transnational Families." *International Migration* 49 (6): 7–24.

Coe, Cati. 2017a. "Returning Home: The Retirement Strategies of Aging Ghanaian Care Workers." In *Transnational Aging and Reconfiguration of Kin Work*, edited by Parin Dossa and Cati Coe, 141–158. New Brunswick, NJ: Rutgers University Press.

Coe, Cati. 2017b. "Transnational Migration and the Commodification of Eldercare in Urban Ghana." *Identities: Global Studies in Culture and Power* 24 (5): 542–556.

Coe, Cati. 2019. *The New American Servitude Political Belonging among African Immigrant Home Care Workers.* New York: New York University Press.

Cohen, Lawrence. 1994. "Old Age: Cultural and Critical Perspectives." *Annual Review of Anthropology* 23 (1): 137–158.

Cohen, Lawrence. 1998. *No Aging in India: Alzheimer's, the Bad Family, and Other Modern Things.* Berkeley: University of California Press.

Collins, Patricia Hill. 1986. "Learning from the Outsider Within: The Sociological Significance of Black Feminist Thought." *Social Problems* 33 (6): S14–S32.

Collins, Patricia Hill. 2000. *Black Feminist Thought: Knowledge, Consciousness, and the Politics of Empowerment.* New York: Routledge.

Conrad, Peter. 2007. *The Medicalization of Society: On the Transformation of Human Conditions into Treatable Disorders.* Baltimore: Johns Hopkins University Press.

Constable, Nicole. 2014. *Born out of Place: Migrant Mothers and the Politics of International Labor.* Berkeley: University of California Press.

Cwerner, Saulo B. 2001. "The Times of Migration." *Journal of Ethnic and Migration Studies* 27 (1): 7–36.

Deeb-Sossa, Natalia, and Jennifer Bickham Mendez. 2008. "Enforcing Borders in Nuevo South: Gender and Migration in Williamsburg, Virginia, and the Research Triangle, North Carolina." *Gender and Society* 22 (5): 613–638.

Deng, Chung-Yeh, and Chia-Ling Wu. 2010. "An Innovative Participatory Method for Newly Democratic Societies: The 'Civic Groups Forum' on National Health Insurance Reform in Taiwan." *Social Science and Medicine* 70 (6): 896–903.

Di Leonardo, Micaela. 1987. "The Female World of Cards and Holidays: Women, Families, and the Work of Kinship." *Signs* 12 (3): 440–453.

Dominguez, Silvia. 2011. *Getting Ahead: Social Mobility, Public Housing, and Immigrant Networks.* New York: New York University Press.

Dossa, Parin, and Cati Coe, eds. 2017. *Transnational Aging and Reconfiguration of Kin Work.* New Brunswick, NJ: Rutgers University Press.

Dreby, Joanna. 2009. "Gender and Transnational Gossip." *Qualitative Sociology* 32 (1): 33–52.

Dreby, Joanna. 2010. *Divided by Borders: Mexican Migrants and Their Children.* Berkeley: University of California Press.

Dreby, Joanna, and Leah Schmalzbauer. 2013. "The Relational Contexts of Migration: Mexican Women in New Destination Sites." *Sociological Forum* 28 (1): 1–31.

Du Bois, William Edward Burghardt. 1903. *The Souls of Black Folk: Essays and Sketches.* Chicago: A. C. McClurg.

Ehrenreich, Barbara, and Arlie Russell Hochschild. 2004. *Global Woman: Nannies, Maids, and Sex Workers in the New Economy.* New York: Henry Holt.

Elder, Glen H., Jr. 1994. "Time, Human Agency, and Social Change: Perspectives on the Life Course." *Social Psychology Quarterly* 57 (1): 4–15.

Elder, Todd E., and Elizabeth T. Powers. 2006. "The Incredible Shrinking Program: Trends in SSI Participation of the Aged." *Research on Aging* 28 (3): 341–358.

Erdal, Marta Bivand, and R. Ezzati. 2015. "'Where Are You From' or 'When Did You Come'? Temporal Dimensions in Migrants' Reflections about Settlement and Return." *Ethnic and Racial Studies* 38 (7): 1202–1217.

Erel, Umut, and Louise Ryan. 2019. "Migrant Capitals: Proposing a Multi-level Spatio-Temporal Analytical Framework." *Sociology* 53 (2): 246–263.

Espiritu, Yen Le. 1996. *Asian American Women and Men: Labor, Laws and Love.* Thousand Oaks, CA: Sage.

Espiritu, Yen Le. 2003. *Homebound: Filipino American Lives across Cultures, Communities, and Countries.* Berkeley: University of California Press.

Estes, Carroll L. 1979. *Aging Enterprise: A Critical Examination of Social Policies and Services for the Aged.* San Francisco: Jossey-Bass.

Estes, Carroll L., Sheryl Goldberg, Chris Wellin, Karen W. Linkins, Sara Shostak, and Renne L. Beard. 2006. "Implications of Welfare Reform on the Elderly: A Case Study of Provider, Advocate, and Consumer Perspectives." *Journal of Aging and Social Policy* 18 (1): 41–63.

Feenstra, Robert C., and Gary G. Hamilton. 2014. *Emergent Economies, Divergent Paths: Economic Organization and International Trade in South Korea and Taiwan.* Cambridge: Cambridge University Press.

Felix, Adrian. 2011. "Posthumous Transnationalism: Postmortem Repatriation from the United States to Mexico." *Latin American Research Review* 46 (3): 157–179, 231, 233.

Fenge, Robert, and Pierre Pestieau. 2005. *Social Security and Early Retirement.* Cambridge, MA: MIT Press.

Field, Marilyn J., Robert L. Lawrence, and Lee Zwanziger, eds. 2000. *Extending Medicare Coverage for Preventive and Other Services.* Washington, DC: National Academy Press.

Fitzgerald, David. 2004. "Beyond 'Transnationalism': Mexican Hometown Politics at an American Labor Union." *Ethnic and Racial Studies* 27 (2): 228–247.

Fitzgerald, David Scott. 2013. "Immigrant Impacts in Mexico: A Tale of Dissimilation." In *How Immigrants Impact Their Homelands*, edited by Susan Eva Eckstein and Adil Najam, 114–137. Durham, NC: Duke University Press.

Fitzpatrick, Jacki, Shu Liang, Du Feng, Duane Crawford, Gwendolyn T. Sorell, and Barbara Morgan-Fleming. 2006. "Social Values and Self-Disclosure: A Comparison of Chinese Native, Chinese Residents (in U.S.) and North American Spouses." *Journal of Comparative Family Studies* 37 (1): 113–127.

Fomby, Paula. 2005. *Mexican Migrants and Their Parental Households in Mexico.* New York: LFB Scholarly.

Foner, Nancy. 1997. "What's New about Transnationalism? New York Immigrants Today and at the Turn of the Century." *Diaspora: A Journal of Transnational Studies* 6 (3): 355–375.

Foner, Nancy, ed. 2009. *Across Generations: Immigrant Families in America.* New York: New York University Press.

Foner, Nancy, and Joanna Dreby. 2011. "Relations between the Generations in Immigrant Families." *Annual Review of Sociology* 37 (April): 545–564.

Fonseca, Claudia. 2004. "The Circulation of Children in a Brazilian Working-Class Neighborhood: A Local Practice in a Globalized World." In *Cross-Cultural Approaches to Adoption*, edited by Fiona Bowie, 165–181. London: Routledge.

Fouron, Georges, and Nina Glick Schiller. 2001. "All in the Family: Gender, Transnational Migration, and the Nation-State." *Identities: Global Studies in Culture and Power* 7 (4): 539–582.

Friedman, Sara L. 2015. *Exceptional States: Chinese Immigrants and Taiwanese Sovereignty*. Oakland: University of California Press.

Friedman, Sara L., and Pardis Mahdavi, eds. 2015. *Migrant Encounters: Intimate Labor, the State, and Mobility across Asia*. Philadelphia: University of Pennsylvania Press.

Fujiwara, Lynn H. 2005. "Immigrant Rights Are Human Rights: The Reframing of Immigrant Entitlement and Welfare." *Social Problems* 52 (1): 79–101.

Gardner, Katy. 2002. *Age, Narratives and Migration: The Life Course and Life Histories of Bengali Elders in London*. Oxford: Berg.

Garey, Anita Ilta, and Karen V. Hansen, eds. 2011. *At the Heart of Work and Family: Engaging the Ideas of Arlie Hochschild*. New Brunswick, NJ: Rutgers University Press.

Giddens, Anthony. 1992. *The Transformation of Intimacy: Sexuality, Love, and Eroticism in Modern Societies*. Stanford, CA: Stanford University Press.

Gilbertson, Greta. 2009. "Caregiving across Generations: Aging, State Assistance, and Multigenerational Ties among Immigrants from the Dominican Republic." In *Across Generations: Immigrant Families in America*, edited by Nancy Foner, 135–159. New York: New York University Press.

Gonzales, Roberto G. 2016. *Lives in Limbo: Undocumented and Coming of Age in America*. Oakland: University of California Press.

Greenhalgh, Susan. 1988. "Intergenerational Contracts: Familial Roots of Sexual Stratification in Taiwan." In *A Home Divided: Women and Income in the Third World*, edited by Daisy Dwyer and Judith Bruce, 39–70. Stanford, CA: Stanford University Press.

Gross, Neil. 2005. "The Detraditionalization of Intimacy Reconsidered." *Sociological Theory* 23 (3): 286–311.

Gu, Chien-Juh. 2006. *Mental Health among Taiwanese Americans: Gender, Immigration, and Transnational Struggles*. New York: LFB Scholarly.

Gu, Chien-juh. 2017. *The Resilient Self: Gender, Immigration, and Taiwanese Americans*. New Brunswick, NJ: Rutgers University Press.

Guo, Man, Ling Xu, Jinyu Liu, Weiyu Mao, and Iris Chi. 2016. "Parent-Child Relationships among Older Chinese Immigrants: The Influence of Co-residence, Frequent Contact, Intergenerational Support and Sense of Children's Deference." *Aging and Society* 36 (7): 1459–1482.

Gustafson, Per. 2001. "Retirement Migration and Transnational Lifestyle." *Ageing and Society* 21 (4): 371–394.

Hägerstrand, Torsten. 1982. "Diorama, Path and Project." *Tijdschrift voor Economische en Sociale Geografie* 73 (6): 323–339.

Hall, Stuart. 1993. "Cultural Identity and Diaspora." In *Colonial Discourse and Post-Colonial Theory: A Reader*, edited by Patrick Williams and Laura Chrisman, 392–401. London: Harvester Wheatsheaf.

Hansen, Karen V. 1996. *A Very Social Time: Crafting Community in Antebellum New England*. Berkeley: University of California Press.

Hansen, Karen V. 2005. *Not-So-Nuclear Families: Class, Gender, and Networks of Care*. New Brunswick, NJ: Rutgers University Press.

Hareven, Tamara K. 1994. "Aging and Generational Relations: A Historical and Life Course Perspective." *Annual Review of Sociology* 20 (August): 437–461.

Haug, Sonja. 2008. "Migration Networks and Migration Decision-Making." *Journal of Ethnic and Migration Studies* 34 (4): 585–605.

Hirsch, Jennifer S. 2003. *A Courtship after Marriage: Sexuality and Love in Mexican Transnational Families*. Berkeley: University of California Press.

Ho, Elaine Lynn-Ee. 2019. *Citizens in Motion: Emigration, Immigration, and Re-migration across China's Borders*. Stanford, CA: Stanford University Press.

Hoang, Kimberly Kay. 2015. *Dealing in Desire: Asian Ascendancy, Western Decline, and the Hidden Currencies of Global Sex Work*. Oakland: University of California Press.

Hochschild, Arlie Russell. 1989. *The Second Shift: Working Parents and the Revolution at Home*. New York: Viking Penguin.

Hochschild, Arlie Russell. 1997. *The Time Bind: When Work Becomes Home and Home Becomes Work*. New York: Henry Holt.

Hochschild, Arlie Russell. 2003. *The Managed Heart: Commercialization of Human Feeling*. Berkeley: University of California Press.

Holmes, Seth M. 2013. *Fresh Fruit, Broken Bodies: Migrant Farmworkers in the United States*. Berkeley: University of California Press.

Holton, Judith A. 2007. "The Coding Process and Its Challenges." In *The Sage Handbook of Grounded Theory*, edited by Antony Bryant and Kathy Charmaz, 265–289. London: Sage.

Hondagneu-Sotelo, Pierrette. 1994. *Gendered Transitions: Mexican Experiences of Immigration*. Berkeley: University of California Press.

Hondagneu-Sotelo, Pierrette. 2007. *Doméstica: Immigrant Workers Cleaning and Caring in the Shadows of Affluence*. Berkeley: University of California Press.

Horn, Vincent, and Cornelia Schweppe, eds. 2015. *Transnational Aging: Current Insights and Future Challenges*. London: Routledge.

Horton, Sarah. 2004. "Differential Subjects: The Health Care System's Participation in the Differential Construction of the Cultural Citizenship of Cuban Refugees and Mexican Immigrants." *Medical Anthropology Quarterly* 18 (4): 472–489.

Huang, Chun Ming. 2009. "Ping Guo De Zi Wei" (The Taste of an Apple). Pp. 41–70 in *Er Zi De Da Wan Ou* (The Sandwich Man). Taipei, Taiwan: UNITAS Publishing Co.

Hudson, Robert B. 2012. "Epilogue-Conflict and Convergence: An American Perspective on the Politics of Ageing Welfare States." In *Ageing Populations in Post-Industrial Democracies: Comparative Studies of Policies and Politics*, edited by Pieter Vanhuysse and Achim Goerres, 248–262. New York: Routledge.

Hunter, Alistair. 2011. "Theory and Practice of Return Migration at Retirement: The Case of Migrant Worker Hostel Residents in France." *Population, Space and Place* 17 (2): 179–192.

Hunter, Alistair. 2018. *Retirement Home? Ageing Migrant Workers in France and the Question of Return: IMISCOE Research Series*. N.p.: Springer Open.

Jackson, James S., Ivy Forsythe-Brown, and Ishtar O. Govia. 2007. "Age Cohort, Ancestry, and Immigrant Generation Influences in Family Relations and Psychological Well-Being among Black Caribbean Family Members." *Journal of Social Issues* 63 (4): 729–743.

Jacoby, Neil Herman. 1966. *U.S. Aid to Taiwan: A Study of Foreign Aid, Self-Help, and Development*. New York: Frederick A. Praeger.

Jamieson, Lynn. 1999. "Intimacy Transformed? A Critical Look at the 'Pure' Relationship." *Sociology* 33 (3): 477–494.

Jamieson, Lynn. 2011. "Intimacy as a Concept: Explaining Social Change in the Context of Globalisation or Another Form of Ethnocentrism?" *Sociological Research Online* 16 (4): 1–13.

Jang, Yuri, Giyeon Kim, David A. Chiriboga, and Soyeon Cho. 2008. "Willingness to Use a Nursing Home: A Study of Korean American Elders." *Journal of Applied Gerontology* 27 (1): 110–117.

Jiménez, Tomás R. 2010. *Replenished Ethnicity: Mexican Americans, Immigration and Identity*. Berkeley: University of California Press.

Jiménez, Tomás R. 2017. *The Other Side of Assimilation: How Immigrants Are Changing American Life*. Oakland: University of California Press.

Kamo, Yoshinori, and Min Zhou. 1994. "Living Arrangement of Elderly Chinese and Japanese in the United States." *Journal of Marriage and Family* 56 (3): 544–558.

Kan, Kamhon, and Yen-Ling Lin. 2009. "The Labor Market Effects of National Health Insurance: Evidence from Taiwan." *Journal of Population Economics* 22 (2): 311–350.

Karl, Ute, and Sandra Torres. 2015. *Ageing in Contexts of Migration*. London: Routledge.

Kasinitz, Philip, John H. Mollenkopf, Mary C. Waters, and Jennifer Holdaway. 2008. *Inheriting the City: The Children of Immigrants Come of Age*. Cambridge, MA: Harvard University Press.

Kibria, Nazli. 1993. *Family Tightrope: The Changing Lives of Vietnamese Americans*. Princeton, NJ: Princeton University Press.

Kibria, Nazli. 1994. "Household Structure and Family Ideologies: The Dynamics of Immigrant Economic Adaptation among Vietnamese Refugees." *Social Problems* 41 (1): 81–96.

Kibria, Nazil. 2002. *Becoming Asian Americans: Second-Generation Chinese and Korean American Identities*. Baltimore: John Hopkins University Press.

Kim, Allen, and Karen Pyke. 2015. "Taming Tiger Dads: Hegemonic American Masculinity and South Korea's Father School." *Gender and Society* 29 (4): 509–533.

Kim, Nadia Y. 2006. "'Patriarchy Is So Third World': Korean Immigrant Women and 'Migrating' White Western Masculinity." *Social Problems* 53 (4): 519–536.

Kim, Nadia Y. 2008. *Imperial Citizens: Korean and Race from Seoul to LA*. Stanford, CA: Stanford University Press.

Kim, Nadia. 2009. "Finding Our Way Home: Korean Americans, 'Homelands' Trips, and Cultural Foreignness." In *Diasporic Homecomings: Ethnic Return Migrants in Comparative Perspective*, edited by Takeyuki Tsuda, 305–324. Stanford, CA: Stanford University Press.

King, Russell. 2012. "Geography and Migration Studies: Retrospect and Prospect." *Population, Space and Place* 18 (2): 134–153.

King, Russell, Eralba Cela, Tineke Fokkema, and Julie Vullnetari. 2014. "The Migration and Well-Being of the Zero Generation: Transgenerational Care, Grandparenting, and Loneliness amongst Albanian Older People." *Population, Space and Place* 20 (8): 728–738.

King, Russell, and Aija Lulle. 2016. "Grandmothers Migrating, Working and Caring: Latvian Women between Survival and Self-Realisation." *Population Horizons* 13 (2): 43–53.

King, Russell, Ajia Lulle, Dora Sampaio, and Julie Vullnetari. 2017. "Unpacking the Ageing-Migration Nexus and Challenging the Vulnerability Trope." *Journal of Ethnic and Migration Studies* 43 (2): 182–198.

King, Russell, Mark Thomson, Tony Fielding, and Tony Warnes. 2006. "Time, Generations, and Gender in Migration and Settlement." In *The Dynamics of International Migration and Settlement in Europe: A State of the Art*, edited by Rinus Penninx, Maria Berger, and Karen Kraal, 233–268. Amsterdam: Amsterdam University Press.

King, Russell, and Julie Vullnetari. 2006. "Orphan Pensioner and Migrating Grandparents: The Impact of Mass Migration on Older People in Rural Albania." *Ageing and Society* 26 (5): 783–816.

Klinenberg, Eric. 2012. *Going Solo: The Extraordinary Rise and Surprising Appeal of Living Alone*. New York: Penguin.

Kronenfeld, Jennie Jacobs. 2011. *Medicare*. Santa Barbara, CA: Greenwood.

Krooks, Bernard A. 2012. "How Gifts Can Affect Medicaid Eligibility." *Forbes*, December 17, 2012. https://www.forbes.com/sites/bernardkrooks/2012/12/17/how-gifts-can-affect-medicaid-eligibility/#46faee74211f.

Kyung-Sup, Chang. 2010. "The Second Modern Condition? Compressed Modernity as Internalized Reflexive Cosmopolitization." *British Journal of Sociology* 61 (3): 444–464.

Lamb, Sarah. 2000. *White Saris and Sweet Mangoes: Aging, Gender and Body in North India.* Berkeley: University of California Press.

Lamb, Sarah. 2009. *Aging and Indian Diaspora: Cosmopolitan Families in India and Abroad.* Bloomington: Indiana University Press.

Lamb, Sarah. 2017. *Successful Aging as a Contemporary Obsession: Global Perspectives.* New Brunswick, NJ: Rutgers University Press.

Lamont, Michèle. 2000. *The Dignity of Working Men: Morality and the Boundaries of Race, Class, and Immigration.* Cambridge, MA: Harvard University Press.

Lan, Pei-Chia. 2002. "Subcontracting Filial Piety: Elder Care in Ethnic Chinese Immigrant Families in California." *Journal of Family Issues* 23 (7): 812–835.

Lan, Pei-Chia. 2006. *Global Cinderellas: Migrant Domestics and Newly Rich Employers in Taiwan.* Durham, NC: Duke University Press.

Lan, Pei-Chia. 2018. *Raising Global Families: Parenting, Immigration, and Class in Taiwan and the US.* Stanford, CA: Stanford University Press.

Lareau, Annette. 2000. "My Wife Can Tell Me Who I Know: Methodological and Conceptual Problems in Studying Fathers." *Qualitative Sociology* 23 (4): 407–433.

Lee, Jennifer, and Min Zhou. 2015. *The Asian American Achievement Paradox.* New York: Russell Sage Foundation.

Levitt, Peggy. 2001. *The Transnational Villagers.* Berkeley: University of California Press.

Levitt, Peggy. 2002. "The Ties that Change: Relations to the Ancestral Home over the Life Cycle." In *The Changing Face of Home: The Transnational Lives of the Second Generation,* edited by Peggy Levitt and Mary C. Waters, 123–144. New York: Russell Sage Foundation.

Levitt, Peggy, and B. Nadya Jaworsky. 2007. "Transnational Migration Studies: Past Developments and Future Trends." *Annual Review of Sociology* 33 (April): 129–156.

Levitt, Peggy, and Narasimhan Rajaram. 2013. "The Migration-Development Nexus and Organizational Time." *International Migration Review* 47 (3): 483–507.

Levitt, Peggy, and Nina Glick Schiller. 2004. Conceptualizing Simultaneity: A Transnational Social Field Perspective on Society." *International Migration Review* 38 (3): 1002–1039.

Levitt, Peggy, Jocelyn Viterna, Armin Mueller, and Charlotte Lloyd. 2017. "Transnational Social Protection: Setting the Agenda." *Oxford Development Studies* 45 (1): 2–19.

Lewinsohn, Mark A., and Paul D. Werner. 1997. "Factors in Chinese Marital Process: Relationship to Marital Adjustment." *Family Process* 36 (1): 43–61.

Ley, David, and Audrey Kobayash. 2005. "Back to Hong Kong: Return Migration or Transnational Sojourn?" *Global Networks* 5 (2): 111–127.

Li, Pei-Fen, and K. A. S. Wickrama. 2014. "Stressful Life Events, Marital Satisfaction, and Marital Management Skills of Taiwanese Couples." *Family Relations* 63 (2): 193–205.

Li, Wei. 2009. *Ethnoburb: The New Ethnic Community in Urban America.* Honolulu: University of Hawai'i Press.

Li, Yingchun. 2015. "Between Tradition and Modernity: 'Leftover' Women in Shanghai." *Journal of Marriage and Family* 77 (5): 1057–1073.

Lien, Pei-te. 2010. "Pre-emigration Socialization, Transnational Ties, and Political Participation across the Pacific: A Comparison among Immigrants from China, Taiwan, and Hong Kong." *Journal of East Asian Studies* 10 (3): 453–482.

Lin, Kuo-Ming. 1997. "From Authoritarianism to Statism: The Politics of National Health Insurance in Taiwan." PhD diss., Yale University.

Litwin, Howard. 1997. "The Network Shifts of Elderly Immigrants: The Case of Soviet Jews in Israel." *Journal of Cross-Cultural Gerontology* 12 (1): 45–60.

Liu, I-Chun. 2010. "The Research of the Impact of Citizens' Medical Experience and Policy Literacy on Health Insurance Policy Satisfaction." *Journal of State and Society* 12 (December): 67–109 (in Chinese).

Liu, Su-Chiu. 2014. "An Analysis of Welfare and Health Policy Changes on the Health Seeking Behavior of Taiwanese Immigrants Residing in the United States." PhD diss., Boston University.

Lock, Margaret. 1993. *Encounters with Aging: Mythologies of Menopause in Japan and North America.* Berkeley: University of California Press.

Loe, Meika. 2011. *Aging Our Way: Lessons for Living from 85 and Beyond.* New York: Oxford University Press.

Louie, Andrea. 2004. *Chineseness across Borders: Renegotiating Chinese Identities in China and the United States.* Durham, NC: Duke University Press.

Lui, Lake. 2013. *Re-negotiating Gender: Household Division of Labor when She Earns More than He Does.* Dordrecht, Netherlands: Springer.

Lui, Lake. 2016. "Gender, Rural-Urban Inequality, and Intermarriage in China." *Social Forces* 95 (2): 639–662.

Macdonald, Cameron Lynne. 2011. *Shadow Mothers: Nannies, Au Pairs, and the Micropolitics of Mothering.* Berkeley: University of California Press.

Mahler, Sarah J., and Patricia R. Pessar. 2006. "Gender Matters: Ethnographers Bring Gender from the Periphery toward the Core of Migration Studies." *International Migration Review* 40 (1): 27–63.

Mahoney, James. 2000. "Path Dependence in Historical Sociology." *Theory and Society* 29 (4): 507–548.

Man, Guida C. 1997. "Women's Work Is Never Done: Social Organization of Work and the Experience of Women in Middle-Class Hong Kong Chinese Immigrant Families in Canada." *Advances in Gender Research* 2:183–226.

Marrow, Helen B. 2011. *New Destination Dreaming: Immigration, Race, and Legal Status in the Rural American South.* Stanford, CA: Stanford University Press.

Marrow, Helen B. 2012. "Deserving to a Point: Unauthorized Immigrants in San Francisco's Universal Access Healthcare Model." *Social Science and Medicine* 74 (6): 846–854.

Marrow, Helen B., and Tiffany D. Joseph. 2015. "Excluded and Frozen Out: Unauthorised Immigrants' (Non)access to Care after US Health Care Reform." *Journal of Ethnic and Migration Studies* 41 (14): 2253–2273.

Mason, Jennifer, Vanessa May, and Lynda Clarke. 2007. "Ambivalence and the Paradoxes of Grandparenting." *Sociological Review* 55 (4): 687–706.

Massey, Douglas S., ed. 2008. *New Faces in New Places: The Changing Geography of American Immigration.* New York: Russell Sage Foundation.

Massey, Douglas S., Joaquin Arango, Graeme Hugo, Ali Kouaouci, Adela Pellegrino, and J. Edward Taylor. 1998. *Worlds in Motion: Understanding International Migration at the End of the Millennium.* Oxford: Oxford University Press.

Matloff, Norman. 1996. "Welfare Use among Elderly Chinese Immigrants." *Testimony to the US Senate Judiciary Committee, Subcommittee on Immigration.* http://heather.cs .ucdavis.edu/pub/Immigration/WelfareUse/WelfareUsageReport/FullNMReport .html.

May, Jon, and Nigel Thrift, eds. 2001. *Timespace: Geographies of Temporality.* London: Routledge.

May, Vanessa, Jennifer Mason, and Lynda Clarke. 2012. "Being There, yet Not Interfering: The Paradoxes of Grandparenting." In *Contemporary Grandparenting: Changing Family Relationships in Global Contexts,* edited by Sara Arber and Virpi Timonen, 139–158. Bristol, UK: Policy Press.

Mazzucato, Valentina. 2007. "Transnational Reciprocity: Ghanaian Migrants and the Care of Their Parents Back Home." In *Generations in Africa: Connections and Conflicts*, edited by Erdmute Alber, Sjaak van der Geest, and Susan Reynolds Whyte, 91–109. Münster: LIT Verlag.

Menjivar, Cecilia. 1997. "Immigrant Kinship Networks: Vietnamese, Salvadorians and Mexicans in Comparative Perspective." *Journal of Comparative Family Studies* 28 (1): 1–24.

Mills, C. Wright. 1959. *The Sociological Imagination*. New York: Oxford University Press.

Moon, Seungsook. 2003. "Immigration and Mothering: Case Studies from Two Generations of Korean Immigrant Women." *Gender and Society* 17 (6): 840–860.

Mui, Ada C. 1996. "Depression among Elderly Chinese Immigrants: An Exploratory Study." *Social Work* 41 (6): 633–645.

Mui, Ada C., and Tazuko Shibusawa. 2008. *Asian American Elders in the Twenty-First Century: Key Indicators of Well-Being*. New York: Columbia University Press.

Näre, Lena, Katie Walsh, and Loretta Baldassar. 2017. "Ageing in Transnational Contexts: Transforming Everyday Practices and Identities in Later Life." *Identities: Global Studies in Culture and Power* 24 (5): 515–523.

Nelson, Margaret K. 2005. *The Social Economy of Single Motherhood: Raising Children in Rural America*. New York: Routledge.

Nelson, Margaret K. 2006. "Single Mothers 'Do' Families." *Journal of Marriage and Family* 68 (4): 781–795.

Neubeck, Kenneth J. 2006. *When Welfare Disappears: The Case for Economic Human Rights*. New York: Routledge.

Newbold, K. Bruce, and John K. Filice. 2006. "Health Status of Older Immigrants to Canada." *Canadian Journal on Aging / La Revue Canadienne du Vieillissement* 25 (3): 305–319.

Newendorp, Nicole. 2020. *Chinese Senior Migrants and the Globalization of Retirement*. Palo Alto, CA: Stanford University Press.

Newman, Katherine S. 2003. *A Different Shade of Gray: Midlife and beyond in the Inner City*. New York: New Press.

Nieswand, Boris. 2011. *Theorising Transnational Migration: The Status Paradox of Migration*. New York: Routledge.

Øien, Cecilie. 2006. "Transnational Networks of Care: Angolan Children in Fosterage in Portugal." *Ethnic and Racial Studies* 29 (6): 1104–1117.

Okafor, Maria C. 2009. "Avenues and Barriers to Access of Services for Immigrant Elders: State and Local Policies for OAA Units on Aging." *Journal of Gerontological Social Work* 52 (5): 555–564.

Olson, Laura Katz. 2010. *The Politics of Medicaid*. New York: Columbia University Press.

Ong, Aihwa. 1999. *Flexible Citizenship: The Cultural Logics of Transnationality*. Durham, NC: Duke University Press.

Orellana, Marjorie Faulstich, Barrie Thorne, Anna Chee, and Wan Shun Eva Lam. 2001. "Transnational Childhoods: The Participation of Children in Processes of Family Migration." *Social Problems* 48 (4): 572–591.

Ornstein, Katherine A., Amy S. Kelley, Evan Bollens-Lund, and Jennifer L. Wolff. 2017. "A National Profile of End-of-Life Caregiving in the United States." *Health Affairs* 36 (7): 1184–1192.

Ortner, Sherry B. 2006. *Anthropology and Social Theory: Culture, Power, and the Acting Subject*. Durham, NC: Duke University Press.

Pachucki, Mark A., Sabrina Pendergrass, and Michele Lamont. 2007. "Boundary Processes: Recent Theoretical Developments and New Contributions." *Poetics* 35 (6): 331–351.

Parikh, Nina S., Marianne C. Fahs, Donna Shelley, and Rajeev Yerneni. 2009. "Health Behaviors of Older Chinese Adults Living in New York City." *Journal of Community Health* 34 (1): 6–15.

Parreñas, Rhacel Salazar. 2001. "Mothering from a Distance: Emotions, Gender, and Intergenerational Relations in Filipino Transnational families." *Feminist Studies* 27 (2): 361–390.

Parreñas, Rhacel Salazar. 2005. *Children of Global Migration: Transnational Families and Gendered Woes*. Stanford, CA: Stanford University Press.

Paul, Anju Mary. 2017. *Multinational Maids: Stepwise Migration in a Global Labor Market*. Cambridge, UK: Cambridge University Press.

Pearman, William A., and Philip Starr. 1988. *Medicare: A Handbook on the History and Issues of Health Care Services for the Elderly*. New York: Garland.

Pedraza, Silvia. 1991. "Women and Migration: The Social Consequences of Gender." *Annual Review of Sociology* 17 (August): 303–325.

Peng, Yinni, and Odalia M. H. Wong. 2013. "Diversified Transnational Mothering via Telecommunication: Intensive, Collaborative, and Passive." *Gender and Society* 27 (4): 491–513.

Pessar, Patricia R. 1999. "Engendering Migration Studies: The Case of New Immigrants in the United States." *American Behavioral Scientist* 42 (4): 577–600.

Portes, Alejandro, Patricia Fernandez-Kelly, and William Haller. 2005. "Segmented Assimilation on the Ground: The New Second Generation in Early Adulthood." *Ethnic and Racial Studies* 28 (6): 1000–1040.

Portes, Alejandro, and Min Zhou. 1993. "The New Second Generation: Segmented Assimilation and Its Variants." *Annals of the American Academy of Political and Social Science* 530:74–96.

Pred, Allan. 1977. "The Choreography of Existence: Comments on Hägerstrand's Time-Geography and Its Usefulness." *Economic Geography* 53 (2): 207–221.

Pugh, Allison J. 2009. *Longing and Belonging: Parents, Children and Consumer Culture*. Berkeley: University of California Press.

Purkayastha, Bandana. 2012. "Intersectionality in a Transnational World." *Gender and Society* 26 (1): 55–66.

Purkayastha, Bandana, Miho Iwata, Shweta Majumdar Adur, Ranita Ray, and Trisha Tiamzon. 2012. *As the Leaves Turn Gold: Asian Americans and Experiences of Aging*. Lanham, MD: Rowman and Littlefield.

Pyke, Karen. 1999. "The Micropolitics of Care in Relationships between Aging Parents and Adult Children: Individualism, Collectivism, and Power." *Journal of Marriage and Family* 61 (3): 661–672.

Pyke, Karen. 2000. "'The Normal American Family' as an Interpretive Structure of Family Life among Grown Children of Korean and Vietnamese Immigrants." *Journal of Marriage and the Family* 62 (1): 240–255.

Pyke, Karen D., and Denise L. Johnson. 2003. "Asian American Women and Racialized Femininities: 'Doing' Gender across Cultural Worlds." *Gender and Society* 17 (1): 33–53.

Qian, Yue, and Liana C. Sayer. 2016. "Division of Labor, Gender Ideology, and Marital Satisfaction in East Asia." *Journal of Marriage and Family* 78 (2): 383–400.

Quek, Karen Mui-Teng, Carmen Knudson-Martin, Deborah Rue, and Claudia Alabiso. 2010. "Relational Harmony: A New Model of Collectivism and Gender Equality among Chinese American Couples." *Journal of Family Issues* 31 (3): 358–380.

Reynolds, Tracey. 2006. "Caribbean Families, Social Capital and Young People's Diasporic Identities." *Ethnic and Racial Studies* 29 (6): 1087–1103.

Reynolds, Tracey. 2010. "Transnational Family Relationships, Social Networks and Return Migration among British-Caribbean Young People." *Ethnic and Racial Studies* 33 (5): 797–815.

Rosenmayr, Leopold. 1968. "Family Relations of the Elderly." *Journal of Marriage and the Family* 30 (4): 672–680.

Roth, Wendy D. 2012. *Race Migrations: Latinos and the Cultural Transformation of Race.* Stanford, CA: Stanford University Press.

Roy, Kevin, and Linda Burton. 2007. "Mothering through Recruitment: Kinscription of Nonresidential Fathers and Father Figures in Low-Income Families." *Family Relations* 56 (1): 24–39.

Sanchez, Gabriel R., and Shannon Sanchez-Youngman. 2013. "The Politics of the Health Care Reform Debate: Public Support of Including Undocumented Immigrants and Their Children in Reform Efforts in the U.S." *International Migration Review* 47 (2): 442–473.

Sarkisian, Natalia. 2006. "'Doing Families Ambivalence': Nuclear and Extended Families in Single Mothers' Lives." *Journal of Marriage and Family* 68 (4): 804–811.

Schiller, Nina Glick, and Ayse Çaglar, eds. 2010. *Locating Migration: Rescaling Cities and Migrants.* Ithaca, NY: Cornell University Press.

Schmalzbauer, Leah. 2014. *The Last Best Place? Gender, Family, and Migration in the New West.* Stanford, CA: Stanford University Press.

Shia, Jiannbin Lee, and Mia H. Tuan. 2008. "'Some Asian Men Are Attractive to Me, but for a Husband . . .': Korean Adoptees and the Salience of Race in Romance." *Du Bois Review: Social Science Research on Race* 5 (2): 259–285.

Shih, Kristy Y., and Karen Pyke. 2010. "Power, Resistance, and Emotional Economies in Women's Relationships with Mothers-in-Law in Chinese Immigrant Families." *Journal of Family Issues* 31 (3): 333–357.

Shih, Kristy Y., and Karen Pyke. 2016. "Seeing Mothers-in-Law through the Lens of the Mothering Ideology: An Interview Analysis of Taiwanese, Taiwanese American, and Mexican American Daughters-in-Law." *Journal of Family Issues* 37 (14): 1968–1993.

Shim, Janet K. 2010. "Cultural Health Capital: A Theoretical Approach to Understanding Health Care Interactions and the Dynamics of Unequal Treatment." *Journal of Health and Social Behavior* 51 (1): 1–15.

Silverstein, Merril, T. Parrott, J. J. Angelelli, and Fay Lomax Cook. 2000. "Solidarity and Tension between Age-Groups in the United States: Challenge for an Aging America in the 21st Century." *International Journal of Social Welfare* 9 (4): 270–284.

Siu, Lok C. D. 2005. *Memories of a Future Home: Diasporic Citizenship of Chinese in Panama.* Stanford, CA: Stanford University Press.

Smith, Robert Courtney. 2006. *Mexican New York: Transnational Lives of New Immigrants.* Berkeley: University of California Press.

Smith, Robert Courtney. 2014. "Black Mexicans, Conjunctural Ethnicity, and Operating Identities: Long-Term Ethnographic Analysis." *American Sociological Review* 79 (3): 517–548.

Sommer, Elena, and Claudia Vogel. 2015. "Intergenerational Solidarity in Migrant Families from Former Soviet Union: Comparing Migrants Whose Parents Live in Germany to Migrants with Parents Abroad." In *Transnational Aging: Current Insights and Future Challenges,* edited by Vincent Horn and Cornelia Schweppe, 45–63. New York: Routledge.

Spitze, Glena, and Russell A. Ward. 1998. "Gender Variations." In *Handbook on Grandparenthood,* edited by Maximiliane E. Szinovacz, 113–127. Westport, CT: Greenwood.

Stack, Carol B. 1997. *All Our Kin: Strategies for Survival in a Black Community*. New York: Basic Books.

Stack, Carol B., and Linda M. Burton. 1994. "Kinscripts: Reflections on Family, Generation, and Culture." In *Mothering: Ideology, Experience and Agency*, edited by Evelyn Nakano Glenn, Grace Chang, and Linda Rennie Forcey, 33–44. London: Routledge.

Stephens, Robert W. 2013. "Medicare." In *Mental Health Practitioner's Guide to HIV/AIDS*, edited by Sana Loue, 305–307. New York: Springer.

Street, Debra, Stephanie Burge, Jill Quadagno, and Anne Barrett. 2007. "The Salience of Social Relationships for Resident Well-Being in Assisted Living." *Journals of Gerontology Series B: Psychological Sciences and Social Sciences* 62 (2): S129–S134.

Sun, Ken Chih-Yan. 2012. "Fashioning Reciprocal Norms of Elder Care: A Case of Immigrants in the United States and Their Parents in Taiwan." *Journal of Family Issues* 33 (9): 1240–1271.

Sun, Ken Chih-Yan. 2014a. "Transnational Kinscription: A Case of Parachute Kids and Their Parents in Taiwan." *Journal of Ethnic and Migration Studies* 40 (9): 1431–1449.

Sun, Ken Chih-Yan. 2014b. "Transnational Healthcare Seeking: How Aging Taiwanese Return Migrants Think about Homeland Public Benefits." *Global Networks* 14 (4): 533–550.

Sun, Ken Chih-Yan. 2014c. "Reconfigured Reciprocity: How Aging Taiwanese Immigrants Transform Cultural Logics of Elder Care." *Journal of Marriage and Family* 76 (4): 875–889.

Sun, Ken Chih-Yan. 2017. "Managing Transnational Ambivalence: How Stay-Behind Parents Grapple with Family Separation across Time." *Identities: Global Studies in Culture and Power* 24 (5): 509–605.

Sun, Ken Chih-Yan. 2018. "Negotiating the Boundaries of Social Membership: The Case of Aging Return Migrants to Taiwan." *Current Sociology* 66 (2): 286–302.

Sunil, T. S., Viviana Rojas, and Don E. Bradley. 2007. "United States' International Retirement Migration: The Reasons for Retiring to the Environs of Lake Chapala, Mexico." *Ageing and Society* 27 (4): 489–510.

Swidler, Ann. 1986. "Culture in Action: Symbols and Strategies." *American Sociological Review* 51 (2): 273–286.

Swidler, Ann. 2001. *Talk of Love: How Culture Matters*. Chicago: University of Chicago Press.

Tam, Sandra, and Sheila Neysmith. 2006. "Disrespect and Isolation: Elder Abuse in Chinese Communities." *Canadian Journal on Aging / La Revue Canadienne du Vieillissement* 25 (2): 141–151.

Thai, Hung Cam. 2014. *Insufficient Funds: The Culture of Money in Low-Wage Transnational Families*. Stanford, CA: Stanford University Press.

Toyota, Mika, and Leng Leng Thang. 2017. "Transnational Retirement Mobility as Processes of Identity Negotiation: The Case of Japanese in South-East Asia." *Identities: Global Studies in Culture and Power* 24 (5): 557–572.

Treas, Judith. 2008. "Four Myths about Older Adults in America's Immigrant Families." *Generations* 32 (4): 40–45.

Treas, Judith, and Jeanne Batalova. 2007. "Older Immigrants." In *Social Structures: Demographic Changes and the Well-Being of Older Persons*, edited by K. Warner Schaie and Peter Uhlenberg, 1–24. New York: Springer.

Treas, Judith, and Daisy Carreon. 2010. "Diversity and Our Common Future: Race, Ethnicity, and the Older American." *Generations* 34 (3): 38–44.

Tseng, Yen-Fen. 1995. "Beyond 'Little Taipei': The Development of Taiwanese Immigrant Businesses in Los Angeles." *International Migration Review* 29 (1): 33–58.

Tsuda, Takeyuki. 1999. "Transnational Migration and the Nationalization of Ethnic Identity among Japanese Brazilian Return Migrants." *Ethos* 27 (2): 145–179.

Tsuda, Takeyuki. 2012. "Whatever Happened to Simultaneity? Transnational Migration Theory and Dual Engagement in Sending and Receiving Countries." *Journal of Ethnic and Migration Studies* 38 (4): 631–649.

Tsuda, Takeyuki. 2014. "'I'm American, not Japanese!': The Struggle for Racial Citizenship among Later-Generation Japanese Americans." *Ethnic and Racial Studies* 37 (3): 405–424.

Tuan, Mia. 1998. *Forever Foreigners or Honorary Whites? The Asian Ethnic Experience Today*. New Brunswick, NJ: Rutgers University Press.

Vallejo, Jody Agius. 2012. *Barrios to Burbs: The Making of the Mexican American Middle Class*. Stanford, CA: Stanford University Press.

Vertovec, Steven. 1999. "Conceiving and Researching Transnationalism." *Ethnic and Racial Studies* 22 (2): 447–462.

Waldinger, Roger. 2015. *The Cross-Border Connection: Immigrants, Emigrants, and Their Homelands*. Cambridge, MA: Harvard University Press.

Walsh, Katie, and Lena Näre, eds. 2016. *Transnational Migration and Home in Older Age*. New York: Routledge.

Wang, Joseph. 2004. *Healthy Democracies: Welfare Politics in Taiwan and South Korea*. Ithaca, NY: Cornell University Press.

Wang, L. Ling-chi. 2007. "The Chinese Diaspora in the United States: International Relations, Ethnic Identity, and Minority Rights in the New Global Economy." *Amerasia Journal* 33 (1): 1–30.

Warikoo, Natasha, and Irene Bloemraad. 2018. "Economic Americanness and Defensive Inclusion: Social Location and Young Citizens' Conceptions of National Identity." *Journal of Ethnic and Migration Studies* 44 (5): 736–753.

Waters, Johanna L. 2005. "Transnational Family Strategies and Education in the Contemporary Chinese Diaspora." *Global Networks* 5 (4): 359–377.

Waters, Johanna L. 2011. "Time and Transnationalism: A Longitudinal Study of Immigration, Endurance and Settlement in Canada." *Journal of Ethnic and Migration Studies* 37 (7): 1119–1135.

Waters, Mary C. 1999. *Black Identities: West Indian Immigrant Dreams and American Realities*. Cambridge, MA: Harvard University Press.

Waters, Mary C. 2014. "Defining Difference: The Role of Immigrant Generation and Race in American and British Immigration Studies." *Ethnic and Racial Studies* 37 (1): 10–26.

Waters, Mary C., and Tomás R. Jiménez. 2005. "Assessing Immigrant Assimilation: New Empirical and Theoretical Challenges." *Annual Review of Sociology* 31 (August): 105–125.

West, Candace, and Don H. Zimmerman. 1987. "Doing Gender." *Gender and Society* 1 (2): 125–151.

Wimmer, Andreas, and Nina Glick Schiller. 2003. "Methodological Nationalism, the Social Sciences, and the Study of Migration: An Essay in Historical Epistemology." *International Migration Review* 37 (3): 576–610.

Wong, William. 1999. "Asian-Americans and Welfare Reform: The Mainstream Press Perpetuates Images but Fails to Report on Real Experiences." *Nieman Reports* 53 (2): 47–48.

Xie, Xiaolin, and Yan Xia. 2011. "Grandparenting in Chinese Immigrant Families." *Marriage and Family Review* 47 (6): 383–396.

Yarris, Kristine Elizabeth. 2017. *Care across Generations: Solidarity and Sacrifice in Transnational Families*. Stanford, CA: Stanford University Press.

Yoo, Grace J. 2001. "Constructing Deservingness: Federal Welfare Reform, Supplemental Security Income, and Elderly Immigrants." *Journal of Aging and Social Policy* 13 (4): 17–34.

Yoo, Grace J. 2008. "Immigrants and Welfare: Policy Constructions of Deservingness." *Journal of Immigrant and Refugees Studies* 6 (4): 490–507.

Yoo, Grace J., and Barbara W. Kim. 2014. *Caring across Generations: The Linked Lives of Korean American Families*. New York: New York University Press.

Zechner, Minna. 2017. "Transnational Habitus at the Time of Retirement." *Identities: Global Studies in Culture and Power* 24 (5): 573–589.

Zelizer, Viviana A. 2005. *The Purchase of Intimacy*. Princeton, NJ: Princeton University Press.

Zelizer, Viviana A. 2012. "How I Became a Relational Economic Sociologist and What Does That Mean?" *Politics and Society* 40 (2): 145–174.

Zhang, Gehui, and Heying Jenny Zhan. 2009. "Beyond the Bible and the Cross: A Social and Cultural Analysis of Chinese Elders' Participation in Christian Congregations in the United States." *Sociological Spectrum* 29 (2): 295–317.

Zhao, Xiaojian. 2010. *The New Chinese America: Class, Economy and Social Hierarchy*. New Brunswick, NJ: Rutgers University Press.

Zhou, Min. 1992. *Chinatown: The Socioeconomic Potential of an Urban Enclave*. Philadelphia: Temple University Press.

Zhou, Min. 1998. "'Parachute Kids' in Southern California: The Educational Experience of Chinese Children in Transnational Families." *Educational Policy* 12 (6): 682–704.

Zhou, Min. 2009. "Conflict, Coping and Reconciliation: Intergenerational Relations in Chinese Immigrant Families." In *Across Generations: Immigrant Families in America*, edited by Nancy Foner, 1–20. New York: New York University Press.

Zhou, Yanqiu Rachel. 2012. "Space, Time, and Self: Rethinking Aging in the Contexts of Immigration and Transnationalism." *Journal of Aging Studies* 26 (3): 232–242.

Zhou, Yu, and Yen-Fen Tseng. 2001. "Regrounding the 'Ungrounded Empire': Localization as the Geographical Catalyst for Transnationalism." *Global Networks* 1 (2): 131–154.

Zinn, Maxine Baca, Pierrette Hondagneu-Sotelo, and Michael A. Messner, eds. 2011. *Gender through the Prism of Difference*. New York: Oxford University Press.

Zontini, Elisabetta. 2015. "Growing Old in a Transnational Social Field: Belonging, Mobility and Identity among Italian Migrants." *Ethnic and Racial Studies* 38 (2): 326–341.

Zuo, Jiping. 2008. "Marital Construction of Family Power among Male-Out-Migrant Couples in a Chinese Village: A Relation-Oriented Exchange Model." *Journal of Family Issues* 29 (5): 663–691.

Zuo, Jiping. 2009. "Rethinking Family Patriarchy and Women's Positions in Presocialist China." *Journal of Marriage and Family* 71 (3): 542–557.

Index

acculturation: as empowerment, 76; intergenerational relations and, 52–53, 60–74, 76; return migration and, 11, 137, 161. *See also* adaptability; Americanization/Westernization; immigrant incorporation

adaptability, x, 2, 9–11; belonging and, 22; education and, 189; gendered relationships and, 85–94, 98, 104–5; intergenerational reciprocity and, 55, 66. *See also* acculturation; Americanization/Westernization; immigrant incorporation

African Americans, 178, 215n6

aging enterprises, 69–74

aging immigrants, 1–6; care for (*see* elder care); communities (*see* economy of belonging; networks of support); family and (*see* conjugality, gender and; grandparenthood; intergenerational reciprocity); health conditions, 46, 195 (*see also* health care; public benefits); recently-arrived, 175–78; "successful aging" discourse, 62; temporalities of migration and, 7–10. *See also* life stages, intimate relations and; return migrants (in Taiwan); Taiwanese immigrant communities (in US)

ambivalence: about family care, 55–57, 77; about staying or returning, 45–46

American dream, 7–8, 26–30, 38, 46–47, 215n5

Americanization/Westernization: elder care and mode of aging, 53, 60–77; family intimacy and, 192–93; gender hierarchies in marriage and, 19, 94–99, 104–5; return migrants and, 134, 151–54. *See also* acculturation; adaptability; immigrant incorporation

Ang, Ien, 213n3

anti-immigrant sentiment, 171, 173, 187, 214n1(ch.6)

Appadurai, Arjun, 28

assimilation, 2; as empowerment, 76; ethnic traditions and, 48, 60–65; identities and, 188; long-term immigrants and, 189; return migrants and, 151–54 (*see also* return migrants in Taiwan). *See also* acculturation; adaptability; Americanization/Westernization; immigrant incorporation

assisted-living facilities: public benefits and, 169–70; in Taiwan, 42–43; in US, 50, 70–72, 76–77

autonomy, 50, 52–53, 66, 77, 97–98. *See also* independence; self-sufficiency

Baldassar, Loretta, 203

Baldock, Cora, 203

belonging: economy of, 21–23, 30, 35, 38, 46–47, 190–92; homeland society and, 137–38, 148–56 (*see also* return migrants); host/receiving societies and, 137–48, 160 (*see also* Taiwanese immigrant communities in US); long-term migration and, 133; national, 6; networks of support and, 161 (*see also* networks of support); public benefits and, 162; social rights and public benefits, 164

Bengtson, Vern, 53

benshengren (native-born Taiwanese), 25, 141–42, 200, 213n1(preface)

Bloemraad, Irene, 163, 172

boundary work, 13–14, 187

bound feet (*guo jiao*), x

Brown, Hana, 170

Calavita, Kitty, 173

Cambodia, 72

Cantonese, 34, 139

careers. *See* paid work

caregivers: paid, 91, 114; women as, 45, 58–60, 73, 91, 101–2, 126. *See also* domestic workers; elder care; family caregiving

chastity, 102–4

Chen, Carolyn, 198

Cherlin, Andrew J., 110, 112, 130

childcare, 58–59. *See also* grandparenthood; parental authority

children of older immigrants: elder care as burden on, 46, 51, 53, 56–63, 70, 96, 134, 169; emotional connections with, 74–75; interactions with, 97–98; resources of, 53, 58–60. *See also* elder care; family; family caregiving; intergenerational conflict; intergenerational reciprocity